THE 4-STAR AND 5-STAR WINNERS *of* 1997

America's Best Hotels and Restaurants

Fodor's Travel Publications, Inc.
http://www.fodor's.com/

Mobil Travel Guide Staff

General Manager: Diane Connolly
Inspection Coordinator: Kristin Schiller
Inspection Assistant: Peggy T. Keane
Editor: Sara D. Hauber
Creative Director: Fabrizio La Rocca

Acknowledgments

We gratefully acknowledge the help of our more than 100 field representatives for their efficient and perceptive inspection of hotels and restaurants; the proprietors of these establishments for their cooperation in showing their facilities and providing information about them; and our many friends and users of the *Mobil Travel Guide* for their time and information.

Mobil and Pegasus 🐎 the Flying Red Horse, are trademarks of Mobil Oil Corporation. All rights reserved. Reproduction by any means including but not limited to photography, electrostatic copying devices, or electronic data processing is prohibited. Use of the information contained herein for solicitation of advertising or listing in any other publication is expressly prohibited without written permission from Mobil Corporation. Violations of reserved rights are subject to prosecution.

Copyright © 1997 by Mobil Corporation.

All rights reserved, including the right of reproduction in whole or in part in any form.

Published in 1997 by Fodor's Travel Publications, Inc.
201 E. 50th St.
New York, NY 10022

ISBN 0-679-03323-8
ISSN 1086-1726

Printed in the United States of America
10 9 8 7 6 5 4 3 2

Contents

A Word to Our Readers v

Understanding the Listings vi

Symbols and Abbreviations x

Mobil Travel Guide 1997
Five-Star Award Winners xiv

Mobil's Five-Star and Four-Star
Winners of 1997 1

Alabama	1	Nevada	146
Arizona	2	New Hampshire	150
California	16	New Jersey	151
Colorado	58	New Mexico	155
Connecticut	68	New York	157
Delaware	70	North Carolina	180
District of Columbia	71	Ohio	184
Florida	76	Oregon	186
Georgia	98	Pennsylvania	190
Idaho	108	South Carolina	195
Illinois	109	Tennessee	197
Kentucky	118	Texas	199
Louisiana	120	Utah	211
Maine	124	Vermont	213
Maryland	127	Virginia	217
Massachusetts	129	Washington	224
Michigan	139	West Virginia	231
Minnesota	141	Wisconsin	233
Missouri	142	Wyoming	235
Montana	145	Canada	237

A Word to Our Readers

Truly fine hotels and restaurants are not easy to find. While many achieve excellence on occasion, the ambitious properties whose goal it is to create a wonderful setting for their guests and provide superb service to each and every one, year in and year out, are unusual; of those that aim for such lofty goals, only a few hundred achieve them. This small book from the editors of the Mobil Travel Guide is your key to this circle of excellence.

The Mobil Travel Guide has been assessing U.S. and Canadian hotels and restaurants using a Star Rating System for nearly 40 years; few accolades are more coveted in the hospitality industry than the Mobil Travel Guide's Four-Star and Five-Star Awards. *America's Best Hotels and Restaurants* gathers together in one volume the exceptional properties that have achieved this status. Here are the very best establishments the country has to offer—places that provide not just a tasteful room for the night or superb food in lovely surroundings, but exquisite establishments whose every detail is polished, professional, and often perfect. All the Mobil Four-Star or Five-Star hotels and restaurants are carefully evaluated every year by professionals with years of experience in assessing such properties. No Four-Star or Five-Star winner rests on its laurels; each earns its award anew for each new addition.

We at the Mobil Travel Guide value your input. Whatever your experiences at our Four-Star and Five-Star properties, please share them with us; address your letter to us at 4709 W. Golf Road, Suite 803, Skokie, IL 60076. We are sure that you'll find these places more than worthy of the stars we've given them.

Sincerely,

THE EDITORS

Understanding the Listings

Winners of the Mobil Travel Guides' Four-Star and Five-Star Awards are all outstanding choices. They have achieved these coveted ratings after an extensive review of inspection reports from experienced field representatives, the written evaluations of experts who stay and dine anonymously at establishments throughout the year, and guest comments received by the Mobil Travel Guide.

A Five-Star lodging or restaurant is one of the best in the country, while a Four-Star property is outstanding and worth a special trip. What separates Four-Star from Five-Star establishments can be subtle. A Four-Star restaurant might lack the consistency or the special little details that set Five-Star dining experiences apart. A Four-Star hotel might fail to achieve the level of perfection in all areas that's demanded of a Five-Star property.

Rating categories reflect both the quality of an establishment and the features it offers its guests and patrons. For lodgings, ratings take into account the number and quality of facilities and guest services, the luxury of appointments, and the attitude and professionalism of staff and management. Restaurant evaluations emphasize quality of food, preparation, presentation, freshness of ingredients, quality of service, and attitude and professionalism of staff and management. Each restaurant is also viewed in terms of its own style, unique characteristics, decor, and ambience. Climate, historic, cultural, and artistic variations representative of regional differences are major factors in each rating.

Lodgings

Each listing provides the lodging's name, address, phone number (local and 800), and fax number. An added description highlights what's special about the property. Also included are details on the number and type of rooms available, room rates, seasons open (if not year-round), recreational and dining facilities on or adjacent to the establishment, the presence of a luxury level, and credit card information. (Note that Mobil Corporation credit cards cannot be used for payment of meals and room charges.) Symbols and abbreviations used in the listings are described in the section that follows. Facilities are on the premises unless otherwise noted.

All prices quoted in this book are expected to be in effect at the time of publication and during the entire year; however, prices cannot be guaranteed. In some localities there may be short-term price variations because of special events or holidays. Whenever possible, these price changes are noted. Certain resorts have complicated rate structures that vary with the time of year; it's a good idea to contact the property to confirm specific rates.

Restaurants

Listings give the name, address, and phone number, followed by a description of what makes the restaurant distinctive. Information provided includes hours and days of operation (if not open daily year-round), reservation policy, cuisine (if other than American), price range for each meal served, children's meals (if offered), specialties, and credit card information. In addition, special features such as chef ownership, ambience, and entertainment are noted. Symbols and abbreviations used in the listings are described in the section that follows.

Special Information for Travelers with Disabilities

The *Mobil Travel Guide* symbol D shown in accommodation and restaurant listings indicates establishments that are at least partially accessible to people with mobility problems.

The *Mobil Travel Guide* criteria for accessibility are unique to our publication. Please do not confuse them with the universal symbol for wheelchair accessibility. When the D symbol appears following a listing, the establishment is equipped with facilities to accommodate persons in wheelchairs as well as on crutches and the aged in need of easy access to doorways and rest room facilities. Persons with severe mobility problems, as well as the hearing and visually impaired, should not assume that there are facilities to meet their needs. We suggest travelers with disabilities phone an establishment before their visit to ascertain if their particular needs will be met.

The following facilities are available at all lodgings bearing our D symbol:

- ISA-designated parking near access ramps
- Level or ramped entryways to building
- Swinging building entryway doors minimum 3'0"
- Public rest rooms on main level with space to operate a wheelchair; handrails at commode areas
- Elevators equipped with grab bars and lowered control buttons
- Restaurants with accessible doorways; rest rooms with space to operate wheelchair; handrails at commode areas
- Minimum 3'0" width entryway to guest rooms
- Low-pile carpet in rooms
- Telephone at bedside and in bathroom
- Bed placed at wheelchair height
- Minimum 3'0" width doorway to bathroom
- Bath with open sink—no cabinet; room to operate wheelchair

- Handrails at commode areas; tub handrails
- Wheelchair accessible peephole in room entry door
- Wheelchair accessible closet rods and shelves

The following facilities are available at all restaurants bearing our D symbol:

- ISA-designated parking beside access ramps
- Level or ramped front entryways to building
- Tables to accommodate wheelchairs
- Main-floor rest rooms; minimum 3'0" width entryway
- Rest rooms with space to operate wheelchair; handrails at commode areas

Symbols and Abbreviations

Quality ratings

★★★★★ One of the best in the country

★★★★ Outstanding—worth a special trip

Type of establishment

- Lodging
- Restaurant

Symbols at end of listings

- **D** Facilities for the disabled
- Pets allowed
- Fishing
- Horseback riding
- Snow skiing nearby
- Golf, 9-hole minimum, on premises or privileges within 10 miles
- Tennis court(s) on premises or privileges within 5 miles
- Swimming
- Exercise equipment or room
- Jogging
- Major commercial airport within 2 miles
- No-smoking rooms
- Smoke detector and/or sprinkler system
- **SC** Senior citizen rates
- Business center
- Smoking allowed (restaurant listings only)
- Heart-healthy entrees on the menu

Terms and Abbreviations

A la carte entrees With a price, refers to entrees/main dishes only.

AP American plan (lodging plus all meals).

Bar Liquor, wine, and beer are served in a bar or cocktail lounge and usually with meals unless otherwise indicated (e.g., "wine, beer").

Business center The property has a business center accessible to all guests.

Business servs avail The property can perform/arrange at least two of the following services for a guest: audiovisual equipment rental, binding, computer rental, faxing, messenger services, modem availability, notary service, obtaining office supplies, photocopying, shipping, and typing.

Cable Standard cable service; (premium) indicates HBO, Disney, Showtime, etc. are available.

Ck-in; ck-out Check-in time (inn and resort listings only); check-out time.

Coin lndry Self-service laundry.

Complete meal Soup and/or salad, entree, dessert, and nonalcoholic beverage.

Continental bkfst Usually coffee and a roll or doughnut.

Cr cds A, American Express; C, Carte Blanche; D, Diners Club; DS, Discover; ER, en Route; JCB, Japanese Credit Bureau; MC, MasterCard; V, Visa.

D Followed by a price, indicates room rate for a "double"—two people in one room (one or two beds; charge may be higher if two double beds are offered).

Downhill/x-country ski Downhill and/or cross-country skiing within 20 miles of property.

Each addl Extra charge for each additional person beyond the stated number of persons for a given price.

EP European plan (lodging only).

Exc Except.

Exercise equipt Two or more pieces of exercise equipment on the premises.

Exercise rm Both exercise equipment and room, with an instructor on the premises.

Fax Facsimile machines available to all guests.

Golf privileges Privileges at a course within 10 miles.

Hols Holidays.

In-rm modem link Every guest room has a connection for a modem that's separate from the phone line.

Kit. or kits. A kitchen or kitchenette that contains stove or microwave, sink, and refrigerator and that is either part of the room or a separate room. If the kitchen is not fully equipped, the listing will indicate "no equipt" or "some equipt."

Luxury level A special section of a hotel, covering at least an entire floor, that offers increased luxury accommodations. Management must provide no less than three of these four services: separate check-in and check-out, concierge, private lounge, and private elevator service (key access). Complimentary breakfast and snacks are commonly offered.

MAP Modified American plan (lodging plus two meals).

Movies Prerecorded videos are available for rental.

No cr cds accepted No credit cards are accepted.

No phones Phones are assumed; only their absence is noted.

Parking There is a parking lot on the premises.

Prix fixe A full meal for a stated price; usually one price is quoted.

Res Reservations.

S Followed by a price, indicates room rate for a "single," i.e., one person.

Semi-a la carte Meals include vegetable, salad, soup, appetizer, or other accompaniments to the main dish.

Serv bar A service bar, where drinks are prepared for dining patrons only.

Serv charge Service charge is the amount added to the restaurant check in lieu of a tip.

Table d'hôte A full meal for a stated price, dependent upon entree selection; no a la carte options are available.

Tennis privileges Privileges at tennis courts within 5 miles.

TV Indicates color television.

Under certain age free Children under that age are not charged for if staying in room with a parent.

Valet parking An attendant is available to park and retrieve a car.

VCR VCRs in all guest rooms.

VCR avail VCRs are available for hookup in guest rooms.

Mobil Travel Guide 1997

Arizona

Marriott's Camelback Inn Resort Golf Club and Spa
Scottsdale

The Phoenician
Scottsdale

The Wigwam
Litchfield Park

California

Beverly Hills Hotel & Bungalows
Beverly Hills

Château du Sureau
Yosemite National Park

Hotel Bel-Air
Los Angeles

The Peninsula, Beverly Hills
Beverly Hills

The Ritz-Carlton, Laguna Niguel
Laguna Beach

The Ritz-Carlton, San Francisco
San Francisco

L'Orangerie
Hollywood

Colorado

The Broadmoor
Colorado Springs

C Lazy U Ranch
Granby

Little Nell
Aspen

Tall Timber
Durango

Connecticut

Mayflower Inn
Washington

Florida

The Ritz-Carlton, Naples
Naples

Georgia

The Cloister
Sea Island

The Dining Room at the Ritz-Carlton, Buckhead
Atlanta

Illinois

Charlie Trotter's
Chicago

Everest
Chicago

Le Français
Wheeling

New York

Carlyle
New York

Four Seasons
New York

The St Regis Hotel
New York

Chanterelle
New York

Five-Star Award Winners

Daniel
New York

Les Célébrités
New York

Lespinasse
New York

Ohio

Maisonette
Cincinnati

Pennsylvania

Le Bec-Fin
Philadelphia

Texas

Mansion on Turtle Creek
Dallas

Restaurant at the Mansion on Turtle Creek
Dallas

Vermont

Twin Farms
Woodstock

Virginia

Williamsburg Inn
Williamsburg

The Inn at Little Washington
Washington

The Inn at Little Washington
Washington

Washington

Four Seasons Olympic Hotel
Seattle

West Virginia

The Greenbrier
White Sulphur Springs

Canada

The Beaver Club
Montréal, Québec

Nuances
Montréal, Québec

Alabama

Birmingham

★★★★
WYNFREY AT RIVERCHASE GALLERIA
1000 Riverchase Galleria, Birmingham AL 35244
☎ *205/987–1600 or 800/476–7006*
FAX *205/988–4597*

This deluxe hotel, filled with marble, brass, and English Chippendale and French Regency furnishings, rises above the Riverchase Galleria, one of the largest malls in the Southeast. *329 rms, 16 story. S, D $125–$189; suites $250–$825; under 12 free; wkend rates. Crib free. Valet parking $6. TV; cable (premium), VCR avail. Pool; poolside serv. Restaurant 6 am–midnight. Rm serv 24 hrs. Piano bar. Ck-out 11 am. Convention facilities. Business servs avail. Concierge. Courtesy car, airport transportation. Golf privileges 10 mi. Exercise equipt; weights, bicycles, steam rm. Bathrm phone, refrigerator in suites. Luxury level. Cr cds: A, C, D, DS, MC, V*

Arizona

Carefree

★★★★ BOULDERS RESORT & CLUB
34631 N Tom Darlington Dr, Carefree AZ 85377
☎ 602/488-9009 or 800/553-1717
FAX 602/488-4118

Dramatic architecture, indigenous materials, and Native American art and furnishings make this large resort, with golf and tennis clubs and a spa, blend into a desert landscape dotted with massive granite boulders. Accommodations are in spacious adobe casitas with wood-burning, kiva-style fireplaces. *160 casitas, 1-2 story; also patio homes. Mid-Jan-Apr & late Dec: S $460; D $495; each addl $25; under 13 free; MAP avail; lower rates rest of yr. Serv charge $16 per rm per day. Closed July-Aug. Crib free. Pet accepted, some restrictions; $50. TV; cable (premium), VCR. 2 heated pools; whirlpool, poolside serv. Dining rm (public by res) 7-10:30 am, noon-2:30 pm, 6-9:30 pm. Box lunches. Snack bar. Rm serv. Bar 11-1 am. Ck-out noon, ck-in 4 pm. Grocery, coin lndry, package store 2 mi. Meeting rms. Business center. Gift shop. Airport transportation. Tennis, pro. 36-hole golf, greens fee $135, pro, putting green, driving range. Entertainment; dancing. Exercise rm; instructor, weights, bicycles, sauna, steam rm. Massage. Refrigerators, fireplaces. Private patios. Cr cds: A, C, D, MC, V*

Litchfield Park

★★★★★ THE WIGWAM
Litchfield & Indian School Rds, Litchfield Park AZ 85340
☎ 602/935-3811 or 800/327-0396
FAX 602/935-3737

This carefully landscaped 75-acre resort is known for its world-class golf. Spacious casitas and guest rooms are dec-

LITCHFIELD PARK

orated in subtle desert tones and feature oversize bathrooms and local artwork. Poolside entertainment and dining are available. The most casual of the restaurants overlooks the golf links, while the Arizona Kitchen serves Southwestern specialties, and the Terrace offers live music and dancing. A tennis center and gym are fully supervised. 🛪 *331 rms & suites in 1–2 story casitas. Jan–Apr: S, D $296–$356; each addl $25; suites $396–$1,446; under 18 free; golf plan; AP & MAP on request; family rates avail hol seasons; lower rates rest of yr. Crib free. Pet accepted, some restrictions. TV; cable (premium). 2 heated pools; poolside serv. Playground. Supervised child's activities (June–Sept & hols); ages 5–12. Dining rm (public by res) 6:30–10:30 am, 11:30 am–2:30 pm, 5–10 pm (also see THE ARIZONA KITCHEN). Rm serv 24 hrs. Box lunches, bkfst rides, steak fries. Bar 11–1 am. Ck-out 1 pm, ck-in 4 pm. Meeting rms. Business center. Valet serv. Gift shop. Barber, beauty shop. Airport transportation $20/person. Lighted tennis, pro. 54-hole golf, pro, greens fee $85–$95 (incl cart), putting greens. Stagecoach, hayrides. Bicycles. Skeet, trapshooting. Indoor, outdoor games. Soc dir; entertainment, dancing; special hol programs for families. Exercise equipt; weights, bicycles, whirlpool, sauna, steam rm. Masseuse. Some refrigerators. Some fireplaces, wet bars, minibars. Library. Private patios. Cr cds: A, C, D, DS, ER, JCB, MC, V*

✕ ★★★★
THE ARIZONA KITCHEN

In the Wigwam
Litchfield & Indian School Rds, Litchfield Park AZ 85340
☎ *602/935–3811*

As you might guess from the name, this restaurant serves Southwestern cuisine amid Southwestern artifacts, a brick floor and fireplace, and an open display kitchen. 🛪 *Hrs: 6–10:30 pm. Closed Sun; Mon in summer; also for 6 wks in July–Aug. Res accepted. Southwestern menu. Bar 4 pm–midnight. Wine list. A la carte entrees: dinner $18–$27. Specialties: smoked corn chowder, grilled sirloin of buffalo, chilean sea bass. Guitarist. Cr cds: A, C, D, DS, ER, JCB, MC, V*

D

ARIZONA

Phoenix

★★★★ ARIZONA BILTMORE

24th St & Missouri Ave, Phoenix AZ 85016
☎ *602/955–6600 or 800/950–0086*
FAX *602/381–7600*

The Biltmore, designed by Frank Lloyd Wright's colleague Albert Chase McArthur, is set on 250 acres of magnificent gardens with numerous varieties of palms, flowers and cacti. Stained-glass skylights and wrought-iron pilasters grace the lobby; rooms are filled with Wright-inspired furniture and tan and off-white marble baths. ✈ *502 rms, 2–4 story. Jan–Apr: S, D $380–$420; each addl $30; suites from $780; AP, MAP avail; golf plan; lower rates rest of yr. Crib avail. TV; cable (premium). Heated pools; wading pool, whirlpool, poolside serv, lifeguard. Supervised child's activities. Restaurants 7 am–midnight. Rm serv. Bar 11–1 am. Ck-out noon, ck-in 4 pm. Concierge. Shopping arcade. Barber, beauty shop. Lighted tennis. 36-hole golf, greens fee $110 (incl cart), putting greens, driving range. Bicycle rentals. Soc dir; entertainment, dancing. Rec rm. Exercise rm; instructor, weight machines, bicycles, sauna, steam machine. Aerobics classes. Refrigerators. Sun decks. Some private patios, balconies. Cr cds: A, MC, V*

★★★★ THE RITZ-CARLTON, PHOENIX

2401 E Camelback Rd, Phoenix AZ 85016
☎ *602/468–0700*
FAX *602/468–9883*

18th- and 19th-century European paintings and china collections decorate the large public rooms of this elegant hotel fronting Biltmore Fashion Square. ✈ *281 rms, 11 story. Jan–May: S, D $205–$255; suites $285–$385; under 12 free; lower rates rest of yr. Crib avail. TV; cable (premium). Heated pool; poolside serv. Restaurant 5–11 pm. Rm serv 24 hrs. Bar 11–1 am; entertainment. Ck-out noon. Convention facilities. Business center. Concierge. Gift shop. Covered parking. Airport, RR station, bus depot transportation; free trans-*

portation to golf courses. Lighted tennis. Golf privileges. Exercise rm; instructor, weight machines, treadmill, sauna. Massage. Bicycle rentals. Bathrm phones, minibars. Luxury level. Cr cds: A, C, D, DS, JCB, MC, V

 ★★★★
CHRISTOPHER'S
2398 E Camelback Rd, Phoenix AZ 85016
☎ *602/957–3214*

A glass-enclosed wine cellar is the focal point of this elegant, cherrywood-trimmed dining room. *Hrs: 6–10 pm; Fri & Sat to 11 pm. Closed Jan 1, Memorial Day, Labor Day; also Mon & Tues in summer. Res accepted. Contemporary French cuisine. Bar. Wine cellar, one of the largest in the state. Semi-a la carte: dinner $22–$32. Prix fixe: dinner $75, with wine $115. Specialties: crêpe foie gras, house-smoked salmon, chocolate mousse tower. Own baking. Valet parking. Chef-owned. Jacket. Totally nonsmoking. Cr cds: A, C, D, DS, MC, V*

D

 ★★★★
VINCENT GUERITHAULT ON CAMELBACK
3930 E Camelback Rd, Phoenix AZ 85018
☎ *602/224–0225*

One of the handful of Southwestern cuisine's originators, Guerithault is among the West's master chefs. Decor is country French. *Hrs: 11:30 am–2:30 pm, 6–10:30 pm; Sat from 5:30 pm. Closed major hols; also Sun June–Sept. Res accepted. Southwestern, Amer menu. Bar. Wine list. A la carte entrees: lunch $5.50–$8.95, dinner $19.25–$22. Specializes in mesquite-grilled lamb, chicken & seafood, homemade ice cream. Own baking. Valet parking. Open-air market on Sats, mid-Oct-mid-Apr. Cr cds: A, D, MC, V*

ARIZONA

Scottsdale

★★★★★
MARRIOTT'S CAMELBACK INN RESORT GOLF CLUB & SPA

5402 E Lincoln Dr, Scottsdale AZ 85253
☏ *602/948–1700 or 800/24-CAMEL*
FAX *602/951–8469*

This vintage desert resort on 125 landscaped acres is centered on a hilltop spa, where even the lap pool has mountain and sunset views. Large casita-style guest rooms and suites are decorated with Southwestern art and artifacts, cacti and rustic wooden furniture, and some rooms have views of the mountains. Several dining rooms are available. ✈ *427 rms in 1–2 story casitas. Jan–May: S, D $305–$355; suites $475–$1,700; AP addl $64 per person; MAP addl $48 per person; Camelback plan (bkfst, lunch) addl $29 per person; under 18 free; wkend rates; golf, tennis, spa, honeymoon and family packages avail; lower rates rest of yr. Crib free. Pet accepted. TV; cable (premium), VCR avail. 3 pools, heated; whirlpool, sauna, steam rm, poolside buffet, poolside serv, lifeguards. Supervised child's activities (June–Aug; also some wkends & hols); ages 3–12. Dining rm 6:30 am–10 pm. Rm serv to midnight. Box lunches. Bars 11–1 am. Ck-out noon, ck-in 4 pm. Coin lndry. Business center. Valet serv. Concierge. Barber, beauty shop. Gift & sport shops. Lighted tennis, pro. 36-hole golf, greens fee $95, electric cart free, teaching pros, putting greens, driving range, golf school. Bicycles. Lawn games. Soc dir; entertainment; movies winter & spring hols. Full service European health spa offers state-of-the-art equipment and training; includes extensive fitness and exercise facilities, body and beauty treatments, specially designed spa cuisine. Refrigerators, minibars. Wet bar, fireplace, private pool in some suites. Private patios; many balconies. Cr cds: A, C, D, DS, ER, JCB, MC, V*

★★★★★
THE PHOENICIAN

6000 E Camelback Rd, Scottsdale AZ 85251
☏ *602/941–8200 or 800/888–8234*
FAX *602/947–4311*

At the base of Camelback Mountain, an imposing main hotel overlooks 130 acres at this resort that masterfully blends nature, elaborate landscaping, fine art and architec-

SCOTTSDALE

ture and handcrafted furnishings. Bridges lead over a goldfish-stocked duck pond, and an upscale shopping mall is on site. Many of the dining rooms, lounges and bars offer panoramic views of downtown Phoenix. ✈ *580 rms: 460 rms in main bldg, 4–6 story, 95 casitas. EP, Sept–mid-June: S, D, casitas $370–$505; each addl $50; suites $1,000–$1,650; villas $1,500–$2,500; under 12 free; golf plans; spa & holiday packages; lower rates rest of yr. Crib free. TV; cable (premium), VCR avail (movies). 6 heated pools; 2 wading pools, poolside serv. Supervised child's activities; ages 5–13. Dining rms (public by res) 6 am–10 pm (also see MARY ELAINE'S). Rm serv 24 hrs. Bar 11–1 am; entertainment. Ck-out noon, ck-in 4 pm. Convention facilities. Business center. In-rm modem link. Bellhops. Valet serv. Concierge. Shopping arcade. Barber, beauty shop. Airport transportation. Sports dir. 12 lighted tennis courts, pro. 27-hole golf, greens fee $130–$160, pro, putting green, driving range. Hiking. Bicycle rentals. Lawn games. Exercise rm; instructor, weight machine, bicycles, whirlpool, sauna, steam rm. Massage. Complete spa center. Bathrm phones, minibars; some refrigerators, wet bars. Balconies. Picnic tables. Cr cds: A, C, D, DS, JCB, MC, V*

🏨 ★★★★
HYATT REGENCY SCOTTSDALE
7500 E Doubletree Ranch Rd, Scottsdale AZ 85258
☎ *602/991–3388*
FAX *602/483–5550*

Located on 640-acre Gainey Ranch, this resort features Sonoran desert landscaping—lagoons plied by gondolas, fountains, waterfalls and date palm trees. ✈ *486 units in main bldg, 4 story, 7 casitas on lake, 1–4 bedrm. Feb–mid-June: S, D $325–$425; suites $450–$2,500; under 18 free; golf packages; lower rates rest of yr. Crib free. TV; cable (premium), VCR avail. 10 heated pools; wading pool, poolside serv; clock tower with waterslide, sand beach. Playground. Supervised child's activities; ages 3–12. 3 restaurants (public by res) 6:30 am–10:30 pm. Rm serv 24 hrs. Bar noon–1 am. Ck-out noon, ck-in 2 pm. Meeting rms. Business center. Concierge. Gift shop. Complimentary valet parking. Airport transportation. Rec dir. 8 tennis courts, 4 lighted, pro. 27-hole golf, greens fee $105, pro, putting green, driving range. Bicycles. Lawn games. Exercise rm; instructor, weights, bicycles, sauna, steam rm. Massage and spa services. Minibars. Balconies. Fireplace, wet bar in casitas. Luxury level. Cr cds: A, C, D, DS, ER, JCB, MC, V*

ARIZONA

🏨 ★★★★
SCOTTSDALE PRINCESS

7575 E Princess Dr, Scottsdale AZ 85255
☎ *602/585-4848 or 800/223-1818*
FAX *602/585-0086*

Situated on 450 elaborately landscaped acres, with a waterfall in the central courtyard, this large resort offers airy rooms in a Spanish style. The golf course here is the site of the Phoenix Open, a yearly stop on the PGA Tour. 🐦 *650 rms, 3-4 story, 75 suites, 125 casitas. Jan-May: S, D $320-$400; each addl $30; suites $490-$2,500; casitas $440-$490; under 12 free; golf & tennis plans; spa & hol packages; lower rates rest of yr. TV; cable, VCR avail. 3 heated pools; poolside serv. Supervised child's activities (Memorial Day-Labor Day & hols); ages 5-12. Dining rms 6:30 am-11 pm (also see LA HACIENDA and MARQUESA). Rm serv 24 hrs. 7 bars 11-1 am; entertainment, dancing. Ck-out noon, ck-in 4 pm. Convention facilities. Business center. Concierge. Shopping arcade. Barber, beauty shop. Valet parking. Airport, RR station, bus depot transportation. Lighted tennis, pro. 36-hole golf, greens fee $55-$155, pro, putting green, driving range. Croquet, badminton. Racquetball, squash, vollyball, basketball. Exercise rm; instructor, weight machines, bicycles, whirlpool, sauna, steam rm. Massage. Stocked lagoons; fishing rods and tackle box avail for guests. Bathrm phones, refrigerators, minibars. Some fireplaces. Private patios, balconies. Cr cds: A, C, D, DS, ER, JCB, MC, V*

🍽 ★★★★
LA HACIENDA

In the Scottsdale Princess
7575 E Princess Dr, Scottsdale AZ 85255
☎ *602/585-4848*

Situated in a tile-roofed hacienda and furnished with carved tables and chairs, this semiformal restaurant offers refined Sonoran cuisine. 🐦 *Hrs: 6-10 pm; Fri & Sat to 11 pm. Res accepted. Mexican menu. Bar from 5 pm. Wine list. A la carte entrees: dinner $15.50-$25. Child's meals. Specialties: filete al chipotle (char-broiled beef tenderloin), ahi steak with chile pesto, suckling pig. Own baking. Strolling mariachis. Valet parking. Outdoor dining. Continental service. Cr cds: A, C, D, DS, ER, JCB, MC, V*

MARQUESA
In the Scottsdale Princess
7575 E Princess Dr, Scottsdale AZ 85255
☏ *602/585-4848*

Portraits of Spanish royalty decorate this elegant yet casual restaurant specializing in Catalan cuisine. 🍽 *Hrs: 6-10 pm; Fri, Sat to 11 pm; Sun brunch 10:30 am-2:30 pm. Closed Sun-Tues Father's Day-Labor Day. Res accepted. Spanish menu. Bar. Wine cellar. A la carte entrees: dinner $23-$32. Sun brunch $31. Child's meals. Specialties: paella Valenciana, sarsuela de marisc, gambes Marquesa. Tapas bar. Flamenco guitarist Sun brunch. Valet parking. Outdoor dining. Cr cds: A, C, D, DS, ER, JCB, MC, V*

MARY ELAINE'S
In the Phoenician
6000 E Camelback Rd, Scottsdale AZ 85251
☏ *602/423-2530*

The round tables in this bilevel dining room on the top floor of the Phoenician's main building offer panoramic views of the Valley of the Sun. Innovative Continental French cuisine uses fresh organic ingredients. 🍽 *Hrs: 6-10 pm; Fri, Sat to 11 pm. Closed Mon-Wed mid-June-mid-Aug. Res accepted. Contemporary French cuisine. Bar. Wine cellar. A la carte entrees: dinner $29-$38. Complete meals: dinner $75-$95. Child's meals. Specializes in fresh seafood from around the world, rack of lamb, veal. Entertainment. Valet parking. Intimate dining in elegant atmosphere. Overlooks valley. Jacket. Cr cds: A, C, D, DS, JCB, MC, V*

Sedona

CANYON VILLA BED & BREAKFAST
125 Canyon Circle Dr, Sedona AZ 86351
☏ *520/284-1226 or 800/453-1166*
FAX *520/284-2114*

Southwestern decor prevails here, but each guest room is individually decorated. 🏠 *11 rms, 2 story. S $125-$205;*

ARIZONA

D $135–$215; each addl $25. Children over 10 yrs preferred. TV; cable, VCR avail. Heated pool. Complimentary full bkfst, tea; afternoon refreshments, evening snacks. Restaurant nearby. Ck-out 11 am, ck-in 3–6 pm. Business servs avail. Tennis privileges. 18-hole golf privileges, greens fee $65–$75. Health club privileges. Patios, balconies. Totally nonsmoking. Cr cds: MC, V

ENCHANTMENT RESORT
525 Boynton Canyon Rd, Sedona AZ 86336
☎ *520/282–2900 or 800/826–4180*
FAX *520/282–9249*

Enchantment is an active resort, set in Boynton Canyon in the heart of Red Rock Country. You have a choice of spacious studios or two- to three-bedroom pueblo-style casitas, which dot the hillsides around the main lodge. Rooms are decorated in authentic Southwestern style; excellent sports facilities are available. *162 units, 56 kit. casitas (2-bedrm). Mar–June, Sept–Nov: S, D $225–$300; suites $365–$425; kit. casitas $565–$650; lower rates rest of yr. Crib free. TV; cable (premium), VCR avail (movies). Heated pool; whirlpool, poolside serv. Playground. Supervised child's activities; ages 4–12. Complimentary coffee in rms. Restaurant 7 am–2:30 pm, 5:30–9:30 pm. Rm serv. Box lunches, snacks, picnics. Bar 11–1 am; entertainment Fri, Sat. Ck-out noon, ck-in 4 pm. Bellhops. Concierge. Valet serv. Guest lndry. Gift shop. Meeting rms. Business servs avail. In-rm modem link. Sports dir. Tennis, pro. Golf privileges. Hiking. Bicycle rentals. Lawn games. Game rm. Exercise rm; instructor, weight machines, treadmills, steam rm, sauna. Massages, facials. Patios; some balconies. Picnic tables. Casitas surround main lodge in Boynton Canyon. Cr cds: A, DS, MC, V*

THE GRAHAM BED AND BREAKFAST INN
150 Canyon Circle Dr, Sedona AZ 86351
☎ *520/284–1425 or 800/228–1425*
FAX *520/284–0767*

Rooms here are individually decorated, some with antiques; each has a scenic view. *6 rms, 2 story. S $94–$214;*

D $109–$229; each addl $20. TV; cable (premium), VCR (movies). Pool; whirlpool. Complimentary full bkfst, afternoon refreshments. Ck-out noon, ck-in 3 pm. Business servs avail. Gift shop. Balconies. Fireplace, whirlpool in some rms. Guest library. Bicycles avail. Totally nonsmoking. Cr cds: DS, MC, V

★★★★
L'AUBERGE DE SEDONA
L'Auberge Ln, Sedona AZ 86336
☏ *520/282–1661 or 800/272–6777*
FAX *520/282–2885*

This romantic French country retreat is situated on beautiful grounds along Oak Creek. 58 units, 2 story, 31 cottages. S, D $200–$265; cottage $275–$385; each addl $20; under 12 free. Crib free. TV; cable (premium), VCR avail. Heated pool; whirlpool. Complimentary coffee in rms, library. Dining rm 7 am–10 pm. Rm serv. Ck-out 11 am. Concierge. Business servs avail. In-rm modem link. Free airport transportation. Tennis privileges. Health club privileges. Lawn games. Refrigerators, minibars. Some balconies. Cr cds: A, C, D, DS, MC, V

Tucson

★★★★
LOEWS VENTANA CANYON RESORT
7000 N Resort Dr, Tucson AZ 85750
☏ *520/299–2020 or 800/234–5117*
FAX *520/299–6832*

Spectacularly sited at 3,013 feet, with city and mountain views, this luxurious desert resort overlooks an 80-ft waterfall whose waters feed a small lake on the 93-acre property. The modern guest rooms are done in soft pastels and light woods. 398 rms, 4 story. Jan-June: S, D $305–$385; each addl $25; suites $750–$2,100; under 18 free; lower rates rest of yr. Crib free. TV; cable (premium), VCR avail. Heated pool; whirlpool, poolside serv. Playground. Supervised child's activities; ages 5–12. High tea service. 4 dining rms (also see VENTANA ROOM). Rm serv 24 hrs. Bar 11–1 am. Ck-out noon, ck-in 3 pm. Meeting rms. Business center. In-rm modem link. Concierge. Shopping arcade. Beauty salon. Lighted tennis. 18-hole golf, greens fee $60–$125, putting green, driving range.

ARIZONA

Pro shop. Lawn games. Exercise rm; instructor, weight machines, bicycles, sauna, steam rm. Bicycle rentals. Massage. Bathrm phones. Minibars, some refrigerators. Private patios, balconies. Picnic tables. Cr cds: A, C, D, DS, JCB, MC, V

★★★★
OMNI TUCSON NATIONAL GOLF RESORT & SPA
2727 W Club Dr, Tucson AZ 85741
☎ 520/297–2271 or 800/528–4856
FAX 520/742–2452

This attractively landscaped resort, with views of the Santa Catalina Mountains, occupies 650 acres dotted with 11 lakes. 167 units, 2 story. Jan–Apr: S, D $265–$325; each addl $10; suites $325–$350; under 18 free; golf plans; lower rates rest of yr. TV; cable (premium), VCR avail. Heated pool; whirlpool, poolside serv. 3 restaurants. Dining rm 6:30 am–10 pm. Rm serv to midnight. Box lunches, snack bar. Bars 10–1 am; Sun from noon. Ck-out noon, ck-in 4 pm. Convention facilities. Business center. Concierge. Gift shop. Barber, beauty shop. Sports dir. Lighted tennis, pro. 27-hole championship golf, greens fee $95–$125, pro, putting green, driving ranges. Soc dir. Entertainment. Exercise rm; instructor, weights, bicycles, sauna, steam rm. Massage. Full service spa. Wet bars, minibars; many fireplaces. Private patios, balconies. Cr cds: A, C, D, DS, MC, V

★★★★
SHERATON EL CONQUISTADOR RESORT & COUNTRY CLUB
10000 N Oracle Rd, Tucson AZ 85737
☎ 520/544–5000 or 800/325–7832
FAX 520/544–1224

A huge copper mural filled with cowboys and cacti, as well as a wide-window view of one of the pools set against a backdrop of the rugged Santa Catalina Mountains, set the mood of this Southwestern resort. 428 rms. Jan–May: S, D $220–$280; suites, studio rms $265–$600; under 17 free; golf, tennis plans; lower rates rest of yr. Crib free. Pet accepted, some restrictions. TV; cable (premium), VCR avail. Heated pools; poolside serv. Supervised child's activities; ages 5–12.

Coffee in rms. 6 dining rms 6 am–11 pm. Rm serv to 2 am. Bar 11:30–1 am, Sun from 10:30 am; entertainment. Ck-out noon, ck-in 4 pm. Convention facilities. Business center. In-rm modem link. Bellhops. Valet serv. Concierge. Shopping arcade. Beauty shop. Pro shop. Sports dir. Lighted tennis, pro. 45-hole golf, greens fee (incl cart) $95–$135 ($45–$60 in summer), pro, putting green, driving range. Bicycles. Bkfst & evening rides; hayrides. Exercise rms; instructor, weights, bicycles, whirlpools, sauna. Raquetball, basketball & volleyball courts. Lawn games. Hiking & nature trails. Minibars; some bathrm phones, wet bars, fireplaces. Private patios, balconies. Cr cds: A, C, D, DS, ER, JCB, MC, V

★★★★
THE WESTIN LA PALOMA
3800 E Sunrise Dr, Tucson AZ 85718
☎ *520/742–6000 or 800/876–3683*
FAX *520/577–5878*

Guest rooms at this family resort on extensive, elaborately landscaped grounds are elegantly decorated in Southwestern colors and copper tones. Antiques and artwork are displayed. 487 units, 3 story. Jan–May: S, D $295–$385; each addl $30; suites from $495; under 18 free; addl resort serv fee of $71 per day; golf, tennis plans; lower rates rest of yr. Crib free. TV; cable (premium). 2 heated pools; whirlpool, poolside serv, waterslide. Supervised child's activities; ages 6 months–12 yrs. Coffee in rms. Dining rm (public by res) 6:30 am–10 pm. Box lunches, snack bar, picnics. Rm serv 24 hrs. Bar 11–1 am. Ck-out noon, ck-in 4 pm. Package store 2 mi. Convention facilities. Business center. Bellhops. Valet serv. Concierge. Beauty shop. Shopping arcade. Valet parking. Airport transportation; mall shuttle. Sports dir. 12 lighted tennis courts (4 clay), pro. 27-hole golf (Jack Nicklaus Signature Design), greens fee $135, pro, putting green, driving range. Lawn games. Horseback privileges 15 mi. Soc dir; entertainment, movies. Rec rm. Exercise rm; instructor, weight machines, steam rm. Massage. Some fireplaces; whirlpool, sauna in suites. Cr cds: A, C, D, DS, ER, JCB, MC, V

ARIZONA

JANOS
150 N Main, Tucson AZ 85701
☎ 520/884–9426

Situated in an adobe home built in 1864, this innovative restaurant is divided into several intimate and elegant dining rooms filled with flowers. *Hrs: 5:30 pm until closing. Closed Sun; Jan 1, Dec 25; also Mon during mid-May–Nov. Res accepted. French-inspired Southwest regional cuisine. Bar. Wine cellar. Semi-a la carte: dinner $19–$31. Summer Samplers menu (May–Sept, Tues–Sat) $12.95. Preperformance menu (during theater season) $22.50. Specialties: pepito-roasted venison, mushroom & brie relleno, lobster bisque. Fresh ingredients; own herb and vegetable garden. Own baking, pastas, brioche. Parking. Outdoor dining. Chef-owned. Cr cds: A, D, MC, V*

THE TACK ROOM
2800 N Sabino Canyon Rd, Tucson AZ 85715
☎ 520/722–2800

The dining room is elegant in this white-adobe hacienda furnished in the Southwestern style in hues of blue, copper and wine. Views take in the nearby mesquite grove and the mountains beyond. *Hrs: from 6 pm. Closed Mon off-season; first 2 wks of July. Res suggested. Southwestern, Amer cuisine. Bar from 5:30 pm. Wine cellar. A la carte entrees: dinner $24.95–$34.75. Child's meals. Specialties: rack of lamb with mesquite honey & lime, roast duckling with pistachio crust & glaze of jalapeño and lime, Arizona four-pepper steak, herb-painted salmon. Own baking. Valet parking. Family-owned. Cr cds: A, C, D, DS, JCB, MC, V*

VENTANA ROOM
In the Loews Ventana Canyon Resort
7000 N Resort Dr, Tucson AZ 85750
☎ 520/299–2020

There's a spectacular view of downtown Tucson and beyond from the picture windows of this elegantly appointed resort restaurant. Sophisticated, contemporary

TUCSON

American seasonal cuisine featuring fresh local and imported ingredients is complemented by harp music.
Hrs: 6–9 pm; Fri & Sat to 10 pm. Res accepted. Bar. Wine cellar. A la carte entrees: dinner $20–$30. Prix fixe: dinner $45–$55. Specialties: pan-seared ahi tuna with coriander crust, grilled rack of lamb with toasted cumin sauce, mesquite-grilled game. Own pastries. Valet parking. Totally nonsmoking. Cr cds: A, C, D, DS, JCB, MC, V

D

California

Avalon (Catalina Island)

⭐⭐⭐⭐
INN ON MT. ADA
398 Wrigley Rd, Avalon (Catalina Island) CA 90704
☎ *310/510-2030 or 800/608-7669*
FAX *310/510-2237*

Occupying historic Wrigley Mansion, this luxury inn offers elegantly decorated guest rooms and spectacular views of the ocean, harbor and mountains. 🐾 *6 rms, 2 story. AP, June-Oct & wkends: D $340-$620; each addl $100; lower wkday rates rest of yr. TV; cable (premium) in library; VCR avail (movies). Full bkfst 8:30-10 am, light deli lunch, full dinner; refreshments, wine. Ck-out 11 am, ck-in 2 pm. Transportation to and from boats and helicopter. Many fireplaces. Balconies. Use of golf cart during stay. Totally nonsmoking. Cr cds: MC, V*

Berkeley

⭐⭐⭐⭐
CHEZ PANISSE RESTAURANT & CAFE
1517 Shattuck Ave, Berkeley CA 94709
☎ *510/548-5525*

Fresh, organically grown vegetables and fruits are hand-picked daily at this local favorite. The upstairs cafe is homey and casual; downstairs dining is a bit more formal. There's an exceptional wine list and delicious home-baked desserts. 🐾 *Hrs: Cafe (upper level) 11:30 am-3 pm, 5-10:30 pm; Fri & Sat 11:30 am-4 pm, 5-11:30 pm; Restaurant dining rm (main floor) 6-9:15 pm. Closed Sun; Dec 25. Res accepted in cafe; required in dining rm. Contemporary continental menu. Beer. Wine list. A la carte entrees: lunch $15-$19, dinner $25-$30. Prix fixe: dinner $35-$65. Own baking. Cr cds: A, DS, MC, V*

Beverly Hills

★★★★★
BEVERLY HILLS HOTEL & BUNGALOWS

9641 Sunset Blvd, Beverly Hills CA 90210
☎ *310/276-2251*
FAX *800/283-8885*

The legendary Pink Palace is back in all its original glory. Renovations are done in the trademark pink, green and white throughout. Guests enter the hotel under a green-and-white striped awning surrounded by lush gardens. The lobby features a huge chandelier, original artwork, three fireplaces and a harpist. No two rooms are alike, and all are lovely. The famous pool and cabanas are magnificent and state-of-the-art health club facilities are available. *203 rms, 37 suites, 53 bungalows, 1-4 story, 12 kits. S, D $275-$350; suites $595-$3,000; 1-4 bdrm kit. bungalows $275-$2,750; under 12 free. Crib free. Valet parking $15. TV; cable (premium), VCR (movies). Heated pool; poolside serv, whirlpool. Restaurants 7-2 am. Rm serv 24 hrs. Ck-out noon. Meeting rms. Business servs avail. In-rm modem link. Concierge. Beauty shop. Shopping arcade. Lighted tennis, pro. Exercise equipt; weights, treadmill. First building in Beverly Hills (1912). Quiet location on 12 acres; elaborate landscaping; gardens. Cr cds: A, C, D, JCB, MC, V*

★★★★★
THE PENINSULA, BEVERLY HILLS

9882 Little Santa Monica Blvd, Beverly Hills CA 90212
☎ *310/551-2888 or 800/462-7899*
FAX *310/788-2319*

Beyond a semicircular driveway, a fountain and an exclusive jewelry shop lies the polished marble lobby of this ultra-luxurious French Renaissance-style hotel. Off the lobby are a clubby bar that needs a velvet rope most nights and a lounge of fat sofas for drinks, tea, hors d'oeuvres and supper. Deep-carpeted, pastel-hued guest rooms are distinguished by high-quality artwork, down-filled duvets, personal fax machines (on request) and oversize bathrooms in polished marble, outfitted with large all-glass shower stalls with two shower heads, plush Frette robes and separated oval tubs. The fifth floor features a full-service spa and rooftop pool surrounded by private bedouin tent cabanas. *200 units, 4*

CALIFORNIA

story, 32 suites, 16 villas (2 story, 1–2 bedrm). S, D $315–$450; each addl $30; suites & villas $600–$3,000; under 12 free; wkend rates. Crib free. Valet parking $17. TV; cable (premium), VCR (movies). Heated rooftop pool; poolside serv. Complimentary beverages on arrival. Restaurant 6:30–11:00 am, 11:30 am–2:30 pm, 6:30–10:30 pm. Rm serv 24 hrs. Bar from 11:30 am; pianist. Ck-out noon. Meeting rms. Business center. In-rm modem link. Concierge. Gift shop. Clothing & jewelry stores. Airport transportation; Rolls-Royce limos avail. Tennis privileges. 18-hole golf privileges, pro, putting green, driving range. Exercise rm; instructor, weight machine, treadmill, whirlpool, sauna. Massage. Aerobics classes. Bathrm phones, stocked minibars; many wet bars. Balconies. Cr cds: A, C, D, DS, ER, JCB, MC, V

★★★★
REGENT BEVERLY WILSHIRE
9500 Wilshire Blvd, Beverly Hills CA 90212
☎ *310/275–5200 or 800/545–4000*
FAX *310/274–2851*

Sited at the south end of Rodeo Drive, this hotel is often home to visiting celebrities. *275 rms, 10 & 12 story, 69 suites. S, D $255–$395; suites $425–$4,000; under 18 free. Covered parking, valet $18. TV; cable (premium), VCR avail (movies). Heated pool; poolside serv. Restaurant (see THE DINING ROOM). Rm serv 24 hrs. Bar 11–2 am; entertainment. Ck-out noon. Convention facilities. Business center. In-rm modem link. Concierge. Gift shop. Beauty shop. Exercise equipt; weights, bicycles, 2 whirlpools, sauna, steam rm. Masseur. Bathrm phones, refrigerators. Some balconies. Cr cds: A, C, D, DS, ER, JCB, MC, V*

✕ ★★★★
THE DINING ROOM
In the Regent Beverly Wilshire
9500 Wilshire Blvd, Beverly Hills CA 90212
☎ *310/275–5200*

In a famous hotel facing Rodeo Drive and the Hollywood Hills, this superb restaurant with a display kitchen is decorated in Grand European style. *Hrs: 7 am–2 pm, 6–11 pm; Sat 10:30 am–2 pm, 6–11 pm. Res accepted. Continental menu. Bar 11–2 am; pianist. Wine cellar. A la carte entrees: bkfst $6–$20, lunch $12–$26, dinner $16–$30.*

Prix fixe: dinner $58. Specializes in mesquite-grilled meats and fish. Own baking. Valet parking. Seasonal menu with daily specials. Dancing Thurs-Sat. Jacket. Cr cds: A, C, D, DS, ER, JCB, MC, V

Big Sur

★★★★
VENTANA
CA 1, Big Sur CA 93920
☎ *408/667-2331 or 800/628-6500*
FAX *408/667-2419*

This secluded hideaway, composed of luxurious wooden lodges, has spectacular views of the Big Sur ocean horizon. 🐾 *59 rms, 1-2 story. S, D $195-$475; each addl $50; suites $475-$970. TV; cable, VCR (movies). 2 heated pools; sauna, Japanese hot baths, poolside beverage serv (summer). Complimentary continental bkfst. Complimentary wine & cheese 4-5:30 pm. Dining rm noon-10 pm. Bar 11 am-midnight. Ck-out 1 pm, ck-in 4:30 pm. Business servs avail. Bellhops. Exercise equipt; weights, treadmill. Spa. Massage. Wet bars; many fireplaces; some whirlpools. Balconies. Sun deck. Cr cds: A, C, D, DS, MC, V*

Borrego Springs

★★★★
LA CASA DEL ZORRO
3845 Yaqui Pass Rd, Borrego Springs CA 92004
☎ *619/767-5323 or 800/824-1884*
FAX *619/767-4782*

This desert resort, surrounded by Anza Borrego State Park, offers a variety of services and amenities. 🐾 *77 units, 19 cottages. Feb-Apr: S, D $95-$220; suites $260-$340; cottages $160-$505; under 8 free; lower rates rest of yr. Crib free. TV; cable (premium), VCR avail (movies). Heated pools; whirlpools. Supervised child's activities hols & special occasions by prior arrangement. Restaurant 7 am-10 pm. Rm serv to 11 pm. Bar 11-2 am; entertainment Thurs-Sat. Ck-out noon, ck-in 4 pm. Meeting rm. Business servs avail. Bellhops. Concierge. Gift shop. Beauty shop. Lighted tennis, pro. Bicycles. Exercise equipt;*

CALIFORNIA

weight machines, bicycles. Massage. Minibar in suites. Some fireplaces. Golf adj. Cr cds: A, C, D, DS, MC, V

Carmel

PACIFIC'S EDGE
In the Highlands Inn
Box 1700, Carmel CA 93921
☎ *408/622–5445*

Dramatic views of cypress trees and surf highlight this restaurant. ✈ *Hrs: 11:30 am–2 pm, 6–10 pm; Fri & Sat to 10:30 pm; Sun brunch 10 am–2 pm. Res accepted. Contemporary regional cuisine. Bar 11–2 am. Wine cellar. A la carte entrees: lunch $11.50–$14.50, dinner $21–$29. Prix fixe: dinner $45; with wine $70. Sun brunch $28. Specialties: Monterey Bay salmon, pancetta-wrapped loin of venison, classic crème brulée. Entertainment evenings. Valet parking. Cr cds: A, C, D, DS, JCB, MC, V*

STONEPINE
150 E Carmel Valley Rd, Carmel CA 93924
☎ *408/659–2245*
FAX *408/659–5160*

Built in 1928 as the estate of a banking family, this inn sits on 330 secluded acres and offers extensive equestrian services. ✈ *15 suites, 2 story. No A/C. S, D $225–$750; each addl $50; 2-day min wkends, 3-day min hols. TV; cable (premium), VCR (free movies). Heated pool. Children's activities may be arranged. Children over 13 yrs only. Complimentary full bkfst; afternoon tea/sherry. Dining rm (by res). 24 hrs rm serv. Ck-out noon, ck-in 3 pm. Business servs avail. In-rm modem link. Concierge serv. Luggage handling. Free Monterey airport transportation. Tennis. Refrigerators. Cr cds: A, MC, V.*

CORONADO

Carmel Valley

CARMEL VALLEY RANCH
1 Old Ranch Rd, Carmel CA 93923
☎ *408/625-9500 or 800/4-CARMEL*
FAX *408/624-2858*

Sited on 1,700 acres in the Santa Lucia Mountains, this hideaway with a guarded front gate offers contemporary California ranch-style suites. Original art and elaborate landscaping add character. 🏷 *100 suites. July-Oct: S, D $325-$850; each addl $20; under 16 free; lower rates rest of yr. Crib free. TV; cable (premium), VCR avail (movies). 2 heated pools; 6 whirlpools, sauna, poolside serv. Supervised child's activities (June-Sept); ages 5-14. Restaurants 7 am-2 pm; dining rm 6-10 pm. Box lunches, snack bar. Bar 11 am-midnight. Ck-out noon, ck-in 4 pm. Meeting rms. Business servs avail. In-rm modem link. Concierge. Gift shop. Exercise equipt; bicycles, treadmill. Tennis, pro. 18-hole golf, pro, putting green, driving range, pro shop. Entertainment Thurs-Sun. Refrigerators, fireplaces. Private decks, balconies. Cr cds: A, C, D, DS, JCB, MC, V*

Coronado

HOTEL DEL CORONADO
1500 Orange Ave, Coronado CA 92118
☎ *619/435-6611 or 800/468-3533*
FAX *619/522-8266*

Built in 1888, this historic and social landmark has rooms and suites in the original ornate Victorian building. The public areas are grand; a lower-level shopping arcade lined with historic photographs is fascinating. 🏷 *692 rms, 311 A/C. S, D from $179; each addl $25; suites from $499; under 18 free. Crib free. Parking $10; valet $14. TV; VCR avail. 2 heated pools; whirlpool, poolside serv. Supervised child's activities (mid-June-Labor Day & major hols). Dining rm 6:30-3 am. Rm serv 24 hrs. Bar 7-2 am; entertainment. Ck-out noon, ck-in 3 pm. Convention facilities. Business center. In-rm modem link. Concierge. Shopping arcade. Barber, beauty shop. Lighted tennis, pro. Game rm. Exercise rm; instructor, weights, bicycles, sauna. Massage. Minibars; many bathrm* phones. Many private patios, balconies. On swimming beach; sail and power boat rentals avail at hotel docks. Cr cds: A, C, D, DS, JCB, MC, V

LE MERIDIEN SAN DIEGO AT CORONADO

2000 2nd St, Coronado CA 92118
☏ *619/435–3000 or 800/543–4300*
FAX *619/435–3032*

Flamingos greet you at the entrance of this luxury resort, and other exotic wildlife roam the 16 acres of landscaped grounds that include koi-stocked streams and lush lagoons. The interior of the hotel reflects its French heritage and California setting. ✈ 300 rms, 3 story, 28 villas. S, D $185–$255; each addl $20; suites, villas $485–$795; under 12 free. Crib free. Covered parking $8; valet. TV; cable (premium), VCR avail. 3 heated pools; poolside serv. Restaurant 6:30 am–10 pm (also see MARIUS). Rm serv 24 hrs. Bar 4 pm–1 am; entertainment Fri & Sat. Ck-out noon. Convention facilities. Business center. In-rm modem link. Concierge. Shops. Lighted tennis, pro, shop, tennis clinic. Exercise rm; instructor, weight machines, bicycles, whirlpool, sauna. Massage. Minibars. Private patios. On bay; scuba, snorkeling, windsurfing classes on request. Bike rental with guide; floral & wildlife tour. European health spa facilities. Pier; 2 slips. Cr cds: A, C, D, DS, ER, JCB, MC, V

LOEWS CORONADO BAY RESORT

4000 Coronado Bay Rd, Coronado CA 92118
☏ *619/424–4000 or 800/235–6397*
FAX *619/424–4400*

Located on a 15-acre peninsula, this full-service resort has a New England seaside ambiance with sweeping views and an 80-slip marina. ✈ 440 rms, 3 story. S, D $195–$245; each addl $20; suites $395–$1,400; under 18 free; tennis & other package plans avail. Crib free. Pet accepted. TV; cable, VCR avail. 3 pools, heated; poolside serv. Supervised child's activities. Restaurant 6–10 pm. Box lunches. Rm serv 24 hrs. Bar 11–2 am; entertainment, dancing. Ck-out noon, ck-in 3 pm. Grocery. Complimentary guest lndry. Package store. Convention facilities. Business center. In-rm modem link. Bellhops. Valet serv. Concierge. Gift shop. Barber, beauty shop. Sports dir. 5 lighted tennis courts, pro. Beach, boats, water skiing, swimming. Bicycles (rentals). Lawn games. Game rm. Exercise equipt; weight machine, treadmill, whirlpools, sauna. Massage. Bathrm phones, minibars; some wet bars. Refrigerator avail. Balconies. Cr cds: A, C, D, DS, JCB, MC, V

MARIUS
In the Le Meridian San Diego at Coronado
2000 2nd St, Coronado CA 92118
☏ *619/435–3000*

Marius has an old-world feel that's supported by antiques, original oil paintings and iron wall lamps with tear-drop glass ornaments. The outstanding wine list is a welcome accompaniment to the excellent food and impeccable presentation. ✈ *Hrs: 6–10 pm. Closed Sun & Mon. Res accepted. French Provençale menu. Serv bar. Wine list. Prix fixe: dinner $49, with wine $69. Complete meals: dinner 3 course $39, 4 course $45, 5 course $50. Specializes in gourmet southern French cuisine. Own pastries. Valet parking. Mediterranean atmosphere. Cr cds: A, C, D, DS, ER, JCB, MC, V*

Del Mar

L'AUBERGE DEL MAR RESORT & SPA
1540 Camino del Mar, Del Mar CA 92014
☏ *619/259–1515 or 800/553–1336*
FAX *619/755–4940*

This resort in the village of Del Mar overlooks the Pacific Ocean, which is just a block away. Some rooms have coastal views. ✈ *120 rms, 3 story. S, D $169–$339; each addl $20; suites $550–$950; package plans. Crib avail. Valet, underground parking (fee). TV; cable, VCR avail (movies). 2 heated pools; poolside serv. Restaurant 6:30–10 am, 11:30 am–2:30 pm, 6–10 pm. Bar 11–1 am. Ck-out noon, ck-in 4 pm. Concierge. Business servs avail. Shopping arcade. Lighted tennis. 18-hole golf privileges. Exercise rm; instructor, weights, stair machine, sauna, steam rm. Massage.*

CALIFORNIA

Full-service European spa. Minibars. Some fireplaces. Cr cds: A, C, D, DS, JCB, MC, V

Fort Ross State Historic Park

★★★★
TIMBERHILL RANCH
35755 Hauser Bridge Rd, Cazadero CA 95421
☎ 707/847–3258
FAX 707/847–3342

At this secluded ranch on 80 wooded acres, the cedar guest cottages are positioned for maximum privacy. *15 cottages. No rm phones. MAP: S $295; D $335–$365; each addl $175; wkly, winter rates; higher rates: Jan 1, Thanksgiving, Dec 25. TV. Pool; whirlpool, poolside serv. Complimentary continental bkfst. Complimentary coffee in rms. Dining rm (public by res) 11:30 am–2:30 pm, 7–9 pm. Rm serv (bkfst delivered to cottages). Ck-out noon, ck-in 4 pm. Meeting rms. Business servs avail. In-rm modem link. Bellhops. Concierge. Gift shop. Tennis. Hiking. Lawn games. Game rm. Masseuse. Refrigerators, minibars, fireplaces. Balconies. Electric carts provide transportation about grounds. Cr cds: A, C, D, MC, V*

Half Moon Bay

★★★★
SEAL COVE INN
221 Cypress Ave, Moss Beach CA 94038
☎ 415/728–4114 or 800/995–9987
FAX 415/728–4116

Rooms in this inn are individually decorated with country antiques and wood-burning fireplaces. A path through an adjacent cypress grove leads to an ocean bluff near protected tidal pools. *8 rms, 2 story, 2 suites. No A/C. S, D $165–$250; each addl $25; suites $250; 2-night min stay hols. TV; VCR (movies avail). Complimentary full bkfst, coffee, tea, wine. Restaurant nearby. Ck-out 11 am, ck-in 3 pm. Meeting rms. Business servs avail. Refrigerators, minibars. Many balconies. Picnic tables. Totally nonsmoking. Cr cds: A, DS, MC, V*

Hollywood (L.A.)

✕ ★★★★★
L'ORANGERIE
903 N La Cienega Blvd, Hollywood (L.A.) CA 90069
☎ *310/652–9770*

L'Orangerie has not gone the casual route of many L.A. restaurants. The atmosphere is as elegantly French as the fine cuisine, thanks to artful lighting, tall Palladian windows, decor reminiscent of a château, a plethora of flowers and greenery and the talent of master chef Gilles Epie. Former owner of Le Miraville in Paris, he keeps the menu modern and interesting, sometimes playful, but always refined. There is also dining outside on the courtyard terrace and patio. ✈ Hrs: 6:30–11 pm. Closed Mon. Res required. Classic French menu. Extensive wine list. Bar. A la carte entrees: dinner $28–$45. Complete meals: dinner $80. Specialty: rack of lamb with walnuts and celery root remoulade. Pianist Wed-Sat. Valet parking. Jacket. Cr cds: A, C, D, DS, JCB, MC, V

✕ ★★★★
FENIX
8358 Sunset Blvd, West Hollywood CA 90069
☎ *213/848–6677*

Inside the historic building is art deco decor, while outside on the terrace is a view overlooking the city. ✈ Hrs: 6:30–10:30 am, 11:30 am–2:30 pm, 6–10:30 pm. Closed Sun. Res accepted. French, California menu. Bar. Extensive wine list. A la carte entrees: bkfst $5.75–$13, lunch $9–$16, dinner $10–$29. Complete meal: dinner $64. Specialties: grilled salmon with cavier and chive sauce, daikon sesame salad, chicken breast in mushroom crust. Valet parking. Outdoor dining. Cr cds: A, C, D, MC, V

✕ ★★★★
PATINA
5955 Melrose Ave, Hollywood (L.A.) CA 90038
☎ *213/467–1108*

This is an intimate setting, decorated with white walls, pale woods, frosted glass and pigmented metals. Candlelight dances across the white linens of the understated dining

CALIFORNIA

room. Hrs: 6–9:30 pm; Tues noon–2 pm, 6–9:30 pm; Fri to 10:30 pm; Sat 5:30–10:30 pm. Closed some major hols. Res accepted; required wkends. California, French menu. Bar. Wine cellar. A la carte entrees: lunch $14–$17.50, dinner $23.95–$27. Complete meals: dinner $49–$65. Specialties: Santa Barbara shrimp, peppered tournedos of tuna. Valet parking. Casual elegance. Cr cds: A, D, DS, MC, V

La Jolla (San Diego)

★★★★

HYATT REGENCY LA JOLLA AT AVENTINE

3777 La Jolla Village Dr, La Jolla (San Diego) CA 92037
☎ *619/552–1234 or 800/233–1234*
FAX *619/552–6066*

Noted architect Michael Graves designed this hotel, which mixes neoclassic, postmodern and Mediterranean elements. The spacious guest rooms feature cherry wood furnishings. 400 rms, 16 story. S, D $150–$200; each addl $25; suites $230–$510; under 18 free. Crib avail. Garage parking $8, valet $15. TV; cable (premium), VCR avail. Pool; whirlpool. Restaurant 6 am–midnight. Bar from noon. Ck-out noon. Convention facilities. Business center. Concierge. Gift shop. Tennis. Golf privileges. Health club privileges. Minibars. Luxury level. Cr cds: A, C, D, DS, JCB, MC, V

★★★★

SHERATON GRANDE TORREY PINES

10950 N Torrey Pines Rd, La Jolla (San Diego) CA
☎ *619/558–1500 or 800/325–3535*
FAX *619/450–4584*

Set on a bluff above La Jolla, this luxury hotel overlooks the sea and the 18th fairway of the Torrey Pines golf course. 400 rms, 4 story. S, D $205–$250; each addl $20; suites $400–$2,500; under 18 free. Crib free. Valet parking $12; in/out $8. TV; cable (premium), VCR avail. Heated pool; poolside serv. Supervised child's activities (Memorial Day–Labor Day); ages 3–12. Restaurant 6:30 am–10:30 pm. Rm serv 24 hrs. Bar 11–2 am; pianist. Ck-out noon. Convention facilities. Business center. In-rm modem link. Concierge. Butler service each floor. Gift shop. Lighted tennis. Exercise equipt; weight machine, bicycles, whirlpool, sauna. Health club privileges. Bicycle rentals. Bathrm phones, minibars. Wet bar in some suites. Balconies. Cr cds: A, C, D, ER, JCB, MC, V

Laguna Beach

★★★★★
THE RITZ-CARLTON, LAGUNA NIGUEL
1 Ritz Carlton Dr, Dana Point CA 92629
☎ *714/240-2000 or 800/241-3333*
FAX *714/240-0829*

This long-established luxury hotel, perched dramatically on a bluff overlooking a 2-mile beach, resembles a huge Palladian villa, with guest rooms in two wings, each surrounding a pool. In the center, picture windows in the long, catwalk-like lounge and deep-carpeted mezzanine library give grandstand views of the Pacific sunset. Thanks to the height of Dana Point, all west-facing rooms have a panoramic ocean view, even though there are only 4 stories. The hotel gardens are elaborately landscaped with an eye to color and seasonal display, and the fountain in the brick-paved central courtyard can be seen from the Terrace restaurant. The French-style, dinner-only Dining Room has plush banquettes, deep carpets, and antiques. *393 rms, 4 story. S, D $275-$485; each addl $50; suites $700-$3,000. Crib free. Valet parking $17. TV; cable (premium), VCR avail. 2 pools, heated; poolside serv. Supervised child's activities (mid-June-Aug); ages 4-12. Restaurant 6:30 am-midnight. Afternoon tea in library 2:30-5 pm. Rm serv 24 hrs. Bars; entertainment, dancing. Ck-out noon, ck-in 4 pm. Convention facilities. Business center. In-rm modem link. Bellhops. Valet serv. Concierge. Shopping arcade. Barber, beauty shop. International currency exchange. Airport transportation. Tennis, pro. 18-hole golf privileges, greens fee Mon-Wed $90, Thurs-Sun $125, pro, putting green. Swimming beach. Lawn games. 2-mi bicycle path. Exercise rm; instructor, weights, bicycles, sauna, steam rm. Massage. Bathrm phones, refrigerators, minibars; fireplace in some suites. Balconies. Shuttle serv to beach. Luxury level. Cr cds: A, C, D, DS, JCB, MC, V*

CALIFORNIA

Los Angeles

★★★★★
HOTEL BEL-AIR

701 Stone Canyon Rd, Los Angeles CA 90077
☎ *310/472-1211*
FAX *310/476-5890*

Set among 12 acres of exotic gardens and a creek, this vintage resort offers serenity, seclusion and a family of resident swans. The famous open-air walkways are lined with wall sconces and paved with brick and glass. Guest rooms are decorated with peach and earth tones in a Mediterranean style, with polished terra-cotta floors and Aubusson-style area rugs. Poolside service in particular is excellent. ✈ *92 rms, some kits. S, D $315-$435; suites $495-$2,500. TV; cable (premium), VCR (movies). Heated pool; poolside serv. Restaurant 7-10:30 am, 11:30 am-2:30 pm, 6:30-10:30 pm. Rm serv 24 hrs. Bar 10-2 am; entertainment. Ck-out 1 pm. Meeting rms. Business servs avail. In-rm modem link. Concierge. Valet parking. Airport transportation. Fitness Center open to guests 24 hrs with private key access; stair machines, treadmills. Bathrm phones; some wood-burning fireplaces. Private patios. Tea service on arrival. Cr cds: A, C, D, JCB, MC, V*

★★★★
CENTURY PLAZA HOTEL & TOWER

2025 Ave of the Stars, Los Angeles CA 90067
☎ *310/277-2000 or 800/228-3000*
FAX *310/551-3355*

Sited on some 10 acres landscaped with tropical plants and reflecting pools, this modern high-rise with a 30-story tower offers well-furnished rooms with ocean or city views. ✈ *1,072 rms, 19-30 story. S $185; D $210; each addl $25; suites $500-$3,000. Tower: S $245; D $265; suites $750-$5,000; each addl $25; under 18 free. TV; cable (premium), VCR avail. Heated pool; poolside serv in summer. Restaurant 6-1 am. Rm serv 24 hrs. 2 bars 11-2 am; entertainment. Ck-out 1 pm. Lndry facilities 24 hrs. Convention facilities. Business center. In-rm modem link. Concierge. Barber, beauty shop. Valet parking. Exercise equipt; weight machine, bicycles, whirlpool. Tennis & health club privileges adj. Bathrm phones. Balconies. Cr cds: A, C, D, DS, ER, JCB, MC, V*

LOS ANGELES

FOUR SEASONS

300 S Doheny Dr, Los Angeles CA 90048
☎ *310/273-2222*
FAX *310/859-3824*

This modern high-rise close to downtown has beautifully landscaped grounds with a terrace pool and open-air gym. Guest rooms feature understated decor, and the comfortable lounge bar is a Hollywood hangout. ✈ *285 rms, 16 story. S $295-$405; D $325-$405; suites $480-$3,000; family, wkend rates. TV; cable (premium), VCR avail. Pool; poolside serv, lifeguard. Restaurant 6:30 am-11:30 pm. Traditional afternoon tea. Rm serv 24 hrs. Bar 11-1 am; pianist. Ck-out 1 pm. Convention facilities. Business center. In-rm modem link. Concierge 24 hrs. Gift shop. Underground parking. Complimentary limo to Beverly Hills, Century City. Tennis privileges. 18-hole golf privileges. Exercise rm; instructor, weights, bicycles, whirlpool. Massage. Bathrm phones, refrigerators. Balconies. Cr cds: A, C, D, ER, JCB, MC, V*

HOTEL NIKKO AT BEVERLY HILLS

465 S La Cienega Blvd, Los Angeles CA 90048
☎ *310/247-0400 or 800/645-5687*
FAX *310/247-0315*

This contemporary hotel, located near Restaurant Row, is marked by bold American architecture and traditional Japanese simplicity. Hotel Nikko offers a state-of-the-art health club and nightly entertainment as well as a wealth of business services. ✈ *296 units, 7 story, 50 suites. S $270-$310; D $295-$395; each addl $25; suites $600-$1,800; under 12 free. Crib $25. Valet parking $16. TV; cable, VCR avail. Pool. Complimentary coffee in rms. Restaurants 6:30 am-10:30 pm. Rm serv 24 hrs. Lobby bar 11:30-1 am; entertainment. Ck-out 1 pm. Business center. In-rm modem link. Concierge. Gift shop. Tennis privileges. Golf privileges. Exercise equipt; weight machine, bicycles. Masseuse. Bathrm phones. Japanese soaking tubs. Minibars. Balconies. Cr cds: A, C, D, DS, JCB, MC, V*

CALIFORNIA

PARK HYATT LOS ANGELES

2151 Avenue of the Stars, Los Angeles CA 90067
☎ *310/277-1234*
FAX *310/785-9240*

All elegant guest rooms here offer scenic views; some overlook 20th Century-Fox's back lot. ✈ *367 rms, 17 story, 189 suites. S $259; D $284; suites $250-$2,500; under 18 free; wkend package plans. Valet parking $16. TV; cable (premium), VCR avail (movies). 2 heated pools, 1 indoor; poolside serv. Restaurant 6:30 am-10:30 pm. Rm serv 24 hrs. Bar 11:30-1:30 am; pianist. Ck-out 1 pm. Meeting rms. Business center. In-rm modem link. Concierge. Shopping arcade. Tennis & golf privileges. Exercise rm; instructor, weight machines, bicycles, whirlpool, sauna, steam rm. Massage. Bathrm phones, refrigerators, minibars. Private patios, balconies. Cr cds: A, C, D, DS, ER, JCB, MC, V*

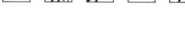

WYNDHAM CHECKERS HOTEL LOS ANGELES

535 S Grand Ave, Los Angeles CA 90071
☎ *213/624-0000*
FAX *213/626-9906*

Having opened in 1927, this residential-style luxury hotel is set in one of this neighborhood's few remaining historical buildings. Guest rooms are furnished with oversize beds, upholstered easy chairs and writing tables, and the lobby features exquisite Oriental and contemporary works of art and antiques. ✈ *188 rms, 12 story. S, D $179-$229; each addl $20; suites $380-$950; under 18 free; wkend rates. Crib free. Valet parking $20. TV; cable (premium), VCR avail. Heated pool; poolside serv. Restaurant 6:30 am-10 pm. Rm serv 24 hrs. Bar 11:30-2 am; entertainment. Meeting rms. Business center. In-rm modem link. Concierge. Airport transportation. Exercise rm; instructor, weight machine, bicycles, whirlpool, sauna, steam rm. Massage. Library. Bathrm phones, minibars. Cr cds: A, C, D, DS, ER, JCB, MC, V*

✕ ★★★★
REX IL RISTORANTE
617 S Olive St, Los Angeles CA 90014
☎ *213/627-2300*

Two floors of a historic art deco building (1928) were remodeled to resemble the dining salon of the 1930s Italian luxury liner *Rex*. 🕊 *Hrs: 6–10 pm; Thurs, Fri also noon–2 pm. Closed Sun; hols. Res accepted. Italian menu. Bar. Wine cellar. Complete meals: lunch $35–$40 (3-course lunch $35), dinner $65–$80 (4-course dinner $60). Specializes in 6-course meals ($75). Own pastries, pasta. Pianist, dancing evenings. Valet parking. Jacket. Cr cds: A, C, D, MC, V*

Marina Del Rey

🏨 ★★★★
THE RITZ-CARLTON, MARINA DEL REY
4375 Admiralty Way, Marina Del Rey CA 90292
☎ *310/823-1700*

Situated on a basin with panoramic views of the Pacific from most balconies, this deluxe high-rise offers well-appointed contemporary guest rooms, access to a marina, and a selection of opulent lounges and dining rooms. 🕊 *306 rms, 12 story. S, D $195–$325; suites $495–$2,000; under 18 free; wkend rates. Crib free. TV; cable (premium), VCR avail. Valet parking $18. Pool; poolside serv. Supervised child's activities; ages 5–13. Restaurant 6 am–11 pm. Rm serv 24 hrs. Bar 11–1 am; pianist in evenings. Ck-out noon. Convention facilities. Business center. In-rm modem link. Concierge. Shopping arcade. Lighted tennis, pro. Golf privileges. Exercise rm; instructor, weights, bicycles, whirlpool. Masseuse. Bathrm phones, refrigerators, minibars. Balconies. Bicycle rentals. Luxury level. Cr cds: A, C, D, DS, ER, JCB, MC, V*

CALIFORNIA

Menlo Park

★★★★
STANFORD PARK
100 El Camino Real, Menlo Park CA 94025
☎ *415/322–1234 or 800/368–2468*
FAX *415/322–0975*

Some guest rooms at this property furnished in French provincial style have balconies. 162 rms, 3–4 story. S $200–$230; D $215–$325; each addl $15; suites $225–$325; under 12 free. Crib free. TV; cable, VCR avail. Heated pool; poolside serv. Restaurant 6:30 am–2 pm, 6–10 pm. Rm serv 24 hrs. Bar 11 am-midnight. Ck-out noon. Meeting rms. Business servs avail. In-rm modem link. Bellhops. Complimentary valet parking. Exercise equipt; weights, bicycles, whirlpool, sauna. Bathrm phones, minibars; some refrigerators. Cr cds: A, C, D, DS, JCB, MC, V

Monterey

★★★★
OLD MONTEREY INN
500 Martin St, Monterey CA 93940
☎ *408/375–8284 or 800/350–2344*
FAX *408/375–6730*

This English country house built in 1929 rests on an oak-studded hillside near the bay. Guest rooms are individually decorated with many antiques, down comforters and pillows and some featherbeds are available. There are 1¼ acres of gardens. 9 rms, 1 cottage. No A/C. No rm phones; cordless phone avail. S, D, cottage $170–$240; 3rd person in suite $50 addl. TV avail. Complimentary full bkfst, wine & afternoon refreshments. Ck-out noon, ck-in 3–7 pm. Business servs avail. Many fireplaces. Totally nonsmoking. Cr cds: MC, V

Newport Beach

FOUR SEASONS
★★★★
690 Newport Center Dr, Newport Beach CA 92660
☎ *714/759-0808*
FAX *714/759-0568*

A short stroll from the Fashion Island shopping mall, this high-rise luxury hotel features a soaring marble lobby and pale, elegant guest rooms with views of the ocean and harbor. 285 rms, 20 story. S, D $285-$325; each addl $30; suites $390-$2,100; under 18 free; wkend rates; honeymoon, anniversary, golf packages. Pet accepted. Valet parking $13.50. TV; cable (premium), VCR avail (movies). Pool; poolside serv. Restaurants 6:30 am-10 pm. Rm serv 24 hrs. Bar 11-1 am; entertainment. Ck-out noon. Convention facilities. Business center. In-rm modem link. Concierge. Gift shop. John Wayne Airport transportation. Lighted tennis, pro. Golf privileges. Bicycles. Exercise rm; instructor, weights, bicycles, whirlpool, sauna. Massage. Bathrm phones, refrigerators. In-rm movies in suites. Balconies. Cr cds: A, C, D, ER, JCB, MC, V

SUTTON PLACE
★★★★
4500 MacArthur Blvd, Newport Beach CA 92660
☎ *714/476-2001 or 800/243-4141*
FAX *714/476-0153*

This hotel is decorated in a distinctive European style. 435 rms, 10 story. S $150-$180; D $160-$195; each addl $15; suites $250-$850; under 16 free, wkend plans. TV; cable (premium), VCR avail (movies). Pool; poolside serv. Restaurant 6:30 am-10:30 pm. Rm serv 24 hrs. Bar 4 pm-2 am; entertainment. Ck-out noon. Meeting rms. Business center. In-rm modem link. Concierge. Gift shop. Free John Wayne Airport transportation. Lighted tennis, pro. Exercise equipt; weights, bicycles, whirlpool and sauna. Health club privileges. Bathrm phones, minibars. Some balconies. Luxury level. Cr cds: A, C, D, DS, ER, JCB, MC, V

Pacific Grove

SEVEN GABLES
555 Ocean View Blvd, Pacific Grove CA 93950
☏ *408/372-4341*

This inn in a landmark Victorian mansion dating from 1886 is elegantly furnished with European antiques; all guest rooms have spectacular views of Monterey Bay. 🐾 *14 rms, 2-3 story. No rm phones. S, D $125-$225. Complimentary full bkfst, afternoon tea. Ck-out noon, ck-in 2:30-10 pm. Some refrigerators. Totally nonsmoking. Cr cds: MC, V*

Palm Desert

HYATT GRAND CHAMPIONS
44-600 Indian Wells Lane, Indian Wells CA 92210
☏ *760/341-1000*
FAX *760/568-2236*

This resort on 35 elaborately landscaped acres features a unique Moorish-style architecture; all guest rooms afford scenic views. 🐾 *316 rms in main building, 5 story, 20 Italian-style garden villas, 1- & 2-bedrm. Mid-Dec-May: S, D $255-$300; each addl $25; villas $760-$970; under 18 free; golf, tennis plans; lower rates rest of yr. Crib free. Valet parking (fee). TV; cable (premium), VCR avail. 4 heated pools; wading pool, poolside serv. Supervised child's activities; ages 3-12. Complimentary coffee in rms. Dining rms 6:30 am-10 pm. Box lunches, snack bar, picnics. Rm serv 6-2 am. Bar 11-1 am. Ck-out 1 pm, ck-in 4 pm. Convention facilities. Business center. In-rm modem link. Beauty shop. Sports dir. 12 tennis courts including 2 clay, 2 grass & 8 hard surface, pro. 36-hole golf, greens fee $80-$110, pro, putting green, driving range. Bicycles. Lawn games. Entertainment, dancing. Exercise rm; instructor, weight machines, bicycles, whirlpool, sauna, steam rm. Aerobics. Massage. Full service health spa. Refrigerators, honor bars. Some fireplaces. Private patios, balconies. Butler serv in villas 6 am-11 pm. Luxury level. Cr cds: A, C, D, DS, ER, JCB, MC, V*

PALM DESERT

★★★★ MARRIOTT'S DESERT SPRINGS RESORT & SPA

74855 Country Club Dr, Palm Desert CA
☎ 760/341–2211 or 800/331–3112
FAX 760/341–1872

This resort, situated on 420 landscaped acres crisscrossed by waterways and punctuated by lakes and a large sunning beach, features an 8-story atrium lobby with waterfall. Boats transport guests to the resort's restaurants and bars. 884 rms, 8 story. Late Dec–Memorial Day: S, D $250–$350; each addl $10; suites $600–$2,000; under 18 free; golf, tennis, spa package rates; lower rates rest of yr. Crib free. Garage: valet parking (fee); public parking free. TV; cable (premium). 5 heated pools; poolside serv. Supervised child's activities; ages 5–13. Dining rms 7 am–10 pm. Box lunches, snack bar, picnics. Bar 11–2 am. Ck-out noon, ck-in 4 pm. Convention facilities. Business center. In-rm modem link. Concierge. Shopping arcade. Barber, beauty shop. Sports dir. 20 hard tennis courts, 7 lighted, 3 clay, 2 grass. 36-hole golf, greens fee $140, pro, championship putting course, putting green, driving range. Boats. Lawn games. Soc dir; entertainment, dancing. Exercise rm; instructor, weight machines, bicycles, whirlpool, sauna, steam rm. Massage. Full service European health spa. Minibars. Private patios, balconies. Cr cds: A, C, D, DS, ER, JCB, MC, V

★★★★ RENAISSANCE ESMERALDA

44–400 Indian Wells Lane, Indian Wells CA 92210
☎ 760/773–4444
FAX 760/773–9250

This 350-acre golf resort nestles in the foothills of the Santa Rosa Mountains. 560 units, 7 story. Jan-May: S, D $290–$390; each addl $25; suites $600–$2,500; under 18 free; tennis, golf plans; honeymoon package; lower rates rest of yr. Crib free. Pet accepted, some restrictions. TV; cable (premium). 2 pools; wading pool, poolside serv. Supervised child's activities; ages 3–12. Dining rms 6:30 am–11 pm. Rm serv 24 hrs. Bar noon–2 am; entertainment. Ck-out noon, ck-in 3 pm. Coin lndry. Meeting rms. Business center. In-rm modem link. Bellhops. Valet serv. Concierge. Gift shops. Airport transportation. Sports dir. Lighted tennis, pro. 36-hole golf, greens fee $100–$110, pro, putting green, driving range. Tennis & golf clinics; equipt rentals. Private

CALIFORNIA

beach. Hiking. Bicycle rentals. Lawn games. Game rm. Fully equipped health/fitness center. Exercise rm; instructor, weight machine, bicycles, whirlpool, sauna, steam rm. Masseuse. Bathrm phones, minibars; some wet bars. Some suites with woodburning fireplace. Balconies. Cr cds: A, C, D, DS, ER, JCB, MC, V

Palm Springs

★★★★
HYATT REGENCY SUITES PALM SPRINGS

285 N Palm Canyon Dr, Palm Springs CA 92262
☎ *760/322–9000*
FAX *760/325–6009*

Adjacent to a downtown shopping plaza, this strikingly asymmetrical hotel has one-, two-, and three-bedroom suites with city or golf course/mountain views.  *192 suites, 6 story. Jan–Apr: suites $205–$425; under 18 free; mid-wk rates; lower rates rest of yr. Crib free. Pet accepted, some restrictions; $25. TV; cable (premium), VCR avail (movies). Pool; poolside serv. Restaurants 7 am–10 pm; Fri–Sun to 11 pm. Bar 11–1 am; entertainment Fri–Sat. Ck-out noon. Meeting rms. Business servs avail. Concierge. Valet parking. Airport transportation. Tennis & golf privileges. Exercise equipt; weight machine, bicycles, whirlpool. Massage. Bathrm phones, refrigerators, wet bars. Private patios, balconies. Cr cds: A, C, D, DS, JCB, MC, V*

★★★★
LA MANCHA PRIVATE POOL VILLAS AND SPA

444 Avenida Caballeros, Palm Springs CA 92263
☎ *760/323–1773 or 800/255–1773*
FAX *760/323–5928*

This Spanish-colonial style resort is a welcome respite from city life, just four blocks from downtown Palm Springs. Villas are luxurious; grounds are lavishly landscaped. Amenities include everything from Nautilus gym, clubhouse sauna and masseuse to tennis courts, bicycles and an abundance of personal services. 53 kit. villas, 1–2 story, 13 minisuites. Dec–Apr: minisuites $195–$225; villas $250–$895; extended stay rates; tennis, golf, honeymoon packages; lower rates rest of yr. Crib $25. TV; cable, VCR avail (movies). Pool; whirlpool, poolside serv. Dining rm 7:30 am–2:30 pm, 5:30–9:30 pm. Box lunches, picnics. Rm serv. Bar 8 am–11 pm. Ck-out noon, ck-in 3 pm. Grocery, coin lndry, package store 1 mi. Meeting rms. Business servs avail. In-rm modem link. Concierge. Gift shop. Free airport transportation. Lighted tennis, pro. Golf privileges, putting green. Bicycles. Lawn games. Exercise equipt; weight machines, bicycles, sauna. Some fireplaces. Private patios, balconies. Grills. Most villas with private pool, whirlpools and/or spa; some villas with private tennis court. Extensive grounds. Cr cds: A, C, D, DS, MC, V

★★★★
MARRIOTT'S RANCHO LAS PALMAS
41000 Bob Hope Dr, Rancho Mirage CA 92270
☎ 760/568-2727
FAX 760/568-5845

Set on spacious grounds with a garden, this resort offers large, luxurious guest rooms and a variety of sports. 450 rms, 2 story. Jan–Apr: S, D $225–$245; suites $330–$1,000; under 18 free; golf & tennis package plan; lower rates rest of yr. Pet accepted, some restrictions. TV; cable (premium), VCR avail (movies). 2 pools, heated; wading pool, poolside serv. Playground. Supervised child's activities; children under 12 yrs. Dining rm 6 am–10 pm. Rm serv; limited serv midnight–6 am. Box lunches, snack bar. Bar 11–2 am. Ck-out noon, ck-in 4 pm. Convention facilities. Business center. In-rm modem link. Concierge. Gift shop. Barber, beauty shop. Lighted tennis, pro. Tennis school. 27-hole golf, greens fee $90, pro, putting green, driving range (free balls). Bicycle rentals. Soc dir. Exercise equipt; weights, bicycles, whirlpool. Massage. Some refrigerators, minibars. Private patios, balconies. Cr cds: A, C, D, DS, ER, JCB, MC, V

CALIFORNIA

THE RITZ-CARLTON, RANCHO MIRAGE

68–900 Frank Sinatra Dr, Rancho Mirage CA 92270
☎ *760/321–8282*
FAX *760/321–6928*

Located on a secluded plateau in the foothills of the Santa Rosa Mountains, this resort includes lush gardens with a gazebo and panoramic views of the desert. *239 rms, 3 story. Jan-mid-June: S, D $275–$425; each addl $25; suites $650–$2,000; lower rates rest of yr. Crib free. TV; cable (premium), VCR avail (movies). Pool; poolside serv. Supervised child's activities; ages 4–12. Dining rm 7 am–11 pm. Box lunches, snack bar, picnics. Afternoon tea 2:30–5 pm. Rm serv 24 hrs. Bar 10:30–1 am. Ck-out noon, ck-in 3 pm. Convention facilities. Business center. In-rm modem link. Shopping arcade. Barber, beauty shop. Valet serv. Concierge. Underground valet parking. Lighted tennis, pro, pro shop. 18-hole golf privileges, greens fee $65–$170. Lawn games. Exercise rm; instructor; weight machines, bicycles, whirlpool, sauna. Massage. Bathrm phones, minibars. Private patios, balconies. Luxury level. Cr cds: A, C, D, DS, ER, JCB, MC, V*

SUNDANCE VILLAS

303 W Cabrillo Rd, Palm Springs CA 92262
☎ *760/325–3888 or 800/455–3888*
FAX *760/323–3029*

Each private villa here has its own whirlpool, swimming pool and two-car garage. *19 kit. villas. Mid-Dec–May: villas $295–$450; wkly rates; lower rates rest of yr. Crib $70/wk. TV; cable (premium), VCR. Pool; whirlpool. Restaurant nearby. Ck-out 1 pm. Business servs avail. Valet serv. Concierge. Free airport transportation. Lighted tennis. Golf privileges. Health club privileges. Wet bars. Fireplaces. Patios. Grills. Cr cds: A, C, D, DS, JCB, MC, V*

THE WESTIN MISSION HILLS

71333 Dinah Shore Dr, Rancho Mirage CA 92270
760/328-5955
FAX *760/321-2955*

Built in classic Moroccan style, this 360-acre resort is landscaped with lagoons, waterways and lush vegetation. Most guest rooms afford panoramic views of the golf course fairways and mountains. *512 units in 16 buildings, 2 story. Jan-May: S, D $289-$329; each addl $25; suites $439-$1,000; under 18 free; golf & tennis plans; lower rates rest of yr. Crib free. Pet accepted, some restrictions. TV; cable (premium), VCR avail (movies). 3 heated pools; poolside serv, lifeguard (main pool); 60-ft waterslide. Playground. Supervised child's activities; ages 4-12. Dining rms 6 am-11 pm. Box lunches. Snack bar. Deli. Rm serv 24 hrs. Bars 10-2 am; entertainment. Ck-out noon, ck-in 4 pm. Convention facilities. Business center. In-rm modem link. Bellhops. Valet serv. Concierge. Gift shop. Clothing shops. Tennis & golf shops. Sports dir. 7 tennis courts, lighted, pro. Pete Dye & Gary Player championship 18-hole golf courses, pro, 6 putting greens, 2 double-sided practice ranges. Bicycles (rentals). Lawn games include croquet, shuffleboard, volleyball. Soc dir. Game rm. Exercise equipt; weight machines, treadmill, whirlpool, steam rm. Health and fitness center; massage, herbal wraps, skin care, beauty salon; aerobics and weight training. Fully stocked minibars. Refrigerators. Cr cds: A, C, D, DS, ER, JCB, MC, V*

Pasadena

THE RITZ-CARLTON HUNTINGTON, PASADENA

1401 S Oak Knoll Ave, Pasadena CA 91106
818/568-3900
FAX *818/568-3700*

Built in 1907 as a fashionable resort and now restored and lavishly decorated with fine art and antiques, this landmark occupies 23 elaborately landscaped acres in the foothills of the San Gabriel Mountains. On the property are themed gardens, such as the Japanese and Horseshoe gardens and the celebrated Picture Bridge, whose murals depict California scenes. Guest rooms are traditionally furnished, with marble-fitted bathrooms. 383 rms, 2-8 story, 6 cottages. S, D $185-$310; suites, cottages $400-$2,000; under 18 free; special package plans. Crib free. Valet parking $15. TV; cable, VCR avail. Heated pool; poolside serv. Supervised child's activities (June-Aug). Restaurants 6:30 am-10 pm. Rm serv 24 hrs. Bar 5 pm-1:30 am; entertainment. Ck-out noon. Convention facilities. Business servs avail. In-rm modem link. Concierge. Gift shop. Barber, beauty shop. Lighted tennis, pro. Golf privileges. Exercise rm; instructor, weight machines, bicycles, whirlpool, sauna. Massage. Lawn games. Bicycle rental. Bathrm phones, minibars; many balconies. Luxury level. Cr cds: A, C, D, DS, ER, JCB, MC, V

Pebble Beach

★★★★
INN & LINKS AT SPANISH BAY

2700 Seventeen Mile Dr, Pebble Beach CA 93953
☎ *408/647-7500 or 800/654-9300*
FAX *408/644-7955*

At this luxury golf resort on 236 acres, guests enjoy preferred tee times at Pebble Beach's prestigious courses. 270 units, 4 story. S, D $275-$385; suites $575-$1,500; children under 18 free; golf, tennis plans. Service charge $17 per day per rm. Crib free. TV; cable, VCR avail. Heated pool; whirlpool, sauna, poolside serv. Dining rm 6:30 am-10 pm. Box lunches. Picnics. Rm serv 24 hrs. Bar 10-2 am. Ck-out noon, ck-in 4 pm. Lndry facility. Package store. Convention facilities. Business center. In-rm modem link. Concierge. Shops, specialty stores. Free valet parking. Free airport transportation. Lighted tennis. 72-hole golf, greens fee $135-$185 (incl cart), pro, putting green. Private beach. Bicycle rentals. Equestrian center. Hiking trails. Exercise rm; instructor, bicycles, treadmills. Minibars. Fireplaces. Private patios, balconies. Picnic tables, grills. Complimentary shuttle service to the lodge and golf courses. Cr cds: A, C, D, DS, JCB, MC, V

THE LODGE AT PEBBLE BEACH

Seventeen Mile Dr, Pebble Beach CA 93953
☎ 408/624–3811 or 800/654–9300
FAX 408/625–8598

This lavish resort on Carmel Bay, with guest rooms overlooking a beach and golf course, includes an equestrian center with 34 miles of trails. ✈ *161 rms, 1–3 story. S, D $335–$550; suites $875–$1,800; under 18 free. Service charge $15 per day per rm. Crib free. Pet accepted. TV; cable (premium), VCR avail. Heated pool; wading pool, poolside serv. Supervised child's activities (June–Aug). Afternoon tea. Restaurants 7 am–3:30 pm, 6:30–10:30 pm. Box lunches, snacks. Rm serv 24 hrs. Bar 11–1 am. Ck-out noon, ck-in 4 pm. Convention facilities. Business servs avail. In-rm modem link. Valet serv. Concierge. Shopping arcade; bank, post office. Barber, beauty shop. Valet parking. Free airport transportation. Tennis. 4 golf courses, par-3 golf, greens fee $150–$275, putting green, 2 driving ranges. Private beach. Exercise equipt; weights, bicycles, whirlpool, sauna, steam rm. Massage. Refrigerators avail, honor bars, fireplaces; some wet bars. Private patios, balconies. Shuttle service throughout resort and to Spanish Bay. Cr cds: A, C, D, DS, JCB, MC, V*

Rancho Santa Fe

RANCHO VALENCIA

5921 Valencia Circle, Rancho Santa Fe CA 92067
☎ 619/756–1123 or 800/548–3664
FAX 619/756–0165

The Spanish architecture at this luxury tennis resort recalls early California haciendas. The spacious, secluded suites occupy red tile-roofed casitas and have private terraces. ✈ *43 suites. S, D $360–$490; 2-bedrm suites $790–$900; 3-bedrm hacienda from $2,500; tennis clinic plans, golf plans. Crib free. Pet accepted. TV; cable (premium), VCR. Heated pool; poolside serv. Complimentary coffee in rms. Restaurant 7 am–2:30 pm, 6–9:30 pm. Box lunches. Picnics. Bar from 10 am. Ck-out noon, ck-in 4 pm. Guest lndry. Meeting rms. Business servs avail. Bellhops. Valet serv. Gift shop. 18 tennis courts, pro. 18-hole golf privileges adj. Exercise equipt; weights, treadmill. Bicycle rentals. Lawn games; professional croquet* *lawn. Soc dir. Bathrm phones, refrigerators, minibars, wet bars, fireplaces. Cr cds: A, C, D, MC, V*

MILLE FLEURS
Country Squire Courtyard, Rancho Santa Fe CA 92067
☎ *619/756–3085*

Portuguese tiles, beamed ceilings and fireplaces create an intimate atmosphere in which to sample the fresh, bold cuisine of chef Martin Woesle. Outdoor dining in an attractive setting is also available. (✈) Hrs: 11:30 am–2:30 pm, 6–10 pm; Sat 5:30–10 pm; Sun 6–10 pm. Closed Jan 1, Dec 25. Res required Fri & Sat. French cuisine. Bar 11:30 am–midnight; Sat from 5:30 pm; Sun from 6 pm. Wine list. Semi-a la carte: lunch $9–$20, dinner $25–$34. Own pastries. Pianist Tues-Sat. Outdoor dining (lunch). Portuguese decor. Menu changes daily. Totally nonsmoking. Cr cds: A, MC, V

San Diego

RANCHO BERNARDO INN
17550 Bernardo Oaks Dr, San Diego CA 92128
☎ *619/487–1611 or 800/542–6096*
FAX *619/675–8501*

This Inn, featuring great golf and fine restaurants, offers an ambience rich with tradition. Large bouquets, plush easy chairs and tile baths distinguish the spacious rooms at this Mission-style golf and tennis resort. (✈) 285 rms, 3 story. Mid-Sept–mid-May: S, D $195–$235; suites $300–$900; under 12 free; golf, tennis plans; lower rates rest of yr. TV; cable (premium), VCR avail. 2 pools, heated; poolside serv. Supervised child's activities (Aug; also major hols); ages 5–15. Dining rm 6 am–10 pm. Snack bar. Rm serv to midnight. Bars 11–1 am. Ck-out 1 pm. Convention facilities. Business center. In-rm modem link. Sundries. Concierge. Gift shop. Airport transportation. Complimentary shuttle service to shopping mall. Lighted tennis, pro. Three 18-hole and one 27-hole golf courses, pro, putting green, driving range. Volleyball. Bicycles. Exercise rm; instructor, weight machine, bicycles, 7 whirlpools, sauna, steam rm. Masseuse. Many honor bars; some bathrm phones. Private patios, balconies. Complimentary tea, sherry, finger sandwiches 4–5 pm. Cr cds: A, C, D, DS, MC, V

SHERATON MARINA
1380 Harbor Island Dr, San Diego CA 92101
☎ *619/291–2900*
FAX *619/296–5297*

This hotel, set at the edge of San Diego Bay, offers extensive business facilities, health and recreation services and easy access to the treasures of the Bay area. Rooms are warm and casual; all have water views. 🐾 *1,048 rms, 12 story. S, D $270–$300; each addl $20; suites $375–$1,100; under 18 free. Crib free. TV; cable (premium). 3 heated pools; 2 wading pools, poolside serv. Playground. Complimentary coffee in rms. Restaurant 6 am–10 pm. Rm serv 24 hrs. Bar 11–1 am. Ck-out noon. Coin lndry. Convention facilities. Business center. In-rm modem link. Concierge. Shopping arcade. Free airport transportation. Lighted tennis, pro. Exercise rm; instructor, weights, bicycles, whirlpool, sauna. Bicycle rentals. Minibars. Bathrm phone in suites. Balconies. All rms with view of marina, city or bay. Elaborate landscaping. Boat dock, beach; bicycles. Cr cds: A, C, D, DS, ER, JCB, MC, V*

THE WESTGATE HOTEL
1055 Second Ave, San Diego CA 92101
☎ *619/238–1818 or 800/221–3802*
FAX *619/557–3737*

This opulent hotel in a modern tower features guest rooms furnished with antiques; views are breathtaking from the seventh floor up. 🐾 *223 units, 19 story, some kits. S, D from $164; each addl $10; suites from $350; under 18 free; wkend rates. Valet parking $10/day. Crib free. TV; cable (premium), VCR avail. Complimentary coffee 6–9 am. Restaurant 6 am–11 pm. Afternoon tea. Rm serv 24 hrs. Bar 11–1 am; entertainment. Ck-out noon. Meeting rms. Business servs avail. In-rm modem link. Concierge. Free airport, RR station, bus depot transportation; downtown transportation on request.*

CALIFORNIA

Exercise equipt; weight machine, bicycles. Bathrm phones, minibars. Cr cds: A, C, D, DS, ER, MC, V

San Francisco

THE RITZ-CARLTON, SAN FRANCISCO
600 Stockton St, San Francisco CA 94108
☎ *415/296-7465*
FAX *415/296-8559*

A landmark neoclassical villa on Nob Hill houses this gracious hotel, which has a crystal chandelier-lit lobby and bar full of antiques, an extensive collection of museum-quality 18th-century oils and impeccable, personalized service. The guest rooms have a European ambiance, thanks to reproduction Louis XVI furniture and jewel-color brocades accenting pastel or white walls. Bathrooms are marble, and the ground-floor health club has a good-size pool as well as a small but well-equipped gym. The Dining Room is among the city's highest-profile restaurants, while the more casual Terrace offers courtyard seating and a breakfast buffet. An art gallery is off the lobby, and the famous San Francisco cable cars can be boarded directly opposite the main entrance. ✱ *336 rms, 9 story, 44 suites. S, D $240-$360; suites $450-$3,000; under 18 free; wkend packages. Crib avail. Garage; valet, in/out $27. TV; cable (premium), VCR avail. Indoor pool. Supervised child's activities; under 13 yrs. Restaurant 6:30 am-11 pm (also see THE DINING ROOM). Rm serv 24 hrs. Bar; entertainment. Ck-out noon. Convention facilities. Business servs avail. In-rm modem link. Concierge. Gift shop. Complimentary limo service within city. Exercise equipt; weight machine, stair machine, treadmills, whirlpool, sauna. European spa service. Bathrm phones, minibars; some wet bars. Luxury level. Cr cds: A, C, D, DS, ER, JCB, MC, V*

CAMPTON PLACE
340 Stockton St, San Francisco CA 94108
☎ *415/781-5555 or 800/235-4300*
FAX *415/955-5536*

Uniformed doormen greet you outside a simple brownstone facade with a white awning, but inside the small luxury hotel is lavish decor punctuated with antiques and artwork. Rooms are done with Asian touches in subtle tones of gold and brown. 🕭 *117 rms, 7–17 story. S, D $225–$335; suites $450–$980; under 18 free. Pet accepted, some restrictions; $25. Valet parking $25. TV; cable, VCR avail (movies). Restaurant 7–10:30 am, 11:30 am–2 pm, 6–10 pm. Rm serv 24 hrs. Bar 10 am–11 pm; Fri, Sat to midnight. Ck-out noon. Meeting rms. Business servs avail. Concierge 24 hrs. Butler services. Health club privileges. Bathrm phones; mini bar. Rooftop garden. Cr cds: A, C, D, DS, JCB, MC, V*

MANDARIN ORIENTAL

222 Sansome, San Francisco CA 94104
☎ *415/885–0999 or 800/622–0404*
FAX *415/433–0289*

Rooms are appealing and have spectacular views thanks to the hotel's location in one of the city's tallest buildings. 🕭 *158 rms, 11 story; on floors 38–48 of the twin towers in the First Interstate Center. S, D $285–$405; suites $625–$1,400; under 12 free; wkend rates. Crib free. Covered parking $23. TV; cable (premium), VCR avail. Restaurant 6:30 am–2 pm, 6–10 pm. Rm serv 24 hrs. Bar 11 am–11 pm; entertainment from 3 pm exc Sun. Ck-out noon. Meeting rms. Business center. In-rm modem link. Concierge. Exercise equipt; weights, bicycles. Bathrm phones, refrigerators, minibars. Cr cds: A, C, D, DS, JCB, MC, V*

MARK HOPKINS INTER-CONTINENTAL

1 Nob Hill, San Francisco CA 94108
☎ *415/392–3434 or 800/327–0200*
FAX *415/421–3302*

This landmark hotel on the site of the old Mark Hopkins mansion offers well-maintained guest rooms decorated in a neoclassical style. The noted Top of the Mark lounge features panoramic views. 🕭 *390 rms, 19 story. S, D $190–$260; each addl $30; suites $375–$2,000; under 14 free; wkend rates. Crib free. Garage, in/out $23/day. TV; cable, VCR avail. Restaurant 6:30 am–11 pm. Bars noon–2 am. Ck-out 1 pm. Convention facilities. Business center. Concierge. Complimentary limo service 7:30 am-noon to Financial District. Exercise equipt; bicycles, treadmill. Minibars. Some bal-*

CALIFORNIA

conies. Complimentary newspaper, shoeshine. Luxury level. Cr cds: A, C, D, DS, ER, JCB, MC, V

★★★★
MONACO

501 Geary St, San Francisco CA 94102
☎ *415/292–0100 or 800/214–4220*
FAX *415/292–0111*

Whimsical, eclectic decor gives this French-inspired hotel a romantic atmosphere. 🛪 *201 rms, 7 story, 34 suites. S, D $135–$215; suites $235–$395; under 16 free; hol rates. Crib free. Valet parking; in/out $20. TV; cable (premium), VCR avail. Restaurant 7 am–10:30 pm. Bar 11:30–1:30 am. Ck-out noon. Meeting rms. Business servs avail. In-rm modem link. Concierge. Exercise rm; instructor, weight machine, treadmill. Masseur. Minibars. Cr cds: A, C, D, DS, ER, JCB, MC, V*

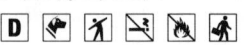

★★★★
PAN PACIFIC

500 Post St, San Francisco CA 94102
☎ *415/771–8600 or 800/533–6465*
FAX *415/398–0267*

This centrally located hotel features a third-floor atrium lobby, decorated mostly in marble (with commissioned sculpture) and highlighted by a spectacular 17-story skylight. 🛪 *330 units, 21 story. S, D $205–$305; suites $350–$1,700; under 18 free; special wkend rates. Crib free. Garage, in/out $24; valet parking. Pet accepted, some restrictions. TV; cable (premium), VCR avail. Supervised child's activities (June–Aug). Restaurant 6:30 am–10 pm. Rm serv 24 hrs. Bar 11 am–11:30 pm; pianist 5–10 pm. Ck-out 4 pm. Meeting rms. Business center. In-rm modem link. Personal valet serv. Concierge. Exercise equipt; weights, bicycles. Minibars, bathrm phones. Complimentary newspaper. Cr cds: A, C, D, DS, ER, JCB, MC, V*

SAN FRANCISCO

★★★★ PARK HYATT

333 Battery St, San Francisco CA 94111
☎ *415/392–1234*
FAX *415/421–2433*

Situated in Embarcadero Center, this hotel is designed with neoclassical formality. ✈ *360 rms, 24 story, 37 suites. S, D $265–$320; each addl $25; suites $350–$2,500; under 18 free; wkend rates. Crib free. Pet accepted, some restrictions. Covered valet parking, in/out $24. TV; cable (premium), VCR avail (movies). Restaurant 6:30 am–9:30 pm. Afternoon tea and evening caviar service. Rm serv 24 hrs. Bar 11–1 am; entertainment. Ck-out noon. Meeting rms. Business center. Concierge. Exercise equipt available for in-rm use. Health club privileges adj. Bathrm phones, minibars. Some balconies. Reference library with national and international publications. Complimentary newspaper, shoeshine. Cr cds: A, C, D, DS, ER, JCB, MC, V*

★★★★ RENAISSANCE STANFORD COURT

Nob Hill, San Francisco CA 94108
☎ *415/989–3500 or 800/227–4736*
FAX *415/391–0513*

This Italianate villa has a circular driveway lit by a domed glass roof and a stained-glass panel at the hotel entrance. Styling throughout evokes the Italian Renaissance, courtesy of antiques, vivid colors, statuary in the lobby area and rooms done in contrasting decors. ✈ *402 rms, 8 story. S, D $235–$315; each addl $30; 1-bedrm suites $365–$1,750; 2-bedrm suites $475–$2,000; under 18 free. Crib free. Valet parking, in/out $24/day. TV; cable (premium), VCR avail. Restaurant 6:30 am–2:30 pm, 5:30–10 pm. Afternoon tea in lobby. Rm serv 24 hrs. Bars 11–1 am. Ck-out noon. Meeting rms. Business center. In-rm modem link. Concierge. Shopping arcade. Exercise equipt; weights, treadmills. Marble bathrms with phone. Cr cds: A, C, D, DS, JCB, MC, V*

CALIFORNIA

★★★★ SHERMAN HOUSE

2160 Green St, San Francisco CA 94123
☎ *415/563–3600 or 800/424–5777*
FAX *415/563–1882*

Occupying a magnificent landmark mansion, this hotel features individually designed guest rooms with Biedermeier, English Jacobean or French Second Empire motifs and antiques. The rooms have working marble fireplaces, four-poster beds with canopies and black-granite bathrooms. 🕊 *14 rms, 4 story. No elvtr. S, D $295–$390; suites $590–$825; under 18 free. Garage $16. TV; cable (premium), VCR (movies). Dining rm (by res) 7 am–2 pm, 5:30–9 pm. Rm serv 24 hrs. Ck-out noon, ck-in 4 pm. Business servs avail. In-rm modem link. Concierge. Butler service. Bathrm phones; many wet bars. Roman tub, whirlpool in some rms. Private patios, balconies. Built 1876. Cr cds: A, D, MC, V*

★★★★ AQUA

252 California St, San Francisco CA
☎ *415/956–9662*

Aqua offers sophisticated dining in a Mediterranean atmosphere. Seafood is the strength here; daily specials and tasting menus feature catches of the day. 🕊 *Hrs: 11:30 am–2:30 pm, 5:30–10:30 pm; Fri & Sat to 11 pm. Closed Sun; most major hols. Res accepted. Bar. A la carte entrees: lunch $14–$18, dinner $24–$39. Complete meals: dinner $60. Specialties: medallions of ahi tuna (rare) with foie gras in wine sauce, Dungeness crab cakes. Valet parking (dinner). Cr cds: A, D, MC, V*

★★★★ THE DINING ROOM

In the Ritz-Carlton, San Francisco
600 Stockton St, San Francisco CA 94108
☎ *415/296–7465*

Replete with antiques, crystal chandeliers and 18th-century oils, the atmospherically lit, flower-bedecked Dining Room offers menus by the number of courses ordered. 🕊 *Hrs: 6–11 pm. Closed Sun. Res accepted. Bar. Wine cellar. Semi-a la carte: dinner $8–$23. Child's meals. Specializes in*

SAN FRANCISCO

regional Northern California and French cuisine. Entertainment. Valet parking. Totally nonsmoking. Cr cds: A, C, D, DS, ER, JCB, MC, V

[D]

FLEUR DE LYS
777 Sutter St, San Francisco CA 94109
415/673-7779

This intimate French provincial dining room has an unusual tapestry ceiling. Hrs: 6-10 pm; Fri, Sat 5:30-10:30 pm. Closed Sun; Jan 1, July 4, Thanksgiving, Dec 25. Res required. French menu. Bar. Wine list. A la carte entrees: dinner $30-$35. Prix fixe: dinner $65. Vegetarian: $52. Specialties: salmon baked in tender corn pancake topped with caviar, oven-roasted rack of lamb in black olive juice, chocolate creme brulée. Valet parking. Jacket. Totally nonsmoking. Cr cds: A, C, D, MC, V

[D]

MASA'S
In Vintage Court
648 Bush St, San Francisco CA 94108
415/989-7154

The artistry of the presentation is as important as the cuisine in this understated, elegant, flower-filled dining spot. Hrs: 6-9:30 pm. Closed Sun & Mon; 2 wks in Jan & 1 wk in July. Res accepted. French menu. Bar. Wine cellar. Prix fixe: dinner $70 & $75. Specialties: foie gras sauté with Madeira truffle sauce, lobster salad with crispy leeks and truffle vinaigrette, sauteéd medallions of New Zealand venison. Valet parking. Cr cds: A, C, D, DS, JCB, MC, V

[D]

POSTRIO
In the Prescott Hotel
545 Post St, San Francisco CA 94102
415/776-7825

Lighting is courtesy of custom Oriental fixtures and a skylight, but the cuisine is courtesy of Wolfgang Puck at this stunning multilevel dining area with open kitchen. Hrs:

CALIFORNIA

7–10 am, 11:30 am–2 pm, 5:30–10 pm; Sat & Sun from 5:30 pm; Sat, Sun brunch 9 am–2 pm. Closed July 4, Thanksgiving, Dec 25. Res required. California, Oriental menu. Bar 11:30–2 am. Wine list. A la carte entrees: bkfst $5–$15, lunch $10–$18, dinner $20–$35. Sat, Sun brunch $6–$10. Specialties: Chinese duck, roasted salmon. Own baking. Valet parking. Cr cds: A, C, D, MC, V

San Jose

★★★★
THE FAIRMONT AT FAIRMONT PLAZA
170 S Market St, San Jose CA 95113
☎ *408/998–1900 or 800/527–4727*
FAX *408/287–1648*

This is a local landmark adjacent to Plaza Park. ✈ 544 rms, 20 story. S $179–$219; D $204–$244; each addl $25; suites $400–$1,500; anniversary, hol packages. Covered parking $12/day. TV; cable (premium), VCR avail. Heated pool; poolside serv. Restaurants 6 am–11 pm; Fri–Sat to 1 am. Rm serv 24 hrs. Bar 11–1:30 am; entertainment. Ck-out 1 pm. Convention facilities. Business center. In-rm modem link. Concierge. Shopping arcade. Barber, beauty shop. Free airport transportation. Exercise rm; instructor, weight machines, bicycles, sauna, steam rm. Massage. Bathrm phones, minibars. Some private patios. Cr cds: A, C, D, DS, JCB, MC, V

★★★★
HOTEL DE ANZA
233 W Santa Clara St, San Jose CA 95113
☎ *408/286–1000 or 800/843–3700*
FAX *408/286–0500*

This hotel was built in art deco style in 1930 and has been restored. ✈ 101 units, 10 story. S, D $175–$190; each addl $15; suites $295–$950; under 18 free; wkend rates. Valet parking $8. TV; cable (premium), VCR (movies). Restaurant 7 am–10 pm. Bar 11–2 am; entertainment. Ck-out noon. Meeting rms. Business center. In-rm modem link. Free airport, RR station, bus depot transportation. Exercise equipt; weight machine, bicycles, stair machine. Health club privileges.

Bathrm phones, refrigerators, minibars; some wet bars. Some balconies. Cr cds: A, C, D, DS, JCB, MC, V

Santa Barbara

🏨 ★★★★
FOUR SEASONS BILTMORE
1260 Channel Dr, Santa Barbara CA 93108
☎ *805/969-2261*
FAX *805/969-4682*

Guest rooms at this 23-acre hotel have views of the ocean, mountains or gardens. 🐾 234 rms, 1-2 story. No A/C. S, D $215-$450; suites from $500; under 18 free. Crib free. Pet accepted. Valet parking $14. TV; cable (premium), VCR. 2 heated pools; wading pool, whirlpool, poolside serv. Supervised child's activities (June-Aug, rest of yr wkends); ages 5-12. Restaurant 7 am-10 pm. Rm serv 24 hrs. Bar 11:30 am-midnight; Fri & Sat to 2 am; entertainment. Ck-out noon. Meeting rms. Business center. In-rm modem link. Concierge. Gift shop. Beauty salon. Free airport transportation. Lighted tennis, pro. Golf privileges, putting green. Exercise rm; instructor, stair machine, treadmill, whirlpool, sauna. Massage & spa treatments. Complete health club. Bicycles. Lawn games. Bathrm phones, minibars; many fireplaces. Many private patios, balconies. Cr cds: A, C, D, DS, ER, JCB, MC, V

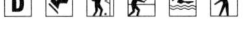

✕ ★★★★
STONEHOUSE
In the San Ysidro Ranch
900 San Ysidro Ln, Santa Barbara CA 93108
☎ *805/969-5046*

Adobe walls, Spanish tile floors and antiques create a contemporary rustic atmosphere. There's outdoor dining as well. 🐾 Hrs: 8 am-10 pm. Res accepted. Bar to midnight. Wine cellar. Semi-a la carte: bkfst $8.95-$12.95, lunch $9.95-$14.95, dinner from $23. Prix fixe: lunch $22.95. Sun brunch $14.95-$22.95. Child's meals. Specialties: cedar plank salmon, lamb shank, vegetarian dishes. Entertainment Thurs-Fri. Valet parking. Totally nonsmoking. Cr cds: A, MC, V

CALIFORNIA

Santa Cruz

INN AT DEPOT HILL
250 Monterey Ave, Capitola-By-The-Sea CA 95010
☎ *408/462–3376 or 800/572–2632*
FAX *408/462–3697*

Guest rooms in this sophisticated seaside inn, which occupies a former railroad depot dating from 1901, are elegant and individually decorated. A reflecting pond is the focal point of the main patio, which is surrounded by flowers, ferns and vines. The dining room creates the illusion of a railroad dining car. 🌣 *9 rms, 2 story, 4 suites. Some A/C. S, D $165–$195; each addl $20; suites $195–$250. TV; cable, VCR (movies). Complimentary full bkfst, wine & hors d'oeuvres, desserts. Complimentary coffee in rms. Restaurant nearby. Limited rm serv. Ck-out 11:30 am, ck-in 3 pm. Business servs avail. In-rm modem link. Concierge serv. Elegant furnishings; each rm with distinctive decor, wood-burning fireplace. 4 rms have whirlpools on private patio. Ocean 2 blks; swimming beach. Totally nonsmoking. Cr cds: A, MC, V*

Santa Monica

SHUTTERS ON THE BEACH
1 Pico Blvd, Santa Monica CA 90405
☎ *310/458–0030 or 800/334–9000*
FAX *310/458–4589*

Named for the distinctive sliding shutter doors of each guest room, this oceanfront hotel has a cozy lobby with a balcony. The contemporary-styled rooms feature marble bathrooms. 🌣 *198 rms in 2 bldgs, 7 story. S, D $295–$500; each addl $50; suites $675–$2,500; under 5 free; wkend plans. Crib $35. Valet parking $18. TV; cable (premium), VCR (movies). Heated pool; poolside serv. Restaurant 6:30 am–11 pm. Rm serv 24 hrs. Bar 11–2 am. Ck-out noon. Meeting rms. Business center. In-rm modem link. Concierge. Gift shop. Exercise equipt; weight machine, bicycles, whirlpool, sauna, steam rm. Minibars. Balconies. Beachfront boardwalk. Cr cds: A, C, D, DS, MC, V*

Solvang

LOS OLIVOS GRAND HOTEL
2860 Grand Ave, Los Olivos CA 93441
☎ *805/688–7788 or 800/446–2455*
FAX *805/688–1942*

There are many antiques among the elegant furnishings of this luxury Santa Ynez Valley hideaway. The extensive landscaping includes an arbor and gazebo. ✈ *21 rms, 2 story. Wkends: S, D $210–$255; suite $325; golf plan; lower rates mid-wk. Crib free. TV; cable, VCR avail. Heated pool; whirlpool, poolside serv. Coffee in rms. Complimentary full bkfst; afternoon refreshments. Dining rm 11:30 am–2:30 pm, 5–9 pm; Sat & Sun 9 am–3 pm, 5–10 pm. Rm serv. Ck-out noon, ck-in 2 pm. Meeting rms. Business servs avail. Bellhops. Valet serv. Free airport transportation. Golf privileges. Fireplaces. Library. Bicycles avail. Totally nonsmoking. Cr cds: A, D, DS, MC, V*

Sonoma

SONOMA MISSION INN & SPA
PO Box 1447, Sonoma CA 95476
☎ *707/938–9000 or 800/862–4945*
FAX *707/938–4250*

San Franciscans once took the cure at this now-restored 1927 Spanish mission-style country inn. Today, guests come for the fitness training and pampering of the high-tech spa. ✈ *169 rms, 2–3 story. Apr-late Oct: S, D $170–$375; each addl $30; suites $475–$650; lower rates rest of yr. Crib free. TV; cable. 2 heated pools; whirlpools. Restaurant 7 am–10 pm. Bar 11–1 am; entertainment. Ck-out noon. Meeting rms. Business servs avail. In-rm modem link. Concierge. Beauty shop. Airport transportation to San Francisco avail. Lighted tennis, pro. 18-hole golf privileges. Exercise rm; instructor, weights, bicycles, sauna, steam rm. Natural hot artesian mineral water in both pools and whirlpools. Full European-style spa. Refrigerators, honor bars. Some private patios, balconies.*

CALIFORNIA

Early morning guided country hikes. Totally nonsmoking. Cr cds: A, C, D, MC, V

St Helena

⭐⭐⭐⭐
AUBERGE DU SOLEIL
180 Rutherford Hill Rd, Rutherford CA 94573
☎ *707/963-1211 or 800/348-5406*
FAX *707/963-8764*

This Mediterranean-style inn nestles in a 33-acre hillside olive grove overlooking the Napa valley. Informal but elegant, it is in the tradition of the finest European inns. 🚭 *50 rms, 2 story. Aug-Nov: S, D $350-$975; lower rates rest of yr, also Mon-Thurs. TV; cable (premium), VCR (movies). Pool; poolside serv. Dining rm (see AUBERGE DU SOLEIL). Rm serv 24 hrs. Bar 11 am-midnight. Ck-out noon, ck-in 3 pm. Meeting rm. Business servs avail. In-rm modem link. Bellhops. Valet serv. Beauty shop. Gift shop. Tennis, pro. Bicycles avail. Exercise equipt; weights, treadmill, sauna, steam rm. Masseuse. Refrigerators. Fireplaces. Private patios, balconies. Cr cds: A, D, DS, MC, V*

⭐⭐⭐⭐
MEADOWOOD
900 Meadowood Lane, St Helena CA 94574
☎ *707/963-3646 or 800/458-8080*
FAX *707/963-3532*

Situated on 256 private wooded acres, this croquet, golf and tennis resort centers on a rambling country lodge; separate bungalow suites cluster on a hillside. 🚭 *99 units, 51 suites. July-mid-Nov: S, D $320-$450; each addl $25; suites $405-$1,812; under 12 free; lower rates rest of yr. Crib free. TV; cable (premium), VCR avail (movies). 2 pools; poolside serv. Coffee in rms. Dining rm 5:30-10 pm. Rm serv. 3 bars 10:30 am-midnight. Ck-out noon, ck-in 4 pm. Meeting rms. Business center. Pro shops. 7 tennis courts, pro. 9-hole golf, pro, putting green. World-class croquet facilities, pro. Exercise rm; instructor, weight machine, bicycles, whirlpool, sauna, steam rm. Masseuse. Spa & fitness center. Refrigerators, honor* bar, fresh fruit; many fireplaces. Private patios, balconies. Bicycle rentals. Cr cds: A, C, D, DS, MC, V

[D] [🚶] [⛷] [≋] [🚶] [🔥] [🚶]

✕ ★★★★
AUBERGE DU SOLEIL
In the Auberge du Soleil
180 Rutherford Hill Rd, Rutherford CA 94573
☎ 707/967–3111

Casually elegant dining in a country atmosphere or al fresco on the terrace with a view of valley and vineyards. ✈ *Hrs: 7–11 am, 11:30 am–2:30 pm, 6–9:30 pm. Res accepted. Bar 11 am–midnight. Wine country cuisine. A la carte entrees: bkfst $8.50–$20, lunch $10–$25, dinner $25–$35. Own baking. Valet parking. Cr cds: A, D, DS, MC, V*

[D]

Walnut Creek

🏨 ★★★★
LAFAYETTE PARK HOTEL
3287 Mt Diablo Blvd, Lafayette CA 94549
☎ 510/283–3700
FAX 510/284–1621

In the style of classical European inns, this property surrounds three separate courtyards. Guest rooms feature fireplaces and vaulted ceilings. ✈ *139 rms, 4 story. S, D $165–$245; suites $225–$350. TV; cable (premium), VCR avail. Heated pool; poolside serv. Restaurant 6:30 am–2 pm, 6–9:30 pm. Evening refreshments. Rm serv 24 hrs. Bar 11 am–midnight. Ck-out noon. Meeting rms. Business servs avail. In-rm modem link. Valet serv. Concierge. Covered parking. Exercise equipt; weight machines, stair machine, whirlpool, sauna. Bathrm phones, refrigerators, minibars. Some private patios. Cr cds: A, C, D, DS, MC, V*

[D] [≋] [🚶] [🧺] [🔥] [SC]

CALIFORNIA

Yosemite National Park

★★★★★ CHÂTEAU DU SUREAU

48688 Victoria Ln, Oakhurst CA 93644
☏ *209/683–6860*
FAX *209/683–0800*

The Château du Sureau is a nine-room fairy-tale-castle inn, complete with stone turret, spiral limestone staircase and circular music tower. Guest rooms are named for herbs and flowers and are furnished with antiques. A stroll through the grounds is full of surprises, including a koi pond, statuary and a larger-than-life checkers-and-chess board, complete with playing pieces. Service is outstanding, and the staff is unfailingly thoughtful. 🕊 *9 rms, 2 story. EP: D $260–$360 and 10% service charge. Cable TV in sitting rm, VCR avail. Pool. Complimentary coffee in rms and in library. Complimentary full bkfst. Restaurant (see ERNA'S ELDERBERRY HOUSE). Ck-out noon, ck-in 2 pm. Luggage handling. Concierge serv. Lawn games. Balconies. Luxurious hillside estate situated on 7 acres; landscaped grounds with several fountains, walking paths. Totally nonsmoking. Cr cds: A, MC, V*

★★★★ ERNA'S ELDERBERRY HOUSE

In the Château du Sureau
48688 Victoria Ln, Oakhurst CA 93644
☏ *209/683–6800*

Offering elegant dining in a European country estate atmosphere, four dining areas are individually decorated with many oil paintings, tapestry and French provincial imported furnishings. A terrace overlooks the Sierra. 🕊 *Hrs: 11:30 am–1 pm, 5:30–8:30 pm; Sat & Sun from 5:30 pm; Sun brunch 11 am–1 pm. Closed Tues; also Mon in winter. Res accepted. French-California cuisine. Bar. Wine cellar. Complete meals: lunch $14.50, dinner $60. Sun brunch $24.50. Menu changes daily. Menu recited. Own baking. Classical harpist special hols. Parking. Cr cds: A, MC, V*

Yountville

DOMAINE CHANDON
1 California Dr, Yountville CA 94599
☎ 707/944-2892

Service at this restaurant is in an architecturally dramatic room with views of the adjacent winery's vineyards. 🍽 *Hrs: 11:30 am-2:30 pm, 6-9:30 pm. Closed Mon & Tues (exc May-Oct open for lunch); Dec 24, 25; also 2 wks Jan. Res accepted. French, California menu. Wine list. A la carte entrees: lunch $13.50-$17.95, dinner $24-$28. Specialties: carmelized scallops with sweet pea sauce, tuna pepper steak, Monterey Bay sardines on basil potatoes. Menu changes daily. Own desserts. Outdoor dining at lunch (May-Nov). Totally nonsmoking. Cr cds: A, C, D, DS, MC, V*

THE FRENCH LAUNDRY
6640 Washington Ave, Yountville CA 94599
☎ 707/944-2380

Patrons will feel like well-tended houseguests in this old converted brick building surrounded by lush gardens, fresh flowers and gentle lighting. The kitchen, wine bar/reception area and patio were recently renovated. The menu changes daily and includes inventive dishes. 🍽 *Hrs: noon-1:30 pm, 5:30-10 pm; Sun to 9 pm. Closed Mon (Nov-May); Jan 1, Dec 25. Res accepted. Wine, beer. Complete meals: lunch 3-course $30, 4-course $38; dinner 5-course $59, 8-course $75. Specializes in American fare with French influence. Menu changes daily. Parking. Outdoor dining in garden. Totally nonsmoking. Cr cds: A, MC, V*

Colorado

Aspen

★★★★★ LITTLE NELL

675 E Durant Ave, Aspen CO 81611
☎ *970/920-4600 or 800/525-6200*
FAX *970/920-4670*

Aspen's only true ski-in, ski-out hotel is worth a visit in summer, too. Looking out on the gondolas of the ski mountain, it has a striking navy-blue swimming pool in back, while, in front, all the shops and restaurants of Aspen are steps away. Off the casual lodge-style lobby, with a sunken bar and lounge where morning coffee is set out, are several shops, including a bookstore that rents videos for the in-room VCRs and a jeweler that specializes in vintage watches. Decor throughout is upscale mountain rustic: exposed beams, and in the guest rooms, stripped-pine gateleg tables. The luxurious bathrooms are stocked with Frette robes, clothes steamers and a generous selection of toiletries. In the oversize closet is a safe and a humidifier to counteract the dry air. The staff of the Little Nell takes great pains to provide a warm atmosphere and gives the impression that nothing is too much trouble for guests. *92 rms, 4 story, 14 suites. S, D $255-$550; suites $350-$2,900; higher rates winter. Crib free. Pet accepted. Garage; valet parking $12. TV; cable (premium), VCR avail (movies $5). Heated pool; poolside serv. Restaurant (see RESTAURANT AT LITTLE NELL). Bar 3 pm-midnight; entertainment Thurs-Sat. Ck-out noon. Meeting rms. Business servs avail. In-rm modem link. Concierge. Shopping arcade. Free airport transportation. Ski shuttle to other mountains. Downhill ski on site. Exercise rm; instructor, weights, bicycles, whirlpool, steam rm. Massage. Bathrm phones, refrigerators, minibars, gas fireplaces. Cr cds: A, C, D, DS, JCB, MC, V*

ASPEN

HOTEL JEROME
★★★★

330 E Main St, Aspen CO 81611
☎ *970/920–1000 or 800/331–7213*
FAX *970/925–2784*

One of Colorado's grand hotels since 1889, the Jerome is grandly Victorian. The sumptuous public areas sport five kinds of wallpapers; guest rooms are individually decorated with period pieces. 🐾 *93 rms, 3–4 story. Mid-Nov–mid-Mar: S, D $245–$495; suites $395–$1,300; lower rates rest of yr. Garage $10. TV; cable (premium), VCR (movies $6). Heated pool; poolside serv. Restaurant 7 am–10 pm. Rm serv 24 hrs. Bar noon–2 am (bar menu to midnight). Ck-out 11 am. Meeting rms. Business servs avail. In-rm modem link. Concierge. Gift shop. Free airport transportation; also ski transportation. Downhill/x-country ski 4 blks. Exercise equipt; weight machines, treadmill, whirlpools. Bathrm phones, refrigerators. Cr cds: A, C, D, MC, V*

THE RITZ-CARLTON, ASPEN
★★★★

315 E Dean St, Aspen CO 81611
☎ *970/920–3300*
FAX *970/925–8998*

The reception area of this imposing redbrick hotel at the base of Aspen Mountain hosts antique clocks, crystal chandeliers and a $5-million art collection. Guest quarters are more casual but still posh. 🐾 *257 rms, 6 story. Early Jan-late Mar & early June-early Oct: S, D $259–$349; each addl $25; suites $349–$595; under 18 free; ski plans; lower rates rest of yr. Crib free. Pet accepted. Valet parking $17. TV; cable (premium), VCR avail (movies). Heated pool; poolside serv (summer). Supervised child's activities (Nov-mid-Apr); ages 3–16. Restaurants 6:30 am–11 pm. Rm serv 24 hrs. Bar 11–1 am; entertainment. Ck-out noon. Convention facilities. Business center. In-rm modem link. Concierge. Gift shop. Beauty shop. Golf privileges. Downhill ski 2 blks, x-country ski 2 mi; rental equipt. Hiking. Bicycles (rentals). Exercise rm; instructor, weight machine, bicycles, whirlpools, saunas, steam rms. Masseuse. Bathrm phones, minibars. Some balconies. Luxury level. Cr cds: A, C, D, DS, ER, JCB, MC, V*

COLORADO

SARDY HOUSE ★★★★
128 E Main St, Aspen CO 81611
☎ 970/920-2525 or 800/321-3457
FAX 970/920-4478

A winding staircase with a magnificent oak balustrade leads to the beautifully appointed guest rooms of this 1892 house, which offer panoramic views of the mountains. 🍴 *20 units, 3 story. Mid-Nov-Mar: D $265-$375; suites $425-$650; higher rates winter hols; lower rates rest of yr. TV; cable (premium), VCR avail (free movies). Pool; whirlpool, sauna, poolside serv. Free full bkfst. Dining rm 7:30-10:30 am, 6-9:30 pm. Rm serv. Bar 4:30 pm-midnight. Ck-out noon, ck-in 4 pm. Business servs avail. In-rm modem links. Luggage handling. Concierge serv. Downhill/x-country ski 5 blks. Health club privileges. Some refrigerators, bathrm phones, in-rm steam baths. Cr cds: A, D, MC, V*

RENAISSANCE ★★★★
304 E Hopkins, Aspen CO 81611
☎ 970/925-2402

The American cuisine here has modern French accents and is served in an intimate peach room with contemporary French decor, pink tablecloths and abstract sculpture. The wine room has 1,000 bottles of wine. 🍴 *Hrs: 6-10:30 pm. Res accepted. Modern French menu. Bar. Extensive wine list. A la carte entrees: dinner $24-$32. Child's meals. Specialties: spinach with crab tart, sea bass with artichokes and shitake mushrooms, fresh sautéed foie gras. Menu changes nightly. Own baking. Valet parking. Outdoor dining. Cr cds: A, MC, V*

RESTAURANT AT LITTLE NELL ★★★★
In Little Nell
675 E Durant Ave, Aspen CO 81611
☎ 970/920-4600

An elegant, bilevel room overlooks a snowscape of the Aspen mountain gondolas during the winter season. Diners are seated in cushioned armchairs in this romantic, wood-trimmed restaurant, which has large picture windows overlooking a pretty courtyard. ⏣ *Hrs: 7–10:30 am, 11:30 am–2:30 pm, 6–10 pm; Fri & Sat to 10:30 pm; afternoon tea 3–6 pm; Sun brunch noon–2:30 pm. Res accepted. American alpine cuisine. Bar 3 pm–2 am. Wine cellar. A la carte entrees: bkfst $7–$13.50, lunch $9.50–$17, dinner $23.50–$31. 3-course dinner $29. Sun brunch $19–$24. Specialties: charred tuna steak, rack of lamb, mustard-crusted trout. Valet parking. Outdoor dining (seasonal). Cr cds: A, C, D, DS, JCB, MC, V*

D

Colorado Springs

 ★★★★★
THE BROADMOOR
Lake Ave at Lake Circle, Colorado Springs CO 80901
☎ *719/634-7711 or 800/634-7711*
FAX *719/577-5700*

This famous 3,500-acre resort resembles a small city. Several buildings—including the Italianate turreted main building, the brand-new West Tower rooms and the two-year-old spa complex—are set around a private lake that's home to flocks of decorative fowl and shoals of carp. Practically every sport is available, including golf on world-class courses, one of which hosted the U.S. Women's Open in 1995. Other entertainment options include dancing in the formal rooftop restaurant, the Penrose Room or the more casual Tavern; listening to live jazz in the bar or taking in a movie. Guest rooms vary greatly in size, decor and aspect; the newest have a European style, oversize white-marble bathrooms and French windows that open onto balconies. ⏣ *700 rms. Mid-May–mid-Oct: S, D $240–$375; suites $280–$1,600; package plans; lower rates rest of yr. Crib free. TV; cable (premium), VCR avail. 4 heated pools, 1 indoor; wading pool, poolside serv, lifeguard. Supervised child's activities (June–Labor Day & Dec 25 hols); ages 3–12. Dining rm open 24 hrs. Rm serv. Box lunches, snack bar. Bars noon–1 am; Sun to midnight. Ck-out noon, ck-in 4 pm. Convention facilities. Business center. In-rm modem link. Concierge. Airport, RR station, bus depot transportation. Tennis (indoor in winter), pro. Recreational facilities (all extra) include: 3 18-hole golf courses, greens fee, pro, putting green, driving range. Boats. Bicycles. Skeet, trap and sporting clay shooting. Horseback riding. Hot-air ballooning. Entertainment, dancing, movie theater. Exercise rm; instructor, weight machine, bicycles, whirlpool, sauna. Masseuse. Fishing/hunting guide ser-*

vice. Minibars; some refrigerators. Balconies. Center for large convention groups. Cr cds: A, C, D, DS, MC, V

Denver

★★★★
BROWN PALACE
321 17th St, Denver CO 80202
☎ *303/297-3111 or 800/321-2599*
FAX *303/293-9204*

Opened in 1892, this grand dame of Colorado hotels has lodged luminaries from President Eisenhower to the Beatles. A dramatic stained-glass window tops the nine-story lobby; rooms are decorated with Victorian flair. 230 rms, 9 story. S $185; D $185-$199; each addl $15; suites $245-$725; under 12 free; wkend package plan. Garage in/out $14. Crib free. TV; cable (premium), VCR avail. Restaurants (see PALACE ARMS). Afternoon tea 2-4:30 pm. Rm serv 24 hrs. Bar 10:30 am-midnight; entertainment exc Sun. Ck-out noon. Meeting rms. Business center. In-rm modem link. Concierge. Gift shop. Barber. Valet parking. Exercise equipt; bicycles, rowing machine. Some refrigerators. Cr cds: A, C, D, DS, JCB, MC, V

★★★★
LOEWS GIORGIO
4150 E Mississippi Ave, Denver CO 80222
☎ *303/782-9300*
FAX *303/758-6542*

A modern steel-and-glass facade conceals an Italian Renaissance-style interior distinguished by magnificent frescoes. Guest rooms are spacious and elegant. 190 rms, 11 story. S $180-$215; D $200-$230; each addl $20; suites $250-$800; under 14 free; wkend packages. Pet accepted, some restrictions. TV; cable (premium), VCR avail (movies). Coffee in rms. Restaurant 6 am-11 pm. Bar 10 am-midnight. Ck-out 11 am. Meeting rms. Business center. In-rm modem link. Concierge. Gift shop. Valet parking. Exercise equipt; treadmills, stair machines. Bathrm phones, minibars; some refrigerators. Complimentary newspaper. Library. Cr cds: A, C, D, DS, JCB, MC, V

DURANGO

✕ ★★★★
PALACE ARMS
In the Brown Palace
321 17th St, Denver CO 80202
☎ *303/297–3111*

Artifacts from the Napoleonic era—among them dueling pistols believed to have belonged to Bonaparte and Josephine—are displayed near the red leather booths of this intimate dining room, which also features a mirrored ceiling and huge chandelier. 🐎 Hrs: 11:30 am–2 pm, 6–10 pm; Sat, Sun from 6 pm. Res accepted. Continental, regional Amer menu. Bar to 1 am. Extensive wine list. Semi-a la carte: lunch $8.50–$16, dinner $19.50–$34. Specializes in rack of lamb, fresh seafood. Own baking. Valet parking. Jacket, tie. Cr cds: A, C, D, DS, JCB, MC, V

[D]

✕ ★★★★
ZENITH AMERICAN GRILL
1750 Lawrence St, Denver CO 80202
☎ *303/820–2800*

This attractive space sports a cool high-tech look—track lighting, striking artwork and black-and-white tables—in addition to courtyard dining. The kitchen produces creative Southwestern variations and lighter versions of traditional Colorado meat-and-potatoes cuisine. 🐎 Hrs: 11 am–10 pm; Sat from 5 pm; Sun 5–9 pm. Closed some major hols. Res accepted. Bar. Wine list. Semi-a la carte: lunch $7–$11, dinner $15–$30. A la carte entrees: lunch $5–$10.50, dinner $13–$24.50. Specializes in fresh game & seafood. Valet parking. Cr cds: A, D, MC, V

[D]

Durango

★★★★★
TALL TIMBER
Box 90M, Silverton Star Rte, Durango CO 81301
☎ *970/259–4813*

This family-run luxury resort, set in 180 secluded acres of high-altitude desert and surrounded by the San Juan National Forest, offers an individualized wilderness vacation. Arrival is either by historic narrow-gauge Old West railroad or by 15-minute helicopter ride over the canyons. Recreational activities range from fishing, tennis, horseback riding and golf to enjoying the library, sun decks with open-air hot tubs or wave-resistance swimming pool, available 24 hours a day. Meals are taken in the dining room with a panoramic view of the valley. Many of the luxury log cabin-style duplex apartments contain stone fireplaces, deep carpets and whirlpool baths, and the lack of phones, TVs and radios guarantees absolute peace and quiet. ✈ 10 suites, 2 story. No A/C. No rm phones. AP, July 2–Sept & mid-Dec–early Jan, wkly: 7 days, 6 nights: S $3,500; D $1,900/person; each addl $1,900; 4 days, 3 nights: S $2,500; D $1,400/person; each addl $1,400; 3–12 yrs 50% less; under 3 yrs $300; transfer from Durango included; lower rates mid-May–July 1, Oct. Closed rest of yr. Crib free. Indoor/outdoor pool; whirlpools, sauna. Coffee in rms. Dining rm 7:30–9:30 am, 12:30–1:30 pm, 6:30–7:30 pm. Box lunches, helicopter picnics. Ck-out 10:30 am, ck-in 3:30 pm. Gift shop. Tennis. 9-hole par-3 golf, putting green, driving range. Stocked pond for children. Downhill ski 3 min by air; x-country ski on site. Hiking trails. Horseshoes. Refrigerators, wet bars. Balconies. Library. Totally nonsmoking. No cr cds accepted.

Granby

C LAZY U RANCH
Box 379, Granby CO 80446
☎ 970/887-3344
FAX 970/887-3917

Family-owned and -run for 64 years (by the Murray family since 1988), the C Lazy U is an apparent contradiction in terms—a luxury dude ranch. Comfortable wood cabins and rooms in the lodge house have log fires, lounge areas and tea/coffee makers. The ranch has 5,000 acres of spectacular Rocky Mountain trails and 150 highly trained, spirited horses, one of which is assigned to you for the duration of your stay. Meals are taken family style in the dining room, and a light entree choice is always available. Cookouts are a regular summer occurrence. Entertainment ranges from live bands and square dancing to concerts, plus impromptu gatherings that are a consequence of the ranch's warm, sociable atmosphere—and its lack of TVs. In the warmer months, there's fly fishing in the stocked creek, complimentary tennis instruction and a program of guided hikes and river-rafting expeditions. Come winter, there's cross-country and downhill skiing and telemarking. 🐎 *4 rms in lodge, 41 1–5 rm units in cottages. No A/C. No rm phones. AP (7-day min), Jun–Aug, wkly: S, D $1,600–$3,200/person; ski package plan; lower rates early June, Sept & mid-Dec–Mar. Closed rest of yr. TV in game rm; VCR avail (free movies). Heated pool; poolside serv, whirlpool, sauna. Playground. Free supervised child's activities; ages 3–18. Complimentary coffee in rms. Dining rm (guests only). Barbecues, outdoor buffets. Bars 11–12:30 am. Ck-out 10 am, ck-in 3 pm. Complimentary lndry facilities. Meeting rms. Business servs avail. Valet serv. Gift shop. Tennis, pro. Paddleboats. Stocked lake. Downhill ski 20 mi; x-country ski on site. Sleighing, tobogganing, ice-skating. Racquetball. Skeet, trap range. Trail rides. Hayrides. Petting zoo. Lawn games. Rec rm. Library. Entertainment, dancing. Exercise equipt; bicycles, stair machine. Fishing guides; cleaning and storage. Some fireplaces. No cr cds accepted.*

Steamboat Springs

🏨 ★★★★
HOME RANCH
Follow signs from CO 129, Clark CO 80428
☎ 970/879-1780
FAX 970/879-1795

This ranch occupies 1,500 evergreen- and aspen-dotted acres in the Elk River Valley. Innovative Southwestern cuisine is served in the vaulted-ceiling lodge house, and guest cabins are furnished with genuine Stickley pieces. 🐎 *6 rms in lodge, 8 cottages. No rm phones. AP, June–Oct & mid-Dec–Apr 1, wkly: D $3,010–$3,885; each addl $205/day. Closed rest of yr. Heated pool; sauna. Hot tub. Playground. Supervised child's activities; ages 6–16. Complimentary coffee in rms. Dining rm 8–9 am, noon–1 pm, dinner (1 sitting) 7 pm; children's dinner 5:30 pm. Box lunches, snacks, picnics. Ck-out 10 am, ck-in 4 pm. Valet serv. Meeting rms. Business servs avail. Free local airport, bus depot, ski transportation. Sports dir. Tennis privileges. Downhill ski 20 mi; x-country ski on site. Sleighing, tobogganing. Guided hiking. Horse riding instruction avail. Lawn games. Soc dir; entertainment, movies. Rec rm. Fishing guides; cleaning & storage. Fly fishing instruction avail. Petting zoo for children. Refrigerators, wood stoves.*

COLORADO

Private hot tub at each cabin. Private porches. Ranch rodeo, barbecue. Library. Cr cds: A, MC, V

★★★★
VISTA VERDE
Seed House Rd, Steamboat Springs CO 80477
☎ *970/879–3858 or 800/526–7433*
FAX *970/879–1413*

Luxurious accommodations and gourmet dining could make you forget that you're on a guest ranch, but a step outside onto the 540 acres of this property will remind you why you came here in the first place. ✈ *8 cabins, 1–2 story, 3 lodge rms. No A/C. Early June–late Sept, AP (7-day min): S, D $1,395–$1,595/person/wk; under 12, $995–$1,095/wk; lower rates mid-Dec–Mar.* Playground. Free supervised child's activities (late May–mid-Sept). Coffee in rms. Dining rm. Box lunches; snack bar; picnics. Meeting rms. Business servs avail. Free guest lndry. Gift shop. Free local airport, bus depot transportation. Lake swimming. X-country ski on site. Sleighing, tobogganing. Mountain bikes. Guided hiking trips. Float & backpack trips; gold-panning expeditions. Rock climbing with guide. Hot-air ballooning. Hayrides. Cattle drives. Dog sledding. Rec rm. Game rm. Lawn games. Entertainment, dancing, movies in lodge. Exercise equipt; rowing machine, bicycles, whirlpool, sauna. Fish/hunt guides. Refrigerators. Wood stoves. Private porches. Totally nonsmoking. No cr cds accepted.

Vail

★★★★
HYATT REGENCY—BEAVER CREEK
136 E Thomas Pl, Beaver Creek CO 81620
☎ *970/949–1234*
FAX *970/949–4164*

This multi-gabled slopeside resort in a traditional mountain setting offers contemporary amenities. The lobby sports an imposing antler chandelier, while guest rooms are decorated in country pine style. ✈ *295 rms, 6 story, 31 suites. Dec-Mar: S, D $390–$565; each addl $25; suites $925–$2,220; under 18 free; ski, golf plans; lower rates rest of yr.* Crib free. Valet parking $10. TV; cable (premium), VCR avail.

VAIL

Heated pool; indoor step-in, poolside serv. Playground. Supervised child's activities; ages 5–12. Complimentary coffee in rms. Dining rm 7 am–10 pm. Box lunches, picnics. Rm serv 6 am–midnight. Bar 11:30–1:30 am; entertainment. Ck-out noon, ck-in 4 pm. Deli. Coin lndry. Convention facilities. Business center. In-rm modem link. Bellhops. Valet serv. Concierge. Shopping arcade. Barber, beauty shop. Recreation dir. Tennis, pro. 18-hole golf privileges, greens fee $100, pro, putting green, driving range. Downhill/x-country ski on site. Hiking. Bicycles (rentals). Lawn games. Exercise rm; instructor, bicycles, stair machine, treadmill, whirlpool, sauna, steam rm. Massage. Spa facilities. Fishing/hunting guides. Minibars. Balconies. Cr cds: A, C, D, DS, ER, JCB, MC, V

★★★★
LODGE AT CORDILLERA
Squaw Creek Rd, Edwards CO 81632
☏ *970/926–2200 or 800/548–2721*
FAX *970/926–2486*

Handcarved Spanish pine woodwork and furnishings create rustic luxury at this palatial mountaintop retreat with sweeping vistas of a pristine wilderness area. ✈ 28 rms, 3 story. S, D $240–$325; suites $320–$595; under 16 free; golf & spa plans. Crib free. TV; cable (premium), VCR avail (movies $5). 2 pools, 1 indoor. Restaurant 7–10 am, 11:30 am–2:30 pm, 6–10 pm. Box lunches. Rm serv 6:30 am–11 pm. Bar; entertainment wkends. Ck-out noon, ck-in 4 pm. Meeting rms. Business center. In-rm modem link. Valet serv. Concierge. Gift shop. Tennis, pro. 18-hole golf, pro, greens fee $125 (inclusive). Downhill ski 8 mi; x-country ski on site; rentals. Hiking. Bicycle rentals. Exercise rm; instructor, weight machine, treadmill, whirlpool, sauna, steam rm. Health/spa facilities. Many fireplaces, sleeping lofts. Many balconies, private decks. Totally nonsmoking. Cr cds: A, C, D, DS, MC, V

Connecticut

Greenwich

✕ ★★★★
JEAN-LOUIS
61 Lewis St, Greenwich CT 06830
☎ *203/622-8450*

Roses, Villeroy & Boch china and crisp, white tablecloths with lace underskirts complement extraordinary food, carefully served. 🍴 *Hrs: 6-9 pm. Closed Sun. Res accepted. French menu. Wine cellar. A la carte entrees: dinner $25-$30. Menu degùstation: dinner $65. Specializes in seafood, poultry. Own baking. Jacket. Cr cds: A, C, D, MC, V*

♥

Washington

🏨 ★★★★★
MAYFLOWER INN
CT 47, Washington CT 06793
☎ *860/868-9466*
FAX *860/868-1497*

Restored in 1992, this gracious inn in the Litchfield Hills resembles a generations-old country mansion, painstakingly decorated with antiques, dried rosebud arrangements, other floral displays (some real, some silk), portraits, framed autographs (including Queen Victoria's), board games (take one to your room and play at will), old magazines and books. There are open porches, magnificently manicured gardens, a compact but state-of-the-art fitness center, a tennis court and a fine dining room (open to the general public) and bar. The mostly youthful staff is well-trained and friendly, and the general manager personally leads guests on a 1½-hour "power walk" through the nearby countryside on Saturdays. 🛏 *25 rms in 3 bldgs, 2-3 story, 7 suites. S, D $230-$375; each addl (1 addl max) $50; suites $395-$550; 2-3-night min wkends. Children over 12 yrs only. Valet parking wkends. TV; cable (premium), VCR avail (movies). Heated pool. Dining rm 7:30-10 am, noon-2 pm, 6-8:30 pm. Rm serv (bkfst only). Ck-out 1 pm, ck-in 3 pm. Meeting rms. Business servs avail. In-rm modem* *link. Luggage handling. Sundries. Gift shop. Tennis, pro. 9-hole golf privileges. Exercise rm; instructor, weight machine, bicycles, sauna, steam rm. Massages. Fitness club. Game rm. Refrigerators, minibars. Balconies. Totally nonsmoking. Cr cds: A, MC, V*

Westport

 ★★★★
INN AT NATIONAL HALL
2 Post Road W, Westport CT 06880
☎ *203/221–1351 or 800/628–4255*
FAX *203/221–0276*

In a historic district on the Saugatuck River, this European manor-style house built in 1873 combines Old World elegance with modern convenience. 🐦 15 rms, 3 story, 7 suites. MAP: S, D $195–$295; each addl $15; suites $295–$450; family rates; 2-day min wkends June–Nov. Crib free. TV; cable (premium), VCR (movies). Complimentary coffee, refreshments in rms. Complimentary full bkfst. Restaurant 7–10 am, noon–2:30 pm, 5:30–10 pm. Rm serv. Ck-out 11:30 am, ck-in 3 pm. Business servs avail. Luggage handling. Concierge serv. Health club privileges. Refrigerators. Totally nonsmoking. Cr cds: A, D, MC, V

Delaware

Wilmington

★★★★
HOTEL DU PONT
11th & Market Sts, Wilmington DE 19801
302/594-3100 or 800/441-9019
FAX *302/656-2145*

The spacious guest rooms in this renovated landmark are furnished with reproductions of 18th-century antiques. 216 rms, 12 story. S, D $139-$239; suites $395-$495; under 12 free; wkend rates. Crib free. Valet parking $12. TV; cable (premium), VCR (movies). Restaurant 6 am-11 pm. Rm serv 24 hrs. Bar; entertainment. Ck-out 1 pm. Meeting rms. Business center. In-rm modem link. Concierge. Shopping arcade. Barber, beauty shop. Tennis privileges. 54-hole golf privileges, greens fee, pro, putting green, driving range. Exercise rm; instructor, weight machine, bicycles. Minibars. Cr cds: A, C, D, DS, ER, JCB, MC, V

District of Columbia

Washington

★★★★
THE CARLTON
923 16th St NW, Washington DC 20006
☏ *202/638-2626*
FAX *202/638-4231*

An Italian Renaissance mansion, bedecked with gilt and carved wood, anchors this quiet hotel two blocks from the White House. Guest rooms are furnished with antiques and reproductions. *195 rms, 8 story. S $250-$290; D $275-$315; each addl $25; suites $550-$2,100; under 18 free; wkend rates. Crib free. Covered valet parking $22. Pet accepted, some restrictions. TV; cable (premium), VCR avail. Pool privileges. Restaurant 7 am-10:30 pm. Afternoon tea 2:30-6 pm. Rm serv 24 hrs. Bar; entertainment. Ck-out 1 pm. Meeting rms. Business servs avail. In-rm modem link. Concierge. Gift shop. Tennis privileges. Exercise equipt; bicycles, treadmill. Massage. Bathrm phones, refrigerators, minibars. Courtyard terrace. Cr cds: A, C, D, DS, ER, JCB, MC, V*

★★★★
FOUR SEASONS
2800 Pennsylvania Ave NW, Washington DC 20007
☏ *202/342-0444*
FAX *202/944-2076*

This highly efficient, midsize hotel on the edge of Georgetown has a strong dedication to guest service. Rooms, which have park views, are comfortably furnished and well-lighted. *196 rms, 6 story. S $305-$355; D $320-$370; each addl $30; suites $675-$2,100; under 18 free; wkend rates. Crib free. Pet accepted. Valet parking $22. TV; cable (premium), VCR avail (movies). Indoor pool. Restaurant 7-2 am. Rm serv 24 hrs. Afternoon tea. Bar from 11 am. Ck-out noon. Meeting rms. Business center. In-rm modem link. Concierge. Complimentary limo serv in DC area. Exercise rm; instructor, weight machine, bicycles, steam rm. Massage. Full service health club & spa. Bathrm phones, minibars. Some

DISTRICT OF COLUMBIA

balconies. Tastefully appointed rooms and public areas. Cr cds: A, C, D, ER, JCB, MC, V

★★★★
JEFFERSON
16th & M Sts NW, Washington DC 20036
☎ *202/347–2200 or 800/368–5966*
FAX *202/331–7982*

The hotel has been in operation since 1923, and the individually decorated rooms feature some four-poster and canopy beds as well as antiques. *100 rms, 8 story. Jan–June, Sept–Nov: S $240–$278; D $255–$295; each addl $25; suites $340–$1,000; under 15 free; wkend plans; lower rates rest of yr. Crib free. Garage, valet parking $20. TV; cable (premium), VCR (movies avail). Pool privileges. Restaurants 6:30 am–11 pm. Rm serv 24 hrs. Afternoon tea 3–5 pm. Bar 10–2 am. Ck-out 1 pm. Business servs avail. In-rm modem link. Concierge. Health club privileges. Some private patios. Cr cds: A, C, D, DS, JCB, MC, V*

★★★★
LOEWS L'ENFANT PLAZA
480 L'Enfant Plaza SW, Washington DC 20024
☎ *202/484–1000*
FAX *202/646–4456*

The center piece of L'Enfant Plaza, you will find an upscale hotel with a pretty lobby and pleasant rooms. The hotel is popular with travelers doing business with nearby government agencies. *370 rms on floors 11–15. S, D $190–$230; each addl $20; suites $370–$1,200; under 18 free; wkend rates. Crib free. Pet accepted. Valet parking $16. TV; cable (premium), VCR (movies avail). Pool; poolside serv, lifeguard. Restaurant 6:30 am–midnight. Bar 11:30–1:30 am. Ck-out 1 pm. Convention facilities. Business center. In-rm modem link. Concierge. Underground shopping arcade with Metro subway stop. Gift shop. Exercise rm; instructor, weights, bicycles. Refrigerators, minibars. Many balconies. Cr cds: A, C, D, DS, MC, V*

WASHINGTON

★★★★ PARK HYATT

24th & M St NW, Washington DC 20037
☎ *202/789-1234*
FAX *202/457-8823*

An impressive collection of modern art distinguishes the interiors of this hotel, softened by touches of bronze and chinoiserie. Guest rooms are furnished with a mix of contemporary and antique pieces as well as museum reproductions of Oriental antiques. 🐾 *224 units, 10 story, 133 suites. S $238-$295; D $263-$320; each addl $25; suites $270-$1,975; under 18 free; wkend rates; lower rates July, Aug. Crib free. TV; cable (premium), VCR avail. Indoor pool; whirlpool, poolside serv. Restaurant 6:30-11 am, 11:30 am-2:30 pm, 6-10:30 pm. Afternoon tea 3-5 pm. Rm serv 24 hrs. Bar 11:30-1 am, Fri & Sat to 2 am; pianist. Ck-out noon. Meeting rms. Business center. In-rm modem link. Concierge. Gift shop. Barber, beauty shop. Covered parking; valet. Golf privileges. Exercise rm; instructor, weight machines, bicycles, steam rm, sauna. Massage. Bathrm phones, refrigerators. Daily newspapers. Cr cds: A, C, D, DS, JCB, MC, V*

★★★★ RENAISSANCE MAYFLOWER

1127 Connecticut Ave NW, Washington DC 20036
☎ *202/347-3000*
FAX *202/466-9082*

This grand hotel opened in 1925 for Calvin Coolidge's inauguration and with its ornate gilded interior, extravagant use of marble and stained-glass skylights, has remained a fixture of Washington life ever since. Rooms are furnished with custom-designed pieces, and suites still have original mantel pieces. 🐾 *660 rms, 10 story, 78 suites. S, D $250-$300; each addl $30; suites $450-$3,500; under 19 free; wkend plans. Crib free. Pet accepted, some restrictions. Garage adj $11.50. TV; cable (premium), VCR avail. Complimentary coffee in rms. Restaurant 6:30 am-11:30 pm. Rm serv 24 hrs. Bar 11-1:30 am; entertainment. Ck-out 1 pm. Convention facilities. Business center. In-rm modem link. Concierge. Exercise rm; instructor, weight machine, bicycles, sauna. Health club privileges. Bathrm phones; refrigerators avail. Foreign currency exchange. Cr cds: A, C, D, DS, ER, JCB, MC, V*

DISTRICT OF COLUMBIA

★★★★ THE RITZ-CARLTON

2100 Massachusetts Ave NW, Washington DC 20008
☎ *202/293-2100 or 800/241-3333*
FAX *202/293-0641*

This intimate hotel has the air of an English hunt club with its classic 18th-century European furnishings and extensive collection of 18th- and 19th-century British oils of horses and dogs. 🐾 *206 rms, 8 story. S, D $250-$375; suites $350-$2,100; under 18 free; wkend rates. Crib free. Valet parking $20. TV; cable (premium), VCR avail. Restaurant 6:30 am-10:30 pm. Bar 11:30-1 am; entertainment. Ck-out noon. Meeting rms. Business servs avail. In-rm modem link. Concierge. Tennis, golf privileges. Exercise equipt; weights, stair machines, sauna. Bathrm phones, minibars; some bathrm TVs. Complimentary newspapers. Elegant ballroom. Within 10 minutes of Georgetown. Luxury level. Cr cds: A, C, D, DS, JCB, MC, V*

★★★★ THE WATERGATE

2650 Virginia Ave NW, Washington DC 20037
☎ *202/965-2300 or 800/424-2736*
FAX *202/337-7915*

With its spacious rooms, striking views and white stepped balconies overlooking the Potomac, this hotel is a Washington landmark. Fine antiques and murals lend an air of English gentility. 🐾 *232 rms, 13 story. S $275-$410; D $300-$435; each addl $25; suites $550-$1,885; under 18 free; wkend, hol rates. Crib free. Valet parking $18. TV; cable (premium), VCR avail (movies). Indoor pool; whirlpool, lifeguard. Restaurant 7 am-10:30 pm. Rm serv 24 hrs. Bar 11:30-1 am; pianist. Ck-out noon. Meeting rms. Business center. In-rm modem link. Concierge. Shopping arcade. Barber, beauty shop. Complimentary downtown & Capitol transportation. Exercise rm; instructor, weight machines, bicycles, sauna, steam rm. Massage. Bathrm phones, minibars. Many extras. Many balconies. Kennedy Center adj. Cr cds: A, C, D, DS, JCB, MC, V*

WILLARD INTER-CONTINENTAL

1401 Pennsylvania Ave NW, Washington DC 20004
☎ *202/628-9100*
FAX *202/637-7326*

This opulent Beaux Arts hotel was host to every president from Franklin Pierce to Dwight D. Eisenhower on the eve of their inaugurations. A faithful renovation has returned elegance to the stately columns, mosaic, floors and turn-of-the-century decor. Guest rooms are furnished with mahogany Queen Anne-style reproductions. *340 units, 12 story, 36 suites. S $305-$395; D $325-$425; each addl $30; suites $700-$3,300; under 14 free; wkend rates. Crib free. Pet accepted, some restrictions. Covered parking, valet $20. TV; cable (premium), VCR avail. Restaurant 6:30 am-11 pm. Rm serv 24 hrs. Bar 11-1 am, Sun 11:30 am-midnight; entertainment. Ck-out noon. Convention facilities. Business center. In-rm modem link. Concierge. Shopping arcade. Exercise equipt; weight machines, treadmill. Bathrm phones, minibars. Famous "Peacock Alley" runs the length of the hotel, connecting Pennsylvania Ave and F St. Cr cds: A, C, D, DS, JCB, MC, V*

KINKEAD'S

2000 Pennsylvania Ave NW, Washington DC 20006
☎ *202/296-7700*

Chef Bob Kinkead has created two distinct but delicious dining options in this multichambered restaurant. Downstairs is a more informal and inexpensive pub-style eatery, while upstairs you can watch Kinkead and company turn out grilled dishes with an emphasis on seafood. *Hrs: 11:30 am-10:30 pm; Sun brunch 11:30 am-2:30 pm. Closed Jan 1, Thanksgiving, Dec 25. Res accepted. Bar to midnight. Semi-a la carte: lunch $12-$16, dinner $14-$20. Sun brunch $8-$12. Specialties: pepita-crusted salmon, pepper-seared tuna, grilled squid. Complimentary valet parking (dinner). Outdoor dining. Jazz pianist Mon-Sat. Two levels of dining areas. Cr cds: A, C, D, DS, MC, V*

Florida

Amelia Island

★★★★ THE RITZ-CARLTON, AMELIA ISLAND
4750 Amelia Island Pkwy, Amelia Island FL 32034
☎ *904/277-1100*
FAX *904/261-9063*

Along with stylish elegance, superb comfort and excellent service comes one of the prettiest and most pristine beaches on Florida's east coast. All rooms have ocean views. 🕊 *449 units, 8 story, 45 suites. Mar-May: S, D $255-$305; suites $440-$695; under 18 free; golf & tennis packages; other packages avail rest of yr. Crib free. Garage parking, valet $10. TV; cable (premium), VCR avail. 2 pools, 1 indoor; poolside serv. Supervised child's activities; ages 5-14. Restaurant 6:30 am-11 pm (also see THE GRILL). Afternoon tea 3-5 pm, Fri & Sat (seasonal). Rm serv 24 hrs. Bar 11-1 am; entertainment. Ck-out noon, ck-in 3 pm. Convention facilities. Business center. In-rm modem link. Bellhops. Valet serv. Concierge. Shopping arcade. Beauty shop. Airport transportation. Lighted tennis, pro. 18-hole golf, pro, putting green, driving range. Exercise equipt; weight machines, bicycles, whirlpool, sauna, steam rm. Bathrm phones, refrigerators, minibars, wet bars. Balconies. Luxury level. Cr cds: A, C, D, DS, JCB, MC, V*

★★★★ THE GRILL
In the Ritz-Carlton, Amelia Island
4750 Amelia Island Pkwy, Amelia Island FL 32034
☎ *904/277-1100*

All of the usual elegance of a Ritz-Carlton dining room is combined with superior cuisine, dedicated service and a relaxed ambiance, plus piano music to help create a romantic evening. If you're seated at one of the floor-to-ceiling windows, the Atlantic Ocean is just over your shoulder. 🕊 *Hrs: 6-10 pm. Closed Sun. Res accepted. Bar to midnight. Wine cellar. A la carte entrees: dinner from $25. Prix fixe: dinner from $45. Specializes in meat & game, fresh*

Florida seafood. Pianist. Valet parking. Club atmosphere; fireplace. Jacket. Cr cds: A, C, D, DS, JCB, MC, V

Boca Raton

★★★★
BOCA RATON RESORT & CLUB
501 E Camino Real, Boca Raton FL 33432
☎ *561/395–3000 or 800/327–0101*
FAX *561/391–3183*

This historic, long-time dazzling resort on 351 landscaped acres has almost everything a vacationer would desire; the tennis and golf facilities are world-renowned. The main buildings and beach club (reachable by car, bus or yacht) are a mecca for conventioneers, and the almost-constant hustle and bustle are fun if you like lots of company. 🕊 *963 units in 4 bldgs, 242 rms in 27-story tower, several villa apts with kit., 214 rms in beach club, 327 cloister rms. Mid-Dec–Apr: S, D $230–$430; suites $460–$5,500; MAP avail; lower rates rest of yr. Maid and bellman service charge $9 per day. Dining facilities: 18% food & beverage service charge at all dining outlets in lieu of gratuities. Crib free. TV; cable. 4 pools; poolside serv, lifeguard. Supervised child's activities. Dining rm 7 am–midnight. Box lunches, snack bar. Rm serv 24 hrs. Bar 11–2 am. Ck-out noon, ck-in 3 pm. Convention facilities. Business center. Barber, beauty shop. Many specialty shops. Airport transportation. Sports dir. 34 tennis courts, 9 lighted, pro. 36-hole golf, 2 putting greens, driving range. Private beach; cabanas. Charter boats. 23 yacht slips. Bicycles. Lawn games. Soc dir. Exercise rm; instructor, weights, bicycles, sauna. Masseur. Some balconies. Luxury level. Cr cds: A, C, D, DS, ER, JCB, MC, V*

✕ ★★★★
LA VIEILLE MAISON
770 E Palmetto Park Rd, Boca Raton FL
☎ *561/391–6701*

This country French oasis just off the beach has many tastefully decorated rooms for quiet dining. Chef Richard Ruiz presents an extensive selection of contemporary French Provencale delicacies; there's a four-course "grand menu" and, every night except Saturday, a three-course "tempta-

FLORIDA

tion menu" in addition to a la carte choices. 🐎 *Hrs: May–Oct 6:30–9:30 pm; Nov–Apr 6–10 pm. Closed July 4, Labor Day. Res accepted; required in season. French menu. Bar. Wine list. A la carte entrees: dinner $17–$38. Prix fixe: dinner $56 excluding beverage. "Temptation" menu (May-Nov 1, Sun-Fri) $36. Specialties: escargot, shrimp Pernod, medallions of lamb and beef, fresh Dover Sole. Own baking. Treetop balcony dining & outdoor courtyard. Patio & private dining area. Valet parking. Jacket. Cr cds: A, C, D, DS, MC, V*

Fort Lauderdale

★★★★
HYATT REGENCY PIER 66

2301 SE 17th St Causeway, Fort Lauderdale FL 33316
☎ *954/525–6666 or 800/327–3796*
FAX *954/728–3541*

Guests at Pier 66 will enjoy a magnificent 3-pool oasis, on-site Aquatics Center, and full-service marina and spa with exercise facilities. The trademark is the rooftop Pier Top Lounge, which revolves every 66 minutes and is accessed by an exterior elevator. 🐎 *388 rms, 17 story. Mid-Dec–Apr: S, D $180–$270; each addl $15; suites $650–$1,000; under 15 free; varied lower rates rest of yr. Crib free. Parking $6; valet parking $8. TV; cable (premium). 2 heated pools; wading pool, poolside serv, hot tub. Dining rm 6:30 am–midnight; 6 restaurants and bars. Rm serv 24 hrs. Bars 11–2 am (1 revolving rooftop); entertainment. Ck-out noon. Coin lndry. Convention facilities. Business center. In-rm modem link. Concierge. Gift shop. Full service hair salon. Transportation shuttle to beach by water or vehicle. Lighted tennis, pro. Golf privileges, greens fee $35, pro. Exercise rm; instructor, weights, bicycles, whirlpool, sauna, steam rm. Full service spa. Refrigerators. Many private patios, balconies. Glass-enclosed outside elvtr. 22 acres on Intracoastal Waterway; marina and marina store. Adj to Port Everglades. Cr cds: A, C, D, DS, JCB, MC, V*

Jacksonville Beach

THE LODGE AND BEACH CLUB AT PONTE VEDRA BEACH

607 Ponte Vedra Blvd, Ponte Vedra Beach FL 32082
☎ *904/273-9500 or 800/243-4304*
FAX *904/273-0210*

The look of this plush resort is Mediterranean villa, appealing to an elite clientele whose passions are golf and tennis. 66 rms, 2 story, 24 suites. Mid-Feb–mid-Nov: S, D $205–$319; each addl $20; suites $289; under 18 free; golf, tennis, honeymoon plans; higher rates: TPC wk, Gator Bowl, FL-GA football game; lower rates rest of yr. Crib free. TV; cable. 3 pools; poolside serv, lifeguard. Supervised child's activities (Memorial Day–Labor Day); ages 3–11. Restaurant 7 am–10 pm. Rm serv 24 hrs. Bar 11–12:30 am. Ck-out noon. Meeting rms. Business servs avail. Concierge. Free valet parking. Tennis, golf privileges. Exercise equipt; weight machines, bicycles, whirlpools, saunas. Bathrm phones, refrigerators; some in-rm whirlpools, minibars, fireplaces. Wet bar in suites. Balconies. On ocean. Cr cds: A, C, D, DS, MC, V

PONTE VEDRA INN & CLUB

200 Ponte Vedra Blvd, Ponte Vedra Beach FL 32082
☎ *904/285-1111 or 800/234-7842*
FAX *904/285-2111*

Established in 1928, this luxurious yet cozy oceanfront resort features third-generation employees serving third-generation guests. 222 units, 2 story, 64 kits. Mar–May: S, D $220–$240; suites $320–$340; golf plans; MAP, AP avail; lower rates rest of yr. Crib $5. TV; cable (premium). 4 pools, 2 heated; wading pool, poolside serv, lifeguard. Playground. Supervised child's activities (June–Sept & hols); ages 4–12. Dining rm 7–10:30 am, 11:30 am–3:30 pm, 6:30–10 pm. Box lunches, snack bar, picnics. Rm serv 24 hrs. Bars 11 am–midnight; entertainment Thurs–Sat. Ck-out noon, ck-in 3 pm. Package store. Convention facilities. Business center. In-rm modem link. Concierge. Gift shops. Valet parking avail. Airport transportation. Tennis, pro, shop. Two 18-hole golf courses, greens fee $85–$95, pro, putting green, driving range, shop. Private beach, swimming; boats, rowboats, sailboats, paddleboats. Bicycles. Lawn games. Soc dir; entertainment. Exercise *rm; instructor, weights, bicycles, whirlpool, steam rm, sauna. Health spa facilities; technicians and therapists. Refrigerators, minibars, wet bars; some fireplaces. Private patios, balconies. Picnic tables. Cr cds: A, C, D, DS, MC, V*

Key West

LITTLE PALM ISLAND
28500 Overseas Hwy, Little Torch Key FL 33042
☎ *305/872-2524 or 800/343-8567*
FAX *305/872-4843*

On beautifully landscaped, palm-fringed Little Munson Island, once a retreat and fishing camp that hosted many a luminary, this small luxury resort consists of an old cypress fishing lodge and thatch-roof villas that stand on stilts 20 feet from the water. Views from the terrace at sunset are spectacular. 🅟 28 suites in 14 villas and 1 in greathouse. No rm phones. Mid-Dec–Apr: S, D $465–$645; 2-day min hols; AP, MAP avail; lower rates rest of yr. Children over 12 yrs only. TV; VCR avail (movies). Heated pool; poolside serv. Complimentary coffee in rms. Dining rm 7:30–10 am, 11:30 am–2:30 pm, 7–10:30 pm. Picnics. Rm serv. Bar; entertainment Thurs–Sun. Ck-out 11 am, ck-in 3 pm. Coin lndry. Bellhops. Valet serv. Business servs avail. Concierge. Gift shop. Airport transportation. Sports dir. Sailing cruises, boat rentals, scuba trips, swimming beach. Social dir. Exercise equipt; weights, bicycles, sauna. Massage avail. Fishing guides; clean & store. Minibars, wet bars. Sun balconies. Picnic tables. Herb garden. The island is a 15-minute boat ride from Little Torch Key; the launch makes the trip each way once an hour. White sand beach; water sports; nature tours. Dockage avail for 3 deep-draft yachts and 8 shallow-draft boats; complete marine center. Cr cds: A, C, D, DS, MC, V

MARCO ISLAND

Longboat Key (& Lido Beach)

★★★★
THE RESORT AT LONGBOAT KEY CLUB

301 Gulf of Mexico Dr, Longboat Key FL 34228
☎ *941/383-8821 or 800/237-8821*
FAX *941/383-5396*

This is not simply a refined luxury hotel on 1,000 elaborately landscaped gulfside acres; it's one of the best places to golf in the state, as well as a great place for tennis. *233 units, 4-10 story, 213 kits. Mid-Jan-Apr: rms $200-$295; suites $300-$610; 1-bedrm suites $335-$440; 2-bedrm suites $445-$610; varied lower rates rest of yr. TV; cable, VCR avail. Heated pool; whirlpool, sauna, poolside serv. Supervised child's activities (June-Sept); ages 5-12. Complimentary coffee in rms. Dining rm 7 am-midnight. Box lunches. Snack bar. Rm serv from 6:30 am. Bar from 11 am; entertainment. Ck-out 11 am, ck-in 3 pm. Meeting rms. Business servs avail. Valet serv. Concierge. Pro shops. Airport transportation; also transportation on site and to local area attractions. Activities dir. 38 tennis courts, 6 lighted, pro. 45-hole golf, greens fee $98 (incl cart), pro, putting green, driving range. Private beach, boardwalk; water sports. Boat cruises. Bicycles. Lawn games. Exercise rm; instructor, weight machines, bicycles. Refrigerators, minibars. Extensive library. Private patios. Bird sanctuary. Cr cds: A, C, D, DS, MC, V*

Marco Island

★★★★
MARCO ISLAND HILTON BEACH RESORT

560 S Collier Blvd, Marco Island FL 33937
☎ *941/394-5000 or 800/443-4550*
FAX *941/394-5251*

The lobby of this hotel sets a tone of luxury with its Oriental antiques and marble floors. It has an abundance of amenities and facilities. *294 rms, 11 story. Mid-Dec-Apr: S, D $189-$339; each addl $25; 1-bedrm suite $389; family rates; special packages; golf, tennis plans; lower rates rest of yr. Crib free. TV; cable (premium). Heated pool; poolside serv.*

FLORIDA

Supervised child's activities; ages 3–14. Coffee in rms. Restaurant 7 am–10 pm. Bkfst buffet on patio in season & wkends. Bar noon–2 am. Ck-out noon. Convention facilities. Business center (Jan–May). In-rm modem link. Concierge. Gift shop. Drugstore. 3 lighted tennis courts, pro. Golf privileges, greens fee $25–$115, pro, putting green, driving range. Exercise rm; instructor, bicycles, weight machines, whirlpool, sauna, steam rm. Massage. Game rm. Bathrm phones & TVs, refrigerators, minibars, wet bars. Private patios, balconies. On gulf, fishing by arrangement; beach, water sports. Bicycles avail. Cr cds: A, C, D, DS, MC, V

Miami

★★★★
DORAL GOLF RESORT AND SPA
4400 NW 87th Ave, Miami FL 33178
☎ *305/592–2000 or 800/71-DORAL*
FAX *305/594–4682*

Site of the annual Doral-Ryder Open Tournament, this luxurious resort hotel on 2,400 elaborately landscaped acres is an inland golf and tennis mecca. Accommodations are in separated 3- and 4-story lodges nestled beside the golf links. ✈ *694 rms in 12 buildings. Dec–Apr: S, D $225–$370; each addl $40; suites $360–$1,500; under 17 free; lower rates rest of yr. Crib free. TV; cable (premium). Heated pool; wading pool, poolside serv. Playground. Supervised child's activities (hols only); ages 3–15. Dining rm (public by res) 6:30 am–midnight; also 3 others. Rm serv 24 hrs (in season). Snack bar; box lunches. 3 bars 11–1:30 am. Ck-out 11 am, ck-in 4 pm. Convention facilities. Business center. Valet serv. 15 tennis courts (4 lighted), pro. Four 18-hole golf courses; 9-hole par-3 golf, 4 putting greens, lighted driving range, golf school, pro. Bicycle rentals. Lawn games. Soc dir; entertainment, dancing, movies. Game rm. Exercise rm; instructor, weights, bicycles, whirlpool, steam rm. Massage. European spa facilities. Bathrm phones, refrigerators, minibars. Private patios, balconies. Free transportation to Doral Ocean Beach Resort Hotel in Miami Beach. Cr cds: A, C, D, DS, JCB, MC, V*

MIAMI

FISHER ISLAND CLUB

1 Fisher Island Dr, Fisher Island FL 33109
☎ *305/535-6020 or 800/537-3708*
FAX *305/535-6003*

Mediterranean-inspired, circa-1925 cottages and guest houses sit amid 200 landscaped acres on an island that was the winter estate of William Vanderbilt. ✈ *60 rms, 1-5 story, 4 kit. cottages. Nov-Apr: S $385-$690; D $385-$1,400; suites, cottages $575-$1,250; under 12 free; golf plan; lower rates rest of yr. Crib free. TV; cable (premium), VCR (movies $3). 4 pools, 1 indoor; poolside serv. Playground. Supervised child's activities; ages 4-10. Complimentary coffee in rms. Dining rm 7 pm-midnight. Rm serv. Bar 11-2 am; entertainment Wed-Sun. Ck-out noon, ck-in 3 pm. Grocery. Coin lndry. Meeting rms. Business servs avail. In-rm modem link. Bellhops. Valet serv. Concierge. Gift shop. Airport transportation. Sports dir. Lighted tennis; pro. 9-hole golf; greens fee $80, pro, putting green, driving range. Boating. Exercise rm; instructor, weight machine, treadmill, whirlpool, sauna. Spa facility. Masseur. Lawn games. Social dir. Minibars. Balconies. Bird aviary. Swimming beach. Marina; dockage avail. Cr cds: A, C, D, MC, V*

GRAND BAY

2669 S Bayshore Dr, Miami FL 33133
☎ *305/858-9600 or 800/327-2788*
FAX *305/858-1532*

This modern high-rise with a stepped facade resembling a Mayan pyramid features traditional furnishings, original art, attentive service and breathtaking views of Biscayne Bay and downtown Miami. ✈ *178 rms, 13 story, 47 suites. S, D $205-$295; each addl $20; suites $350-$1,100; under 15 free; wkend rates. Crib free. TV; cable (premium), VCR (movies avail). Heated pool; poolside serv. Restaurant 7 am-11 pm. Rm serv 24 hrs. Bar 11:30-2 am; entertainment exc Sun. Ck-out noon. Meeting rms. Business center. In-rm modem link. Concierge. Hair salon. Airport transportation. Exercise equipt; weights, bicycles, whirlpool, sauna. Massage. Bathrm phones, minibars. Private balconies. Cr cds: A, C, D, MC, V*

FLORIDA

MAYFAIR HOUSE ★★★★
3000 Florida Ave, Miami FL 33133
☎ *305/441-0000 or 800/433-4555*
FAX *305/447-9173*

This European-style luxury hotel sits within Mayfair Shops at the Grove, an exclusive open-air shopping mall. Public areas have Tiffany windows, polished mahogany, marble walls and floors, imported ceramics and crystal and a glassed-in elevator. 🐾 *185 suites, 5 story. Mid-Dec–Apr: S, D $230–$900; each addl $35; under 12 free; wkend, honeymoon plans; lower rates rest of yr. Crib free. Valet parking $10. TV; cable (premium), VCR (movies avail). Rooftop pool. Restaurant 7 am–11 pm. Rm serv 24 hrs. Bars from noon. Ck-out 1 pm. Meeting rms. Business center. Concierge. Shopping arcade. Airport transportation. Health club privileges. Bathrm phones, refrigerators, honor bars. Private patios, all with hot tub. Cr cds: A, C, D, DS, ER, JCB, MC, V*

TURNBERRY ISLE RESORT & CLUB ★★★★
19999 W Country Club Dr, Aventura FL 33180
☎ *305/932-6200 or 800/327-7028*
FAX *305/933-6560*

This luxurious, gracious and comfortable resort consists of the European-style Marina hotel, the Yacht Club, the Mizner-style Country Club Hotel and the new Mediterranean-style annex, all on 300 secluded acres with subtropical gardens. 🐾 *340 rms in 3 bldgs, 3–7 story. Late Dec–Apr: Country Club: S, D $375–$475; each addl $30; suites $675–$2,100; Yacht Club: S, D $295; each addl $30; Marina Wing: S, D $335; each addl $30; under 12 free; golf, tennis and spa plans; lower rates rest of yr. Crib free. TV; cable, VCR (movies avail). 4 pools; poolside serv. Dining rm for guests 7 am–10 pm. Box lunches, snack bar, picnics. Rm serv 24 hrs. Bars 11–1 am. Ck-out noon, ck-in 4 pm. Grocery, package store 1 blk. Coin lndry. Convention facilities. Business center. In-rm modem link. Lighted tennis, pro. 36-hole golf, greens fee $80 ($40 in summer), pro, putting green. Beach, boats, diving, water sports. Entertainment. Rec rm. Exercise rm; instructor, weights, bicycles, whirlpool, sauna, steam rm. Massage. Refrigerators; many in-rm whirlpools, hot tubs. Cr cds: A, C, D, DS, ER, MC, V*

MIAMI BEACH

✕ ★★★★
CHEF ALLEN'S
19088 NE 29th Ave, Aventura FL 33137
☎ *954/935–2900*

In this art-deco world of glass block, neon trim, fresh flowers and gallery art, your gaze nevertheless remains riveted on the kitchen. Chef Allen Susser designed it with a picture window 25 feet wide, so you can watch him create new American masterpieces with the help of a wood-burning mesquite grill. 🍴 *Hrs: 6–10:30 pm. Res accepted. Bar. Wine cellar. A la carte entrees: dinner $24.95–$32.95. Specializes in fresh local seafood, veal chops, dessert soufflés. Own baking. Valet parking. Cr cds: A, D, MC, V*

✕ ★★★★
MARK'S PLACE
2286 NE 123rd St, North Miami FL 33181
☎ *305/893–6888*

Behind the adobe facade lies a stylish, deco-detailed dining room, a work of art itself, while in the kitchen, owner-chef Mark Militello cooks regional Florida gourmet fare in a special oak-burning oven imported from Genoa. The changing menu is based on the availability of fresh ingredients. 🍴 *Hrs: 6:30–10 pm; Fri, Sat 6–11 pm; Sun to 10:30 pm. Closed Dec 25. Res accepted. Serv bar. Semi-a la carte: dinner $15–$32. Specializes in fresh Florida seafood, pasta. Cr cds: A, C, D, MC, V*

Miami Beach

✕ ★★★★
PACIFIC TIME
915 Lincoln Rd, Miami Beach FL 33140
☎ *305/534–5979*

This cool California-style restaurant is packed even on nights something special isn't happening. Twenty-foot cathedral ceilings, abstract paintings, accents of mahogany and brass, plank floors and an open kitchen give this restaurant a special flair. 🍴 *Hrs: 6–11 pm; Fri & Sat to midnight; early-bird dinner to 7 pm. Closed Thanksgiving. Res accepted. Asian, Amer menu. Bar. Wine list. A la carte entrees:*

FLORIDA

dinner $14.50–$24.50. Child's meals. Specialties: Szechwan grilled grouper, shiitake grilled beef, shrimp Peking pancake. Parking. Outdoor dining. Cr cds: A, C, D, DS, MC, V

Naples

THE RITZ-CARLTON, NAPLES

280 Vanderbilt Beach Rd, Naples FL 33941
☎ *941/598–3300 or 800/241–3333*
FAX *941/598–6690*

This imposing hotel sits like an impregnable fortress on the Gulf of Mexico, but it exudes comfort, friendliness and relaxation despite its elegant imperial presence inside and out. Rooms are spacious and tastefully furnished. There's a large outdoor swimming pool and veranda, from which plank paths lead through lush tropical growth to the broad beach, great for a sunset stroll. Service is virtually impeccable, aimed at making each and every guest feel not just satisfied, but very special. ✈ *463 units, 14 story. Late Dec–Apr: S, D $325–$595; each addl $15; suites $850–$3,345; under 17 free; monthly, honeymoon plans; MAP avail; lower rates rest of yr. Crib free. TV; cable (premium), VCR avail. Heated pool; poolside serv. Supervised child's activities (late Dec–early Apr); ages 3–16. Dining rms 6:30 am–10 pm. Rm serv 24 hrs. Bar 9–1:30 am; entertainment. Ck-out noon, ck-in 3 pm. Convention facilities. Business center. In-rm modem link. Valet serv. Concierge. Gift shop. Barber, beauty shop. Covered parking, valet. Airport transportation. Lighted tennis, pro. 18-hole golf privileges, greens fee (incl cart) $100, pro, putting green, driving range. On white sand beach; water sports. Complimentary bicycles avail. Lawn games. Activities dir. Rec rm. Exercise rm; instructor, weights, bicycles, whirlpool, sauna, steam rm. Massage therapy. Nutrition & fitness program. Bathrm phones, minibars. Balconies. Luxury level. Cr cds: A, C, D, DS, ER, JCB, MC, V*

REGISTRY RESORT NAPLES
★★★★

475 Seagate Dr, Naples FL 33940
☎ *941/597-3232 or 800/247-9810*
FAX *941/597-3147*

From the atrium lobby with a 2-story fountain and the sumptuously decorated rooms to the free-form swimming pools with waterfalls and the exceptional service, this high-rise on 21 lush tropical acres is the essence of luxury. *424 rms in main building, 18 story, 50 villas. Late Dec-mid-Apr: S, D $295-$385; each addl $25; suites $495-$675; villas $495; under 18 free; tennis, golf plans; honeymoon packages; lower rates rest of yr. Crib free. TV; cable (premium), VCR avail (movies). 3 heated pools; poolside serv. Supervised child's activities; ages 5-12. 4 dining rms 7 am-11 pm. Box lunches. Snack bar. Rm serv 24 hrs. Bar 11-2 am. Ck-out noon, ck-in 3 pm. Convention facilities. Business center. Valet serv. Concierge. Shopping arcade. Barber, beauty shop. Valet parking. Activities dir. 15 tennis courts, 5 lighted, pro, instruction avail, pro shop. Golf privileges, greens fee (incl cart) $110; putting green. Swimming beach. Boating; water sports avail. Bicycle rentals. Lawn games. Health club and spa; 3 instructors, weights, bicycles, whirlpool, steam rm, sauna. Massage therapy. Entertainment. Wet bars; mini honor bars. Private patios, balconies. All tower rms with view of gulf. Trolley to beach. Cr cds: A, C, D, DS, ER, JCB, MC, V*

Orlando

PEABODY ORLANDO
★★★★

9801 International Dr, Orlando FL 32819
☎ *407/352-4000 or 800/PEABODY*
FAX *407/351-9177*

This is an impressive high-rise with sweeping views and extensive grounds. Famous are the resident ducks who parade to the lobby fountain each morning at 11, splash around in it all day and return to their duck palace with fanfare at 5 pm. *891 units, 27 story. S, D $185-$270; each addl $15; suites $400-$1,350; under 18 free; some package plans May-Sept. Crib free. Valet parking $7. TV; cable (premium). Heated pool; wading pool, poolside serv. Restaurant open 24 hrs (also see DUX). Bar 11-2 am; entertainment exc Sun. Ck-out noon. Convention facilities. Business center. In-rm*

FLORIDA

modem link. Shopping arcade. Beauty shop. Lighted tennis, pro shop. 18-hole golf privileges, greens fee. Exercise rm; instructor, weight machines, bicycles, whirlpool, sauna, steam rm. Massage therapy. Game rm. Refrigerators avail. Luxury level. Cr cds: A, C, D, DS, ER, JCB, MC, V

★★★★
DUX
In the Peabody Orlando
9801 International Dr, Orlando FL 32819
☎ 407/345–4550

Expert service and innovative cuisine are the hallmarks of this hotel dining room. The room itself is warm and comfortable, adorned with flowers and crystal chandeliers; around the perimeter is a mural painted with—what else—ducks. 🕹 *Hrs: 6–10 pm; Fri & Sat to 11 pm. Closed Sun; also month of Aug. Res accepted. Continental menu. Bar. Wine cellar. Semi-a la carte: dinner $23–$40. Child's meals. Specializes in wild game, seafood. Valet parking. Jacket. Totally nonsmoking. Cr cds: A, C, D, DS, ER, JCB, MC, V*

Palm Beach

★★★★
THE BREAKERS
1 South County Rd, Palm Beach FL 33480
☎ 561/655–6611
FAX 561/659–8403

Blending formality with tropical resort ambience, this historic and palatial Italian Renaissance hotel on 140 splendid acres has been frequented by wealthy socialites and celebrities for most of this century. 🕹 *572 rms, 7 story. Mid-Dec–mid-Apr: S, D $295–$545; each addl $25; suites $515–$2,100; MAP avail; golf, tennis package plans; lower rates rest of yr. Crib avail. TV; cable, VCR avail (movies). Heated pool; wading pool, poolside serv, lifeguard. Playground. Supervised child's activities; ages 3 and up. Dining rm (open to public) 7–10:30 am, 6–10 pm; beach club lunch from 11:30 am. Box lunches; snack bar; picnics. Rm serv 24 hrs. Bar 11–2 am. Ck-out noon, ck-in 4 pm. Convention facilities. Business center. In-rm modem link. Valet serv. Concierge. Shopping arcade. Barber, beauty shop. Valet parking. Airport* transportation. 14 tennis courts, 5 lighted, pro. 36-hole golf, greens fee $85, pro, putting green, driving range. Scuba diving instructor. Bicycle rentals. Lawn games. Soc dir; entertainment, movies. Rec rm. Exercise rm; instructor, weights, bicycles, sauna. Masseurs. 24 languages spoken. Refrigerators, minibars. On ocean, private beach; cabanas, beach club. Gourmet food and extensive recreational and relaxation facilities. Cr cds: A, C, D, DS, ER, JCB, MC, V

CHESTERFIELD HOTEL
363 Cocoanut Row, Palm Beach FL 33480
☏ *561/659–5800 or 800/243–7871*
FAX *561/659–6707*

With a little pretense, a lot of chintz and brass and a super-abundance of service, this hotel may be a Mizner copy, but it has an English-country-style elegance all its own. ✈ 53 rms, 3 story, 11 suites. Mid-Dec–Apr: S, D $185–$280; suites $375–$800; lower rates rest of yr. Crib free. TV; cable, VCR avail. Heated pool; whirlpool, poolside serv. Restaurant 7 am–10 pm, Fri & Sat to 11 pm. Afternoon tea and scones. Rm serv 24 hrs. Bar 11–1 am; pianist. Ck-out noon. Meeting rms. Business center. In-rm modem link. Concierge. Free valet parking. Cigar club rm. Library/reading rms. Ocean 3 blks. Cr cds: A, C, D, DS, ER, MC, V

THE FOUR SEASONS
2800 S Ocean Blvd, Palm Beach FL 33480
☏ *561/582–2800 or 800/332–3442*
FAX *561/547–1557*

This beachside property combines contemporary design with the luxurious detailing of a traditional Floridian resort. There are views of the Atlantic Ocean from many rooms. ✈ 210 rms, 4 story. Mid-Dec–mid-Apr: S, D $325–$525; suites $750–$1,800; under 17 free; lower rates rest of yr. Crib free. Valet parking $10. TV; cable (premium), VCR avail (movies). Heated pool; poolside serv. Supervised child's activities; from age 3. Restaurant 7 am–10 pm (also see THE RESTAURANT AT FOUR SEASONS). Rm serv 24 hrs. Bar 4 pm–midnight; pianist. Ck-out noon. Meeting rms. Business center. In-rm modem link. Concierge. Barber, beauty shop. Airport transportation. Tennis, pro. 18-hole golf privileges, greens fee

$50, pro. Exercise rm; instructor, weight machine, bicycles, whirlpool, sauna, steam rm. Massage. Bathrm phones, minibars; refrigerators avail. Balconies. On beach. Cr cds: A, C, D, DS, JCB, MC, V

THE RITZ-CARLTON, PALM BEACH
100 S Ocean Blvd, Manalapan FL 33462
☎ *561/533–6000 or 800/241–3333*
FAX *561/588–4201*

Three towers rise above this modern Mediterranean-style beachfront hotel. 🐾 *270 rms, 6 story, 56 suites. Mid-Dec–Apr: S, D $330–$650; suites $890–$3,000; under 12 free; golf plans; lower rates rest of yr. Crib free. Garage $12/day. TV; cable (premium), VCR avail (movies). Heated pool; poolside serv. Supervised child's activities. Restaurant 6 am–11 pm (also see THE RESTAURANT). Rm serv 24 hrs. Bar; entertainment. Ck-out noon. Meeting rms. Business center. In-rm modem link. Concierge. Shopping arcade. Barber, beauty shop. Airport transportation. Lighted tennis. 18-hole golf privileges, greens fee $85–$120, pro, putting green, driving range. Exercise rm; instructor, weight machine, bicycles, whirlpool, steam rm. Massage. Bathrm phones, minibars. Balconies. Luxury level. Cr cds: A, C, D, DS, ER, JCB, MC, V*

THE RESTAURANT
In the Ritz-Carlton, Palm Beach
100 S Ocean Blvd, Manalapan FL 33462
☎ *561/533–6000*

Elegant decor features hand-strung crystal chandeliers and museum-quality works of art. And the dining room overlooks the Atlantic Ocean. 🐾 *Hrs: 6 am–10 pm; Sun brunch 10:30 am–3:30 pm. Res required. Continental menu. Bar. Extensive wine list. A la carte entrees: lunch $8.50–$18, dinner $18–$28. Sun brunch $36. Fri seafood buffet (6–11 pm) $33. Child's meals. Pianist. Valet parking. Jacket (dinner). Cr cds: A, C, D, DS, ER, JCB, MC, V*

THE RESTAURANT AT FOUR SEASONS
In the Four Seasons
2800 S Ocean Blvd, Palm Beach FL 33480
☎ 561/582–2800

Trend-setting cuisine is based on the history and heritage of the Southeast, and a garden on the premises provides fresh fruits and herbs. The dining area overlooks pool and ocean. Hrs: 6–10:30 pm. Closed Mon & Tues late May–Nov. Res required. Southeast regional menu. Bar. Extensive wine list. A la carte entrees: dinner $24–$39. Specialties: Indian River blue crab, guava-braised short ribs of beef, yellow-tail snapper. Pianist. Valet parking. Jacket. Cr cds: A, C, D, DS, JCB, MC, V

Pompano Beach

CAFE MAXX
2601 E Atlantic Blvd, Pompano Beach FL
☎ 954/782–0606

New-wave epicurean dining had its south Florida start here in the early '80s, and the restaurant is still very popular. The setting, in a little strip of stores, is ordinary, but the fare, prepared in an open kitchen, is fine gourmet cuisine. Hrs: 5:30–10:30 pm; wkdays off-season from 6 pm. Closed July 4, Dec 25; Super Bowl Sunday. Res accepted. Semi-a la carte: dinner $16.95–$31.95. Specialties: caviar pie, grilled veal chop, Norwegian salmon. Own ice cream. Valet parking. Cr cds: A, C, D, DS, MC, V

FLORIDA

St Pete Beach Area

★★★★
DON CESAR BEACH RESORT & SPA
3400 Gulf Blvd, St Pete Beach FL 33706
☎ *813/360-1881 or 800/637-7200*
FAX *813/367-6952*

The sprawling, sybaritic "Pink Palace" still echoes with ghosts of Scott and Zelda Fitzgerald, and its beachfront buzzes with activity. The elaborate landscaping features a courtyard and flower gardens. ✈ *275 rms, 1-10 story. Jan-Apr: S, D $230-$343; each addl $15; suites $295-$725; penthouse $1,200-$1,700; under 18 free; lower rates rest of yr. Crib free. TV; cable (premium), VCR avail (movies). 2 heated pools. Supervised child's activities; ages 4-12. Restaurant 5:30-10 pm. Rm serv 24 hrs. Bars 11-1 am; Sun from 1 pm. Ck-out noon. Convention facilities. Business center. In-rm modem link. Coin Lndry. Concierge. Shopping arcade. Valet parking. Tennis privileges. Golf privileges. Exercise equipt; weight machine, bicycles, whirlpool, sauna. Game rm. Lawn games. Spa. Massage therapy. Sailboat rentals. Watersport clinics & rentals. Beach cabanas, boardwalk. Lawn games. Some refrigerators, minibars. Some balconies. Cr cds: A, C, D, DS, ER, JCB, MC, V*

St Petersburg

★★★★
RENAISSANCE VINOY RESORT
501 Fifth Ave NE, St Petersburg FL 33701
☎ *813/894-1000*
FAX *813/822-2785*

This 1925 landmark on the National Register of Historic Places has been imaginatively renovated for '90s lifestyles. ✈ *360 units, 7 story. Mid-Jan-May: S, D $249-$309; suites $510-$1,700; under 18 free; wkend packages; golf & tennis plans; lower rates rest of yr. Crib free. Garage, overnight; valet parking $10, self-park $7. TV; cable (premium), VCR avail. 2 heated pools; poolside serv. Supervised child's activities (June-Aug); ages 4-12. Complimentary coffee & newspaper in rms. Restaurants 6 am-11 pm. Rm serv 24 hrs. Bar 10-2 am, Sun 1 pm-midnight; entertainment. Ck-out noon. Lndry facilities. Convention facilities. Business center. In-rm modem link.*

Concierge. Gift shops. 14 tennis courts, 11 lighted, 4 different surfaces, incl grass and clay. 18-hole golf, greens fee $85 (incl cart), pro, putting green, driving range. Exercise rm; instructor, weight machine, bicycles, whirlpool, sauna, steam rm. Masseuse. Day spa and salon. Croquet courts. Minibars. Wet bar in suites. Stenciled cypress beams in lobby; leaded-glass windows, hand-painted ceilings and wall murals in the original dining wing; tropical gardens. Situated on a 14-acre site overlooking Tampa Bay; swimming beach; 74-slip private marina. Cr cds: A, C, D, DS, ER, JCB, MC, V

Tampa

★★★★
HYATT REGENCY WESTSHORE

6200 Courtney Campbell Causeway, Tampa FL 33607
☎ *813/874–1234*
FAX *813/281–9168*

This large business-oriented luxury hotel is well placed, nestled next to a 35-acre nature preserve on Tampa Bay. A courtyard with fountains highlights the elaborate landscaping. 400 rms in main bldg, 14 story, 45 casita villas. Sept–May: S $179–$204; D $199–$224; each addl $25; suites $300–$640; casita villas: S $179; D $204; suites (1–3 bedrm) $300–$640; under 18 free; wkend rates; lower rates rest of yr. Crib free. Covered parking; valet parking $8/night. TV; cable (premium), VCR avail. 2 heated pools; whirlpool, poolside serv. Restaurant 6:30 am–11 pm. Rm serv 24 hrs. Bar noon–1 am; pianist. Ck-out noon. Convention facilities. Business center. In-rm modem link. Concierge. Gift shop. Free airport transportation. Tennis. Exercise equipt; weights, bicycles, sauna. Massage. Lawn games. Some refrigerators, minibars. Boat dock. Luxury level. Cr cds: A, C, D, DS, ER, JCB, MC, V

★★★★
SADDLEBROOK RESORT

5700 Saddlebrook Way, Wesley Chapel FL 33543
☎ *813/973–1111 or 800/729–8383*
FAX *813/973–4504*

Arguably one of Florida's premier tennis and golf resorts, it rests on 480 secluded acres of woodlands, lakes and rolling

FLORIDA

hills. 542 units, 2 story, 411 with kits., 131 hotel rms, 163 1-bedrm condos, 248 2-bedrm condos. Mid-Jan–Apr: S, D $210–$340; each addl $20; under 13 free; lower rates rest of yr. TV; cable. 4 pools, 2 heated; whirlpool, poolside serv. Playground. Free supervised child's activities; ages 3–12. Dining rm (public by res) 6:30 am–10:30 pm. Rm serv to 1 am. Bar 11–1 am; entertainment. Ck-out noon, ck-in 3 pm. Convention facilities. Business center. In-rm modem link. Concierge. Grocery 1 mi. Package store. Gift shop. Barber, beauty shop. Valet parking. Airport transportation. Sports dir. Tennis, 45 courts, 5 lighted, pro. Home of Harry Hopman Tennis Academy. 36-hole golf course designed by Arnold Palmer & Dean Refram, pro, putting green, driving range. Home of Arnold Palmer Golf Academy. Nature walks. Bicycle rentals. Game rm. Exercise rm; instructor, weight machines, bicycles, sauna, steam rm. Massage therapy. Minibars. Many refrigerators. Private patios, balconies. Accommodations and activities center designed as a walking village. Cr cds: A, C, D, DS, MC, V

Tarpon Springs

★★★★
INNISBROOK HILTON RESORT
36750 N US 19, Palm Harbor FL 34684
☎ *813/942–2000 or 800/456–2000*
FAX *813/942–5576*

In a 1,000-acre wooded setting with elaborate landscaping, this resort is popular with golfers because of its top-rated championship courses. 1,000 condo units in 28 lodges, 2–3 story. Jan–Apr: 1-bedrm, 2-bedrm $187–$360; under 18 free; AP, MAP, family rates; package plans; monthly rates; lower rates rest of yr. Deposit required. Crib free. TV; cable (premium). 6 pools, heated; poolside serv. Supervised child's activities; ages 4–14. Coffee in rms. 4 dining rms. Rm serv. 2 snack bars. 4 bars; entertainment. Ck-out noon, ck-in 3 pm. Package store. Free lndry facilities. Convention facilities. Business center. Concierge. Gift shop. Beauty shop. Complimentary beach shuttle. Airport transportation. 15 tennis courts, 7 lighted, pro shop. 63-hole golf, pro, 4 putting greens, lighted driving range. Instructional tennis and golf. Miniature *golf. Bicycle rentals. Lawn games. Rec dir. Game rm. Exercise rm; instructor, weights, bicycles, sauna. Honor bars. Private patios, balconies. Wildlife sanctuary with nature walk. Freshwater stocked lake. Tram service around grounds. Cr cds: A, C, D, DS, ER, JCB, MC, V*

Walt Disney World

★★★★
DISNEY'S GRAND FLORIDIAN BEACH RESORT

4401 Floridian Way, Walt Disney World FL 32830
☎ *407/824–3000*
FAX *407/824–3186*

On the shores of the Seven Seas Lagoon, this looks like a turn-of-the-century summer resort, thanks to a gabled red roof, rambling verandas, cupolas and gingerbread porches and an open-cage elevator. 🐕 *900 rms: 65 rms in main bldg, 9 suites; 817 rms, 16 suites in 5 lodge bldgs, 4 & 5 story. Mid-Dec–Jan 1, mid-Feb–late Apr, early June–mid-Aug: S, D $290–$490; each addl $15; suites $870–$1,600; under 18 free; special package plans; lower rates rest of yr. Crib free. TV; cable (premium), VCR avail (movies). Heated pool; wading pool, whirlpool, poolside serv, lifeguard. Supervised child's activities (June–Aug); ages 3–12. Dining rm 7 am–11 pm; five addl dining rms. Afternoon high tea. Rm serv 24 hrs. Bar 11–1 am. Ck-out 11 am, ck-in 3 pm. Coin lndry. Convention facilities. Business center. In-rm modem link. Valet parking. Barber, beauty shop. Monorail to Magic Kingdom, Epcot Center & Disney/MGM Studios. Tennis, clay courts, pro. 99-hole golf privileges, greens fee, pro. Private beach; waterskiing, sailing, marina, boat rentals. Lawn games. Game rm. Exercise rm; instructor, weight machines, bicycles, steam rm. Massage. Fishing guides. Bathrm phones, minibars; wet bar in suites. Balconies. Kennels avail. Complimentary newspaper daily. Palatial vaulted lobby. Aviary, palms and ferns. On 40 acres. Bldgs #6, #7 and #9 (431 rms) are totally nonsmoking. Luxury level. Cr cds: A, MC, V*

FLORIDA

DISNEY'S YACHT CLUB RESORT
★★★★

1700 Epcot Resort Blvd, Lake Buena Vista FL 32830
☎ *407/934–7000*
FAX *407/934–3450*

This refreshingly unstuffy property designed by noted architect Robert A.M. Stern is just right for families. Set on a 25-acre man-made lake, it has a gray clapboard facade, evergreen landscaping and a lighthouse on its pier, recalling the turn-of-the-century New England seacoast. 🐾 *635 rms, 5 story. Mid-Feb–mid-Apr, mid-June–late Aug: S, D $244–$315; each addl $15; suites $425–$880; under 18 free; Disney packages; higher rates hols; lower rates rest of yr. Crib free. TV; cable (premium), VCR avail. Pool. Supervised child's activities; ages 4–12. Dining rm 7 am–10 pm. Rm serv 24 hrs. Bar 11–1 am. Ck-out 11 am, ck-in 3 pm. Coin lndry. Convention facilities. Business center. In-rm modem link. Bellhops. Valet serv. Concierge. Sundries. Gift shop. Barber, beauty shop. Free Disney transportation, including water taxi, to Disney-MGM Studios Theme Park & Epcot Center. Lighted tennis, pro. Golf privileges. Mini waterpark; boating, marina. Lawn games. Game rm. Exercise rm; instructor, weight machine, bicycles, whirlpool, sauna, steam rm. Massage. Bathrm phones, minibars; wet bar in suites. DISNEY'S YACHT CLUB RESORT meets with DISNEY'S BEACH CLUB RESORT (see) in a central courtyard with a "quiet pool" and shares a Fantasy Lagoon with poolside serv. Luxury level. Cr cds: A, MC, V*

HYATT REGENCY GRAND CYPRESS
★★★★

1 Grand Cypress Blvd, Orlando FL 32836
☎ *407/239–1234*
FAX *407/239–3800*

Part of what is perhaps the Orlando area's most spectacular resort, this hotel offers virtually every resort amenity and then some. 🐾 *750 units, 18 story, 75 suites. Jan–May: S, D $260–$440; suites $650–$4,500; golf plans; lower rates rest of yr. Crib free. Valet parking $9. TV; cable (premium), VCR avail. Heated pool; poolside serv. Supervised child's activities (Memorial Day–Labor Day); ages 3–17. Dining rms 11:30 am–2:30 pm, 6–11 pm. 5 restaurants. Rm serv 24 hrs. Bar; entertainment. Ck-out noon, ck-in 4 pm. Convention facilities. Business center. In-rm modem link. Valet serv. Concierge. Shopping arcade. Personal care salon. Airport, Walt Disney*

World transportation. 12 tennis courts, 6 lighted, pro, instruction avail. 45-hole golf, Academy of Golf, pro, putting green, driving range, pitch & putt. Sailing, canoes, paddleboats; rentals avail. Lake with white sand beach. Nature area, Audubon walk; jogging trails. Bicycle rentals. Lawn games. Game rm. Equestrian center; Western and English trails. Exercise rm; instructor, weights, bicycles, whirlpool, sauna, steam rm. Massage therapy. Minibars. Bathrm phone, refrigerator in some suites. Some private patios. Balconies. Elegant decor. Extensive art collection and artifacts; hotel tours avail. On 1,500 landscaped acres. Van transport throughout property. Luxury level. Cr cds: A, C, D, DS, ER, JCB, MC, V

West Palm Beach

★★★★
PGA NATIONAL RESORT & SPA
400 Ave of the Champions, Palm Beach Gardens FL 33418
☎ *561/627–2000 or 800/633–9150*
FAX *561/622–0261*

This elegant landscaped resort is the focus of the 2,340-acre PGA National community, which contains 39 neighborhoods and 4,250 residences, PGA headquarters and limitless sports facilities, including championship golf courses and croquet courts adorned with 25,000 flowering plants amid a nature preserve. ✈ *339 units, 4 story. Early Jan–mid-Apr: S, D $279–$309; each addl $15; kit. cottages $350; each addl $50; under 17 free; lower rates rest of yr. Crib free. TV; cable, VCR avail (movies). Heated pool; wading pool, poolside serv. Supervised child's activities (June–Sept); ages 5–12. Dining rm 5:30–10 pm. Bar 11–2 am. Ck-out noon, ck-in 3 pm. Convention facilities. Business center. In-rm modem link. Valet serv. Concierge. Barber, beauty shop. Pro shops. Valet parking. Airport transportation. 19 tennis courts, 12 lighted, pro. 5 golf courses, greens fee $70–$115, pro, 3 putting greens, 3 driving ranges. Boating. Beach volleyball. 5 croquet courts, pro. 3 indoor racquetball/handball courts. Exercise rm; instructor, weight machines, bicycles, whirlpool, sauna, steam rm. Massage. Spa building with gardens; also 6 pools that contain various minerals and salts imported from around the world. Refrigerators, minibars. Balconies. 26-acre lake for sailing; sand beach. Cr cds: A, C, D, DS, ER, JCB, MC, V*

Georgia

Atlanta

★★★★ THE GRAND HOTEL

75 Fourteenth St, Atlanta GA 30309
☎ *404/881–9898 or 800/952–0702*
FAX *404/873–4692*

Occupying the first 20 floors of the Grand Building, this luxury hotel combines Old World traditions with New South hospitality. *246 rms, 19 story. S, D $175–$305; each addl $25; suites $450–$1,900; under 16 free; wkend rates. Crib free. Pet accepted, some restrictions; deposit required. Garage parking, valet $15. TV; cable (premium), VCR avail. Indoor pool; poolside serv. Restaurant 6 am–11 pm. Rm serv 24 hrs. Bar 11:30–1 am; entertainment. Ck-out noon. Convention facilities. Business center. In-rm modem link. Concierge. Gift shop. Barber, beauty shop. Exercise rm; instructor, weight machine, bicycles, whirlpool, sauna, steam rm. Masseuse. Spa/health club. Refrigerators, minibars. Complimentary newspaper. Three-story grand entry with dramatic grand staircase. Grand ballroom on 4th floor. A 5th-floor terrace provides scenic view of skyline. Cr cds: A, C, D, DS, ER, JCB, MC, V*

★★★★ HOTEL NIKKO

3300 Peachtree Rd, Atlanta GA 30305
☎ *404/365–8100*
FAX *404/233–5686*

The focus of the dual-height lobby is the adjacent tri-level Japanese garden and 35-foot cascading waterfall. The spacious, comfortable and understated rooms have a style that's more American than Japanese. *440 rms, 25 story. S $165–$255, D $185–$275; each addl $20; suites $435–$1,500; wkend rates. TV; cable (premium), VCR avail. Pool. Restaurants 6:30 am–11 pm. Rm serv 24 hrs. Bars 11–1 am; entertainment, pianist. Ck-out noon. Convention facilities. Business center. In-rm modem link. Concierge. Gift shop. Garage, valet parking. Tennis & golf privileges. Exercise equipt;*

ATLANTA

bicycles, treadmill, sauna. Bathrm phones, minibars. Luxury level. Cr cds: A, C, D, DS, ER, JCB, MC, V

🏨 ★★★★
RENAISSANCE WAVERLY
2450 Galleria Pkwy, Atlanta GA 30339
☎ *770/953-4500*
FAX *770/953-0740*

One of northwest Atlanta's most luxurious hotels is especially good for conventioneers and shoppers: The Galleria Specialty Mall makes up the building's west half. The ample rooms are appealingly decorated in earth tones and pastels and have 19th-century English reproductions. ✈ *521 rms, 14 story. S $169–$234; D $189–$254; each addl $20; suites $700–$1,400; under 18 free; wkend rates. Crib free. TV; cable (premium), VCR avail. 2 pools, 1 indoor. Complimentary coffee in rms. Restaurant 6 am–10 pm. Rm serv 24 hrs. 3 bars 11:30–1 am. Ck-out noon. Convention facilities. Business center. In-rm modem link. Concierge. Shopping arcade. Exercise rm; instructor, weight machines, bicycles, whirlpool, sauna, steam rm. Racquetball. Bathrm phones; refrigerator in suites. Luxury level. Cr cds: A, C, D, DS, ER, JCB, MC, V*

🏨 ★★★★
THE RITZ-CARLTON
181 Peachtree St NE, Atlanta GA 30303
☎ *404/659-0400*
FAX *404/688-0400*

This quiet retreat in downtown Atlanta has all the important facilities for business travelers and vacationers. The mood at this luxuriously decorated hotel is set by traditional afternoon tea served in an intimate sunken lobby beneath an 18th-century chandelier. ✈ *447 rms, 25 story. S, D $175–$265; suites $450–$1,165; under 12 free; wkend, hol rates. Crib free. Valet parking $16, in/out $10. TV; cable (premium), VCR avail. Restaurant (see THE RESTAURANT). Rm serv 24 hrs. Bar 11:30–2 am; entertainment. Ck-out noon. Convention facilities. Business center. In-rm modem link. Concierge. Gift shop. Exercise equipt; weight machine, treadmill, steam rm. Massage therapy. Health club privileges.*

Refrigerators, minibars. Luxury level. Cr cds: A, C, D, DS, ER, JCB, MC, V

THE RITZ-CARLTON, BUCKHEAD
3434 Peachtree Rd NE, Atlanta GA 30326
☎ *404/237–2700 or 800/241–3333*
FAX *404/239–0078*

Here is a busy but elegant and eminently comfortable place where you can unwind after a busy day. Decorated with the Ritz's signature 18th- and 19th-century antiques, this elegant gem bids a discreet welcome both to visitors and to locals who come to enjoy its many nice bars and restaurants, including the Dining Room, which serves haute cuisine. ✈ *553 rms, 22 story. S, D $170–$295; suites $365–$1,200; under 12 free; wkend plans. Crib free. Valet parking $14; self-park in/out $8. TV; cable (premium), VCR avail. Indoor pool; poolside serv. Restaurants 6:30 am–midnight (also see THE DINING ROOM). Rm serv 24 hrs. Bar 11–2 am; entertainment. Ck-out noon. Convention facilities. Business center. In-rm modem link. Concierge. Shopping arcade. Airport transportation. Tennis privileges, pro. Golf privileges, greens fee $40–$100. Exercise rm; instructor, weight machines, bicycles, whirlpool, sauna, steam rm. Massage. Bathrm phones, minibars. Luxury level. Cr cds: A, C, D, DS, ER, JCB, MC, V*

THE DINING ROOM
In the Ritz-Carlton, Buckhead
3434 Peachtree Rd NE, Atlanta GA 30326
☎ *404/237–2700*

Set in Atlanta's poshest hotel in the heart of its most exclusive neighborhood, The Dining Room exudes the simple elegance of a comfortable private club. Wood paneling and fabric-covered walls, oil paintings of animals and aristocrats and large dining chairs set around well-spaced tables add to the elegant serenity of the place. Chef Guenter Seeger exploits seasonal ingredients to create meals that both surprise and delight. ✈ *Hrs: 6–10 pm. Closed Sun; major hols. Res accepted. Traditional European menu with American regional influences. Bar. Wine cellar. Prix fixe: dinner $58–$86. Specializes in light contemporary cuisine. Own baking,* *pasta, ice cream. Menu changes daily. Valet parking. Jacket, tie. Cr cds: A, C, D, DS, ER, JCB, MC, V*

BACCHANALIA
3125 Piedmont Rd, Atlanta GA 30305
☎ *404/365-0410*

Angels highlight the walls and tables of this small restaurant, one of Atlanta's most charming. Austrian crystal chandeliers, Oriental rugs and original art and antiques add to the ambience. Baking is done on the premises. 🐾 *Hrs: 6–9:30 pm; Fri & Sat to 10 pm. Closed Sun, Mon; some major hols. Res required. Wine, beer. Prix fixe: dinner $35. Specializes in seafood, game. Parking. Totally nonsmoking. Cr cds: A, D, MC, V*

CANOE
4199 Paces Ferry Rd NW, Atlanta GA 30339
☎ *770/432-2663*

Wonderfully landscaped grounds dotted with walkways and benches add to the outdoor dining experience here. Inside, brick walls, wrought-iron and splashes of Southwestern upholstery accent the dining areas. 🐾 *Hrs: 10:30 am–2:30 pm, 5:30–10:30 pm; Fri to 11:30 pm; Sat 5:30–11:30 pm; Sun 10 am–2:30 pm (brunch), 5:30–9 pm. Closed Jan 1, Thanksgiving, Dec 25. Res accepted. Bar. Wine list. Semi-a la carte: lunch $5.95–$13.95, dinner $12.95–$19.95. Sun brunch $7.95–$13.50. Specialties: slow-roasted pork with gorgonzola polenta and spicy escarole, Florida grouper with roasted sweet corn and lobster succotash, chocolate hazelnut praline cake. Valet parking. Outdoor dining. Cr cds: A, C, D, MC, V*

GEORGIA

✕ ★★★★★
HEDGEROSE HEIGHTS INN
490 E Paces Ferry Rd NE, Atlanta GA 30305
☎ *404/233-7673*

Named for a local sub-division, this restored 1915 house caters to a well-heeled, loyal clientele. Warm peach tones alternate with deep green, and tables are well separated; the intimate bar is a perfect spot for sipping. ✈ *Hrs: 6-10 pm. Closed Sun, Mon; major hols. Res accepted. Continental menu. Bar. Wine cellar. A la carte entrees: dinner $17-$25. Specializes in seafood, seasonal game dishes, veal. Own pastries. Parking. Jacket. Totally nonsmoking. Cr cds: A, C, D, MC, V*

✕ ★★★★★
THE RESTAURANT
In the Ritz-Carlton
181 Peachtree St NE, Atlanta GA 30303
☎ *404/659-0400*

A private club atmosphere reigns at this hotel restaurant decorated with objets d'art. ✈ *Hrs: 6-10 pm. Closed Sun. Res accepted. French, continental menu. Wine cellar. A la carte entrees: dinner $26-$30. Prix fixe: dinner $33. Specialties: grilled fresh duck foie gras, seared baby red snapper, grilled Sonoma lamb rack. Own baking, ice cream, pasta. Valet parking. Jacket. Cr cds: A, C, D, DS, ER, JCB, MC, V*

Atlanta Hartsfield Airport Area

🏨 ★★★★★
HILTON & TOWERS
1031 Virginia Ave, Atlanta GA 30354
☎ *404/767-9000*
FAX *404/559-6828*

This sleek high-rise comes with an incredible array of facilities and services unusual in airport hotels. ✈ *503 rms, 17 story. S $127-$186; D $142-$206; each addl $15; suites $350-$450; family, wkend rates. Crib free. TV; cable (premium), VCR avail. 2 pools, 1 indoor; poolside serv. Coffee in rms. Restaurant 6 am-midnight. Rm serv 24 hrs. Bar 11:30-1 am; entertainment. Ck-out noon. Convention facilities. Busi-*

ness center. In-rm modem link. Concierge. Gift shop. Barber, beauty shop. Valet parking. Free airport, RR station, bus depot transportation. Lighted tennis. Exercise rm; instructor, weight machines, bicycles, whirlpool, sauna. Massage. Minibars; some bathrm phones, wet bars. Refrigerators avail. Luxury level. Cr cds: A, C, D, DS, ER, JCB, MC, V

RENAISSANCE-AIRPORT
1 Hartsfield Centre Pkwy, Atlanta GA 30354
☎ *404/209–9999*
FAX *404/209–7031*

Conveniently located, this is the only hotel that has been built on the airport's property. Each room opens up to a dramatic 11-story interior atrium that serves as the hotel's center of activity. ✈ *387 rms, 11 story. S $152–$192; D $172–$212; each addl $20; suites $245–$1,025; family, baseball wkend rates. Crib free. Valet parking $5. TV; cable (premium), VCR avail. 2 pools, 1 indoor; poolside serv. Complimentary coffee in rms. Restaurant 6 am–11 pm. Rm serv 24 hrs. Bar 11–1 am; entertainment exc Sun. Ck-out 1 pm. Convention facilities. Business center. In-rm modem link. Concierge. Gift shop. Exercise rm; instructor, weight machine, bicycles, whirlpool, sauna. Health club privileges. Refrigerators, minibars. Balconies. Luxury level. Cr cds: A, C, D, DS, ER, JCB, MC, V*

Buford

INN AT CHATEAU ELAN
100 Rue Charlemagne, Braselton GA 30517
☎ *770/932–0900 or 800/233–9463*
FAX *770/271–6000*

This 16th-century chateau-style building on 2,400 acres includes its own vineyards and winery. The interior is designed as an open-air French street market. ✈ *310 rms, 5 story. Mid-Mar–June & mid-Aug–mid-Nov: S, D $149–$184; suites $189–$349; wkend & hol rates; golf plan; lower rates rest of yr. Crib free. TV; cable (premium), VCR avail. 4 pools, 1 indoor; whirlpools, poolside serv. Playground. Supervised child's activities (May-Aug). Complimentary coffee in*

GEORGIA

rms. Restaurant 6–10 pm. Rm serv. Bar 11 am–11:45 pm; entertainment in season. Ck-out 11 am, ck-in 3 pm. Gift shop. Convention facilities. Business center. In-rm modem link. Bellhops. Concierge. Valet serv. Hartsfield airport transportation. Lighted tennis; pro. 54-hole golf; 9-hole par-3 golf; greens fee $65–$115, pro, putting green, driving range. Exercise rm; instructor, weight machine, treadmill, sauna. Masseur. Bicycle rentals. Hiking trails. Lawn games. Rec rm. Game rm. Minibars. Picnic tables. Gift shop. Art gallery. Cr cds: A, C, D, DS, JCB, MC, V

🏨 ★★★★
RENAISSANCE PINEISLE RESORT
9000 Holiday Rd, Lake Lanier Islands GA 30518
☎ 770/945-8921
FAX 770/945-0351

On an island in Lake Lanier, this relaxed resort features a wide array of recreational activities and lovely lakeside scenery. 250 rms, 5 story. Apr–Oct, EP: S $119–$156; D $139–$176; each addl $20; 1–2 bedrm suites $329–$785; under 18 free; MAP, golf, tennis, other plans avail; lower rates rest of yr. Crib free. TV; cable (premium), VCR avail. Indoor/outdoor pool; poolside serv & grill (in season). Supervised child's activities (late Mar–late Nov); ages 4–18. Complimentary coffee, newspaper. Dining rm 6:30–10 pm. Rm serv 24 hrs. Box lunches; snack bar. Bar 11–2 am, Sat to midnight, Sun 12:30 pm–midnight. Afternoon tea. Ck-out noon, ck-in 3 pm. Concierge. Lndry avail. Complimentary shoeshine serv. Valet parking. Convention facilities. Business center. In-rm modem link. Gift shop. Tennis, pro. 18-hole golf, greens fee $59–$69 (incl cart), pro, driving range, putting green. Swimming, private beach, waterskiing; water park adj. Boats, motors, sailboats, canoes, pontoon boats, houseboats, docks; instruction avail. Complimentary sunset cruises. Bicycles; horseback riding lessons. Lawn games. Soc dir; entertainment. Game rm. Exercise rm; instructor, weight machine, bicycles, whirlpool, sauna. Masseuse. Picnic tables. Private patios, balconies. Many decks. Some private enclosed spas. Cr cds: A, C, D, DS, ER, JCB, MC, V

Macon

1842 INN
353 College St, Macon GA 31201
☎ *912/741–1842 or 800/336–1842*
FAX *912/741–1842, ext. 41*

The 1842 Inn offers the amenities of a grand hotel with the charm of a country inn and gracious Southern hospitality. The Greek-Revival antebellum house is filled with fine English antiques, Oriental carpets, tapestries and paintings. Rooms are individually decorated and strikingly beautiful. *21 rms, 2 story. S $95–$155; D $105–$155; each addl $10. Children over 12 yrs only. TV; cable (premium), VCR (movies). Complimentary continental bkfst, coffee & tea. Restaurant nearby. Serv bar 8 am–midnight. Ck-out 11 am, ck-in 3 pm. Business servs avail. Valet serv. Health club privileges. Some in-rm whirlpools. Cr cds: A, MC, V*

Pine Mountain (Harris Co)

CALLAWAY GARDENS
US 27, Pine Mountain (Harris Co) GA 31822
☎ *706/663–2281 or 800/282–8181*
FAX *706/663–8114*

This 14,000-acre family golf and tennis resort is best known for its impressive gardens and its butterfly conservatory, where more than 1,000 varieties fly free. *349 rms, 1–3 story, 155 cottages (2-bedrm), 55 villas. Inn: S, D $89–$118; each addl $15; suites $275–$350; luxury villas (1–4 bedrm) $150–$485; under 18 free; MAP, golf, tennis plans; monthly rates off season. Crib free. TV; cable. 3 pools; wading pool, lifeguard in summer. Playground. Supervised child's activities (June–mid-Aug); ages 6 months–18 yrs. 6 dining rms 6:30 am–10 pm. Box lunches, snack bar. Bar 5 pm–1 am, closed Sun. Ck-out noon, ck-in 4 pm. Grocery 1 mi. Coin lndry. Package store. Convention facilities. Business center. Bellhops. Valet serv. Concierge. Local airport transportation. Lighted tennis, pro. Golf (63 holes): three 18-hole, one 9-hole, greens fee $75–$90 (incl cart), pros. Swimming, private beach, waterskiing. Canoes, sailboats. Bicycles avail; 7-mi bicycle trail. Horseback riding nearby. Skeet & trap shooting. Soc dir; enter-*

tainment, movies. Rec rm. Exercise rm; instructor, weights, bicycles, sauna. Refrigerators avail. Private patios, balconies. Picnic tables, grills. Free admission (for overnight guests) to Callaway Gardens opp, all facilities avail. Cr cds: A, D, DS, MC, V

Savannah

★★★★

THE KEHOE HOUSE

123 Habersham St, Savannah GA 31401
912/232–1020 or 800/820–1020
FAX *912/231–0208*

Built in 1892 for an iron-mill owner, this Victorian mansion is furnished with many antiques and reproductions. *15 rms, 3 & 5 story, 2 suites. S, D $150–$250; each addl $35. Crib free. TV; cable, VCR. Complimentary full bkfst, evening refreshments. Restaurant opp noon–10 pm. Ck-out 11 am, ck-in 3 pm. Concierge serv. Luggage handling. Meeting rm. Business servs avail. Totally nonsmoking. Cr cds: A, C, D, DS, JCB, MC, V*

★★★★

ELIZABETH ON 37TH

105 E 37th St, Savannah GA
912/236–5547

This elegant dining room, accented with Oriental rugs, marble fireplaces and classical music, is booked weeks in advance. Chef Elizabeth Terry's ingredients are always fresh and baking is done on the premises. *Hrs: 6–10 pm. Closed Sun; major hols. Res accepted. Semi-a la carte: dinner $21.50–$28.50. Specializes in local seafood, poultry, lamb. Own baking. Converted turn-of-the-century home; 1800s decor. Totally nonsmoking. Cr cds: A, D, DS, MC, V*

Sea Island

THE CLOISTER
★★★★★
Sea Island GA 31561
☎ 912/638-3611 or 800/SEA-ISLA
FAX 912/638-5159

This grand Atlantic Coast resort has flourished for nearly seven decades. Its beginning is marked by a giant Constitution Oak, which began from an acorn that President Calvin Coolidge planted in 1928. Since then, many other oaks have been planted and thrived—the gifts of notable guests ranging from U.S. presidents to Queen Juliana of the Netherlands and former Prime Minister Margaret Thatcher. The Cloister has long been a prime playground for Americans of good breeding, where they bring the family and relax amid good manners and good taste. There's a choice of dining options, from the main dining room (jackets and ties for gentlemen over 12 at dinner) to the more casual Beach Club with its nightly seafood buffet, and several snack bars and clubs. 🐕 *262 rms, 1-3 story, 500 kit. cottages. AP, mid-Mar-Nov: S $234-$462; D $294-$522; each addl $72; 6-12 yrs, $26; 3-5 yrs, $18; under 2 free; spa package, golf, tennis, honeymoon, anniversary plans avail. Serv charge 15% per rm per day. Garage avail; free parking. TV; cable, VCR avail (movies $3). 2 pools, 1 heated; wading pool, whirlpool, poolside serv, lifeguard. Free supervised child's activities; ages 3-11. Dining rm 7:30-9:30 am, noon-2 pm, 7-9:30 pm. Box lunches, snack bar, outdoor buffets. Rm serv 6:30 am-midnight. Bar 2:30 pm-12:30 am, closed Sun. Ck-out noon, ck-in 4 pm. Convention facilities. Business center. In-rm modem links. Valet serv. Package store. Grocery 1 mi. Airport, RR station, bus depot transportation. Sports dir. Tennis, pro, shop. 54-hole golf, greens fee $50, carts required $18 per person, pro, shop, putting greens, driving range. Private beach. Sailboats, charter boats; dock. Nature walks. Bicycles. Lawn games. Trap & skeet shooting & instruction. Soc dir; entertainment, dancing (instruction), movies on Sun. Extra fee for most sports. Rec rm. Exercise rm; instructor, weights, bicycles, sauna, steam rm. Complete spa facilities. Beach club; lockers avail; masseur; steam bath. Private patios, balconies. No cr cds accepted.*

Idaho

Coeur d'Alene

★★★★
COEUR D'ALENE RESORT ON THE LAKE
115 S 2nd St, Coeur d'Alene ID 83814
☎ *208/765-4000 or 800/688-5253*
FAX *208/667-2707*

With its 6½ acres of private beachfront park and floating boardwalk abutting a marina, this is a favorite getaway for Pacific Northwesterners. The pricier tower rooms offer more space than the smaller standard accommodations. 338 rms, 18 story. Mid-June-Sept: S, D $150-$350; each addl $10; suites $350-$2,750; under 18 free; lower rates rest of yr. Crib free. TV; cable (premium), VCR avail (movies). 2 heated pools, 1 indoor; wading pool, poolside serv, lifeguard. Playground adj. Supervised child's activities (Apr-Oct). Restaurants 6-2 am. Rm serv. Bars; entertainment exc Sun. Ck-out noon, ck-in after 3 pm. Convention facilities. Business center. Valet serv. Shopping arcade. Airport, bus depot transportation. Tennis. 18-hole golf. Marina. Boat rentals. Tour boats. Seaplane rides. X-country ski on site. Bowling. Exercise rm; instructor, weights, bicycles, whirlpool, sauna, steam rm. Massage. Refrigerators. Balconies. Atrium areas. City park adj, tennis courts. Cr cds: A, C, D, DS, MC, V

Illinois

Chicago

★★★★ THE DRAKE

140 E Walton Place, Chicago IL 60611
312/787-2200 or 800/553-7253
FAX *312/787-1431*

An historic building of classic design overlooks the lake, with a public beach opposite.  *535 rms, 10 story. S $225-$325; D $255-$325; suites $295-$1,950; family rates; wkend package plans. Crib free. Valet parking $22.50/night; in/out privileges. TV; cable (premium), VCR avail. Restaurant 7 am-11 pm. Rm serv 24 hrs. Bar 11-2 am; piano bar. Ck-out noon. Convention facilities. Business center. In-rm modem link. Concierge. Shopping arcade. Barber. Exercise equipt; rower, stair machine. Minibars; wet bar in some suites. Complimentary newspaper. Luxury level. Cr cds: A, C, D, DS, ER, JCB, MC, V*

★★★★ FAIRMONT

200 N Columbus Dr, Chicago IL 60601
312/565-8000 or 800/527-4727
FAX *312/856-1032*

An international collection of art and antiques grace the interior of this neo-classical pink granite tower. Guest rooms are exceptionally spacious with windows that open on dramatic lake and city views.  *692 rms, 42 story. S, D $199-$299; each addl $25; suites from $500; under 18 free. Crib free. Valet parking, in/out $23. TV; cable (premium), VCR avail. Pool privileges. Restaurant 5:30-10:30 pm. Rm serv 24 hrs. Bar 11-2 am; entertainment Tues-Sat. Ck-out 1 pm. Convention facilities. Business center. In-rm modem link. Concierge. Health club privileges. Bathrm phones, minibars. Cr cds: A, C, D, DS, ER, JCB, MC, V*

ILLINOIS

FOUR SEASONS
★★★★

120 E Delaware Place, Chicago IL 60611
☎ *312/280-8800 or 800/332-3442*
FAX *312/280-1748*

From the spacious English country manor-style lobby of this sparkling hotel, it's easy to forget that you're on the 7th floor of a 66-story skycraper, just above a chic shopping mall on Chicago's fashionable North Michigan Avenue. Many of the guest rooms, which begin on floor 30, have spectacular views of the city and/or Lake Michigan and all the necessities and comforts for work or relaxation. ✈ 343 rms, 66 story building, guest rms on floors 30-46, 157 suites. S $305-$375; D $335-$405; each addl $30; suites $690-$865; wkend rates; special packages. Crib free. Self-park adj, in/out $24. TV; cable (premium), VCR avail (movies). Indoor pool. Restaurant (see SEASONS). Rm serv 24 hrs. Bar 11:30-1 am; entertainment. Ck-out noon. Convention facilities. Business center. In-rm modem link. Concierge. Shopping access to 900 North Michigan Mall. Barber, beauty shop. Extensive fitness facility. Exercise rm; instructor, weight machine, stair machine, treadmill, bicycles, whirlpool, sauna, steam rm. Masseuse. Bathrm phones, minibars; some wet bars. Lake 3 blks. Cr cds: A, C, D, DS, ER, JCB, MC, V

HOTEL NIKKO CHICAGO
★★★★

320 N Dearborn St, Chicago IL 60610
☎ *312/744-1900 or 800/645-5687*
FAX *312/527-2650*

The polished granite, black lacquer and mahogany interior of this Japanese-owned hotel has an understated elegance. Floor-to-ceiling windows look out on a rock garden. Guest rooms are furnished in either contemporary or traditional Japanese style. ✈ 422 rms, 20 story. S $245-$285; D $270-$310; each addl $25; suites $450-$2,500 under 18 free; special packages. Crib free. Pet accepted, some restrictions. Valet parking $24 in/out. TV; cable (premium), VCR avail. Restaurant 6:30 am-11 pm. Rm serv 24 hrs. Bar 11-1:30 am; jazz trio 6 days. Ck-out noon. Convention facilities. Business center. In-rm modem link. Concierge. Tennis privileges. Racquetball privileges. Exercise rm; instructor, weights, bicycles, sauna. Masseuse.

Bathrm phones, minibars. Complimentary shoeshine. Cr cds: A, C, D, DS, ER, JCB, MC, V

★★★★
OMNI CHICAGO HOTEL
676 N Michigan Ave, Chicago IL 60611
☎ *312/944–6664 or 800/THE-OMNI*
FAX *312/266–3015*

This hotel, with its marble floors, vaulted ceilings and art deco touches of dark wood, occupies the first 25 floors of the 40-story City Place building, an office and retail complex.  *347 rms, 25 story. S $275; D $295; suites $320–$2,000; under 12 free. Crib free. Parking in/out $24. TV; cable (premium), VCR avail. Indoor pool. Coffee in rms. Restaurant 6:30 am–10 pm. Rm serv 24 hrs. Bar 11 am–midnight; entertainment. Ck-out noon. Meeting rms. Business center. In-rm modem link. Concierge. Exercise equipt; weight machine, bicycles, whirlpool, sauna. Sun deck. Minibars, wet bars. Cr cds: A, C, D, DS, JCB, MC, V*

★★★★
RENAISSANCE
1 W Wacker Dr, Chicago IL 60601
☎ *312/372–7200 or 800/HOTELS–1*
FAX *312/372–0093*

The interior of this white-stone and glass hotel evokes a grand 19th-century hotel with its multiple fountains, crystal chandeliers, marble and grand staircase. Guest rooms all have sitting areas and many dramatic river views.  *553 units, 27 story. S $210–$295; D $230–$315; each addl $20; suites $450–$750; under 18 free; wkend plans. Crib free. Pet accepted, some restrictions. Garage; valet parking in/out $24. TV; cable (premium), VCR avail. Indoor pool; poolside serv. Restaurants 6 am–midnight. Rm serv 24 hrs. Bar 11–2 am; pianist & jazz trio. Ck-out 1 pm. Convention facilities. Business center. In-rm modem link. Concierge. Shopping arcade. Gift shop. Tennis privileges. Exercise equipt; weight machine, bicycles, whirlpool, sauna. Minibars. Bathrm phone in suites. Luxury level. Cr cds: A, C, D, DS, ER, JCB, MC, V*

ILLINOIS

★★★★ THE RITZ-CARLTON

160 E Pearson St, Chicago IL 60611
☎ *312/266–1000 or 800/621–6906*
FAX *312/266–1194*

Magnificent flower arrangements, a fountain, wicker and palms set the tone in the 2-story greenhouse lobby here. The guest rooms upstairs are spacious with mahogany furniture, cherry-wood armoires and wingback chairs. 🐾 *429 rms, 31 story, 84 suites. S, D $290–$360; each addl $30; suites $375–$995; under 12 free; special packages, wkend plans. Crib free. Parking in/out $25.25/day. TV; cable (premium), VCR avail. Heated pool $8; lifeguard. Restaurant 6:30–1 am (also see RITZ-CARLTON DINING ROOM). Rm serv 24 hrs. Bar 11–1 am, Fri & Sat to 2 am. Ck-out 1 pm. Convention facilities. Business center. In-rm modem link. Concierge. Shopping opp in Water Tower Mall. Tennis privileges. Exercise rm; instructor, weights, bicycles, whirlpool, sauna, steam rm. Masseuse. Bathrm phones, minibars; refrigerators avail. Kennels avail. Cr cds: A, C, D, DS, ER, JCB, MC, V*

★★★★ WHITEHALL

105 E Delaware, Chicago IL 60611
☎ *312/944–6300 or 800/948–4255*
FAX *312/573–6250*

This newly renovated landmark hotel offers all the style and grace of a fine European establishment. Modern conveniences have been incorporated without sacrificing the traditional decor. 🐾 *221 rms, 21 story. S, D $245–$335; each addl $25; suites $375–$995; under 12 free; wkly & wkend rates. Crib free. Pet accepted. Valet parking $21.50. Restaurant 6:30–2 am. Rm serv 24 hrs. Bar from 11 am. Ck-out noon. Meeting rms. Business servs avail. In-rm modem link. Concierge. Exercise equipt; weight machines, treadmills. Health club privileges. Minibars. Luxury level. Cr cds: A, C, D, DS, MC, V*

CHARLIE TROTTER'S

816 W Armitage Ave, Chicago IL
☎ *312/248-6228*

At this tastefully renovated town house, the eponymous Charlie Trotter, a young culinary wizard who is the restaurant's chef and owner, sets high goals and achieves them. There are two six-course dinner menus, one of them vegetarian. Although portions are small, all the food is artistically arranged and delicious, due in part to artful eccentricity. Asian flavors often infuse classic European dishes. The lower dining room is small, while the upper one is more private and less visible. *Hrs: 5:30–10 pm. Closed Sun, Mon; major hols. Res required. American menu with French and Asian influences. Bar. Wine cellars. A la carte entrees: dinner $32–$40. Table d'hôte (dégustation menu): dinner $65–$85. Specialties: hand-harvested sea scallop, organic beef strip loin, artichoke & goat cheese terrine. Two dégustation menus available nightly. Own baking. Valet parking. Chef-owned. Jacket. Totally nonsmoking. Cr cds: A, C, D, JCB, MC, V*

D

EVEREST

440 S La Salle St, Chicago IL
☎ *312/663–8920*

Most diners come to Everest for the fine Alsatian cooking of chef/owner Jean Joho, who brings a light, nouvelle touch to that traditionally hearty cuisine. Food is enhanced by an extensive assortment of accompanying wines and, if you get one of the few tables at or near a window, by the spectacular view of downtown Chicago, where this 40th-floor restaurant is perched. The art deco-influenced aerie is lined with African safari murals. *Hrs: 5:30–9:30 pm (last sitting); Fri & Sat to 10 pm (last sitting); Closed Sun, Mon; major hols. Creative French cuisine with Alsatian influence. Res required. Serv bar. Extensive wine list; specializes in wines from Alsace. A la carte entrees: dinner $23–$35. Prix fixe: 8-course dinner $76. Pretheater menu (5:30–6:30 pm): 3-course dinner $39. Specialties: le tournedos de cabillaud de petite pêche au Pinot Noir d'Alsace, composition of Pennsylvania farm-raised lamb, New York state foie gras roasted with suri rueve colmar style. Complimentary valet parking. Chef-owned. Jacket. Cr cds: A, C, D, DS, JCB, MC, V*

D

ILLINOIS

AMBRIA

In the Belden-Stratford Hotel
2300 N Lincoln Park West, Chicago IL
☎ *312/472–5959*

The mood is retro elegance at this restaurant housed in a turn-of-the-century hotel and decorated with dark wood and Art Nouveau fixtures. Hrs: 6–9:30 pm; Fri & Sat to 10:30 pm. Closed Sun; major hols. Res accepted. French, continental menu. Bar. Wine list. A la carte entrees: dinner $22–$30. Prix fixe: dinner $48 & $64. Specializes in fresh seafood, seasonal offerings. Menu changes seasonally; daily specialties. Own baking. Valet parking. Chef-owned. Totally nonsmoking dining rm. Cr cds: A, C, D, DS, JCB, MC, V

D

ARUN'S

4156 N Kedzie Ave, Chicago IL
☎ *312/539–1909*

This bi-level dining room has lots of natural wood, complemented by Thai art and a small art gallery—world's apart from the typical storefront ethnic restaurant. Seafood is a must; daily specials supplement the extensive basic menu. Hrs: 5–10 pm; Sun to 9 pm. Closed Mon; major hols. Res accepted. Thai menu. Bar. A la carte entrees: dinner $11.95–$24.95. Specialties: phad Thai, three-flavored red snapper, spicy roast eggplant. Thai art display. Cr cds: A, C, D, DS, MC, V

RITZ-CARLTON DINING ROOM

In the Ritz-Carlton
160 E Pearson St, Chicago IL 60611
☎ *312/227–5866*

Burled wood paneling, crystal chandeliers and forest green banquettes lend elegance to this split-level dining room classic. Hrs: 6–11 pm; Sun to 10:30 pm; Sun brunch 10:30 am–2:30 pm. Res accepted. French-inspired menu. Bar. A la carte entrees: dinner $26–$37. Sun brunch $42. Specialties: lobster with seafood ravioli, New Zealand venison with asparagus, Colorado rack of lamb with lavender honey, sautéed halibut with grilled sweet onions. Own pastries.

Pianist. Valet parking. Menu changes daily. Cr cds: A, C, D, DS, ER, JCB, MC, V

SEASONS
In Four Seasons
120 E Delaware Place, Chicago IL 60611
☎ *312/649-2349*

Walnut paneling and old porcelains grace this refined dining room. 🕊 *Hrs: 6:30-9:30 am, 11:30 am-2 pm, 6-10 pm; Sun brunch 10:30 am-1:30 pm. Res accepted. American menu. Bar 11:30-1 am. A la carte entrees: bkfst $8.95-$13.50, lunch $12-$22, dinner $24-$36. Prix fixe: 3-course lunch $19.50, 5-course dinner $59. Sun brunch $42. Child's meals. Specialties: pan-roasted red snapper, rack of lamb with garlic-roasted artichoke, Nantucket stew of lobster, crab & sunchokes, vegetarian menu. Menu changes seasonally. Own baking. Pianist, jazz trio Fri-Sat. Valet parking $15; validated self-parking $5. Jacket. Cr cds: A, C, D, DS, ER, JCB, MC, V*

SPIAGGIA
980 N Michigan Ave, Chicago IL
☎ *312/280-2750*

Elegant, modern decor—complete with 2-story atrium, arches and Italian marble colonnades—adds to the luxurious dining experience at Spiaggia. There are breathtaking views of Lake Michigan through 34-foot-high windows. Elaborate filled pasta dishes, delightful desserts and remarkable wines add adventure. 🕊 *Hrs: 11:30 am-2 pm, 5:30-9:30 pm; Fri, Sat to 10:30 pm; Sun 5:30-9 pm. Closed major hols. Res accepted. Italian menu. Bar to 11 pm; Fri & Sat to midnight; Sun to 10 pm. Extensive wine list. A la carte entrees: lunch $8.95-$17.95, dinner $16.95-$29.95. Specialties: wood-roasted veal chops, skewered boneless quail, scallops with porcini mushrooms. Own pastries, pasta. Pianist (dinner). Seasonal menu. Parking. Jacket (dinner). Cr cds: A, C, D, DS, JCB, MC, V*

ILLINOIS

✗ ★★★★
TOPOLOBAMPO

445 N Clark St, Chicago IL
☏ *312/661–1434*

This restaurant shares owners, kitchen and the same dedication to quality as its less-expensive next-door neighbor, the Frontera Grill. The menu changes constantly and features game and seasonal fruits and vegetables. Outdoor dining is available. *Hrs: 11:30 am–2 pm, 5:30–9:30 pm; Fri & Sat 5:30–10:30 pm. Closed Sun, Mon. Res accepted. Regional Mexican menu. Bar. Wine list. A la carte entrees: lunch $8–$14, dinner $15.50–$22. Specializes in gourmet cuisine featuring complex sauces, exotic wild game. Own pastries. Valet parking. Outdoor dining. Intimate dining. Cr cds: A, C, D, DS, MC, V*

[D]

Evanston

✗ ★★★★
TRIO

1625 Hinman Ave, Evanston IL 60201
☏ *847/733–8746*

A signature of Trio is its unusual presentation of food—artistically arranged on slabs of marble and mirror, in huge deep bowls, in bamboo baskets, in a double-tiered triangle of glass, in a lacquer box, as well as on decorative plates. *Hrs: 5:30–9:30 pm; Sat 5–10:30 pm; Sun 5–9 pm. Closed Mon; some major hols. Res recommended. Continental menu. Serv bar. Wine cellar. Complete meal: dinner $60–$75. Own baking. Jacket. Totally nonsmoking. Cr cds: A, C, D, DS, JCB, MC, V*

[D]

Oak Brook

🏨 ★★★★
OAK BROOK HILLS

3500 Midwest Rd, Oak Brook IL 60521
☏ *630/850–5555 or 800/445–3315*
FAX *630/850–5569*

This elegantly-furnished hotel sits on 150 acres of manicured grounds including duck ponds and a challenging golf course. 382 rms, 11 story, 38 suites. S $167–$197; D $177–$207; each addl $15; suites $275–$650; under 16 free. Crib free. TV; cable (premium), VCR avail (movies). 2 pools, 1 indoor; poolside serv. Restaurants 6:30 am–10:30 pm. Rm serv 24 hrs. Bars 10–1 am, wkends to 2 am; entertainment. Ck-out 1 pm. Convention facilities. Business center. In-rm modem link. Concierge. Shopping arcade. Barber, beauty shops. Lighted tennis. 18-hole golf, greens fee $65–$75, pro, putting green. X-country ski on site. Exercise rm; instructor, weights, bicycles, whirlpools, saunas. Lawn games. Refrigerators, minibars, bathrm phones. Balconies. Luxury level. Cr cds: A, C, D, DS, JCB, MC, V

Wheeling

LE FRANÇAIS
★★★★★

269 S Milwaukee Ave (IL 21), Wheeling IL 60090
☎ *847/541–7470*

While the meals served in this reproduction of a French country inn are sure to satisfy your palate, the warm welcome and superb service make you feel very special, combining to produce an extraordinary culinary adventure. Le Français is sophisticated and somewhat formal, yet quick to put you at ease. Service is carefully timed and impeccable. The captain explains the menu in detail; he and waiters even bring over mock appetizer samples embedded in clear aspic on a large silver tray so that you can see in advance the intriguing options that await your order. There is a wide range of hot and cold hors d'oeuvres and combinations of both, and many light sauces are used. Hrs: 11:30 am–2 pm, 5:30–10 pm; Sat 2 dinner sittings, 6–6:30 pm & 9–9:30 pm; Mon from 5:30 pm; early-bird dinner 5–6 pm. Closed Sun; major hols; also 1st wk Jan. Res accepted. Contemporary French menu. Serv bar. Extensive wine list. A la carte entrees: lunch $13.75–$15.50, dinner $27.50–$30.50. Prix fixe: lunch (Tues–Fri) 4-course $28, dinner (Mon–Thurs) 10-course $75. Specialties: nage de homard et snapper a l'huile de noisettes, magret de canard du jour, tian de boeuf avec son jus naturel, white chocolate Delice with fresh raspberries; also daily specialties. Menu changes frequently. Own desserts, pastries, chocolates. Valet parking. Chef-owned. Jacket (dinner). Cr cds: A, D, DS, MC, V

Kentucky

Lexington

★★★★ MARRIOTT'S GRIFFIN GATE RESORT

1800 Newtown Pike (KY 922), Lexington KY 40511
☎ *606/231–5100*
FAX *606/255–9944*

This gleaming, contemporary resort caters to those who like a mix of activities and comfort. The lobby has an atrium with waterfalls, mahogany tables and leather chairs. *409 rms, 7 story. S $125–$145; D $137–$157; suite $250–$850; under 18 free; golf plans. Crib free. Pet accepted, some restrictions; $40. TV; cable (premium). 2 pools, 1 indoor; poolside serv, lifeguard. Playground. Supervised child's activities (summer). Dining rm 6 am–11 pm. Rm serv. Bar 11–1 am. Ck-out noon. Coin lndry. Convention facilities. Business center. In-rm modem link. Valet serv. Gift shop. Barber, beauty shop. Package store 1 mi. Airport transportation. Sports dir. Lighted tennis, pro. 18-hole golf $28–$62, pro, putting green. Seasonal activities include walking tours, pool activities. Game rm. Exercise rm; instructor, weights, bicycles, whirlpool, sauna. Refrigerator in suites. Private patios, balconies. Picnic tables. Luxury level. Cr cds: A, C, D, DS, JCB, MC, V*

Louisville

★★★★ THE CAMBERLEY BROWN

335 W Broadway, Louisville KY 40202
☎ *502/583–1234 or 800/866–7666*
FAX *502/587–7006*

This elegantly restored 1923 hotel has Old English-style furnishings, artwork, atmosphere and service. *294 rms, 16 story. S $165–$200; D $180–$215; each addl $15; suites from $425; family rates; wkend package plans. Crib free. Covered parking $7/night; valet $10. TV; cable. Restaurants 6:30 am–11 pm. Rm serv 24 hrs. Bar 11–1 am. Ck-out 11 am. Convention facilities. Business servs avail. In-rm modem link. Shopping arcade. Barber, beauty shop. Airport transportation.*

Exercise equipt; weights, stair machine. Refrigerator in suites. Luxury level. Cr cds: A, C, D, DS, ER, JCB, MC, V

★★★★
SEELBACH
500 Fourth Ave, Louisville KY 40202
☎ *502/585–3200 or 800/333–3399*
FAX *502/585–9239*

The lobby in this restored hotel, originally opened in 1905, has eight murals by Arthur Thomas depicting Kentucky pioneers and Native Americans. Rooms have four-poster beds, armoires and marble baths. ✈ *321 rms, 11 story. S $152–$210; D $180–$210; each addl $10; suites $210–$510; under 18 free; wkend package plans. Crib free. Pet accepted; $50 deposit. Parking $8, valet $13. TV; cable, VCR avail. Pool privileges. Restaurants 6:30 am–midnight. Bar 4 pm–2 am; entertainment. Ck-out 1 pm. Convention facilities. Business center. In-rm modem link. Concierge. Shopping arcade. Free airport transportation. Health club privileges. Luxury level. Cr cds: A, C, D, DS, MC, V*

✕
LILLY'S
1147 Bardstown Rd, Louisville KY 40204
☎ *502/451–0447*

The menu here changes biweekly and is filled with inventive dishes made with fresh, homegrown ingredients. The vaguely art deco-style dining room is decked in shades of green, black and purple. ✈ *Hrs: 5–9 pm. Closed Sun, Mon; most major hols. Res accepted. Semi-a la carte: dinner $25–$36. Specialties: pork tenderloin marinated and grilled in an apricot-sage beurre blanc, butterflied leg of lamb with roasted tomato-olive sauce. Cr cds: A, MC, V*

Louisiana

Baton Rouge

CHALET BRANDT
7655 Old Hammond Hwy, Baton Rouge LA
☎ *504/927-6040*

Cypress beams, a 17-foot fireplace, Oriental rugs and antique copper pots lend character to this elegant eatery. *Hrs: 5:30-10 pm; Thurs-Fri also 11:30 am-2 pm. Closed Sun & Mon; some major hols; also wk of July 4. Res accepted. Continental menu with Louisiana flair. Serv bar. Semi-a la carte: lunch $9-$16.75, dinner $9.75-$30. Child's meals. Specializes in fresh seafood, veal, duck, lamb, beef, chicken. Own pastries. Chef-owned. Parking. Jacket. Cr cds: A, C, D, MC, V*

Covington

LA PROVENCE
US 190E, Lacombe LA 70445
☎ *504/626-7662*

This one-story house with sitting room and authentic French furnishings evokes the experience of dining in a fine tavern in the French countryside. On the north shore of Lake Ponchartrain, it's about an hour's drive from central New Orleans. *Hrs: 5-11 pm; Sun 1-9 pm. Closed Mon, Tues; Dec 25. Res required. French, regional menu. Serv bar. Wine list. Semi-a la carte: dinner $17-$28. Prix fixe: dinner $23.95. Specialties: canard à l'ail, duck l'orange, carré d'agneau aux herbes de Provence. Own baking. Pianist Fri-Sun. Parking. Cr cds: A, MC, V*

New Orleans

🏨 ★★★★
INTER-CONTINENTAL
444 St Charles Ave, New Orleans LA 70130
☎ *504/525–5566 or 800/327–0200*
FAX *504/523–7310*

Pale golden marble and lush landscaping greet guests of this modern high-rise. Most rooms are decorated in contemporary style, but some suites have antiques. 🐎 *482 units, 15 story. S $190–$230; D $210–$250; each addl $20; suites $350–$2,000; under 14 free; wkend plans. Valet parking $14. TV; cable (premium), VCR avail. Heated pool; poolside serv. Restaurant 6 am–11 pm. Rm serv 24 hrs. Bars 11–1 am; entertainment. Convention facilities. Business center. In-rm modem link. Concierge. Gift shop. Beauty shop. Airport transportation. Exercise equipt; weight machine, bicycles. Massage. Bathrm phones, TVs; some refrigerators, minibars. Some balconies. Luxury level. Cr cds: A, C, D, DS, ER, JCB, MC, V*

🏨 ★★★★
OMNI ROYAL ORLEANS
621 St Louis St, New Orleans LA 70140
☎ *504/529–5333 or 800/843–6664*
FAX *504/529–7089*

Built in 1960, this property re-creates a grand hotel of the 1800s. Gilt mirrors and Italian marble abound in guest rooms and public areas alike; three magnificent lobby chandeliers were imported from France. 🐎 *346 rms, 7 story. S, D $139–$329; each addl $20; suites $369–$1,000; under 17 free; package plans. Crib free. Valet parking $14. TV; cable (premium), VCR avail. Rooftop heated pool; poolside serv. Restaurant 6:30 am–3 pm, 6–11 pm. La Riviera poolside restaurant 9 am–8 pm (Apr-Oct). Rm serv 24 hrs. Bars 11–2 am; entertainment. Ck-out noon. Meeting rms. Business center. In-rm modem link. Concierge. Barber, beauty shop. Exercise equipt; weights, bicycles. Bathrm phones, minibars; some whirlpools. Some balconies. Observation deck. Cr cds: A, C, D, DS, ER, JCB, MC, V*

LOUISIANA

WINDSOR COURT ★★★★

300 Gravier St, New Orleans LA 70140
☎ 504/523-6000 or 800/262-2662
FAX 504/596-4513

This gracious hotel is full of notable art and antiques (art tours are Saturday at 4 pm), yet features exceptionally friendly service. The famous Grill Room is one of the city's best restaurants, and guest rooms feature a muted, elegant decor, with parquet floors and travertine and marble bathrooms. ✈ *315 units, 23 story, 275 suites. S, D $235–$320; suites $310–$990, each addl $25; under 18 free. Crib free. Valet parking $17. TV; cable (premium), VCR avail. Heated pool; poolside serv. Restaurant (see GRILL ROOM). British high tea daily (2–6 pm), Sat & Sun brunch. Rm serv 24 hrs. 2 bars from 9 am; entertainment. Ck-out 1 pm. Convention facilities. Business servs avail. In-rm modem link. Concierge. Gift shop. Airport transportation. Indoor tennis privileges adj, pro. 18-hole golf privileges, greens fee $35, pro, putting green, driving range. Exercise rm; instructor, weights, bicycles, whirlpool, sauna, steam rm. Massage. Bathrm phones, refrigerators, minibars; wet bar in suites. Balconies. Cr cds: A, C, D, DS, MC, V*

BAYONA ★★★★

430 Rue Dauphine, New Orleans LA 70140
☎ 504/525-4455

Chef Susan Spicer presents "New World" cuisine in this century-old Creole cottage in the French Quarter. There's outdoor dining in a well-planted courtyard with fountain. The homemade soups and ice cream are worth a trip. ✈ *Hrs: 11:30 am–2 pm, 6–10 pm; Fri to 11 pm; Sat 6–11 pm. Closed Sun; Mardi Gras, Easter, Dec 25. Res accepted. French, Mediterranean menu. Bar. Semi-a la carte: lunch $8–$13, dinner $11–$19. Specializes in grilled duck, fresh fish. Cr cds: A, D, DS, MC, V*

NEW ORLEANS

EMERIL'S
800 Tchoupitoulas St, New Orleans LA 70140
☏ *504/528-9393*

This is a large, noisy, renovated warehouse, conveniently located near the convention center. It's contemporary in style with brick and glass walls, gleaming wood floors, burnished-aluminum lamps and a huge abstract-expressionist oil painting. Emeril's is considered by many to be the pacesetter for Creole cuisine in the '90s. ✈ *Hrs: 11:30 am–2 pm, 6–10 pm; Sat 6–10:30 pm. Closed Sun; Mardi Gras, most major hols. Res accepted. Creole, Amer menu. Bar. Wine list. A la carte entrees: lunch $15–$20, dinner $19–$30. Menu changes seasonally. Cr cds: A, C, D, DS, MC, V*

GRILL ROOM
In the Windsor Court
300 Gravier St, New Orleans LA 70140
☏ *504/522-1992*

Rejuvenated Creole classics are elegantly served on the covered terrace or in the deep-carpeted dining rooms outfitted with British furnishings and paintings spanning several centuries. ✈ *Hrs: 7–10:30 am, 11:30 am–2:30 pm, 6:30–10:30 pm; Sat, Sun from 10 am, brunch to 2 pm. Res accepted. Continental, regional cuisine. Bar 11 am–midnight. Wine cellar. A la carte entrees: bkfst $8–$13, lunch $9.75–$19.75, dinner $19.50–$45. Sun brunch $25–$27.50. Specialties: oysters polo, rack of lamb, mandarin coffee-glazed duck. Own baking. Valet parking. Jacket. Cr cds: A, C, D, DS, MC, V*

Maine

Bar Harbor

★★★★☆
BAR HARBOR HOTEL-BLUENOSE INN
90 Eden St, Bar Harbor ME 04609
☎ *207/288-3348 or 800/445-4077*
FAX *207/288-2183*

This service-oriented property has a premiere location atop a granite-terraced hillside that provides beautiful views of Frenchman Bay. Two elegant guest buildings, Mizzentop and Stenna Nordica, offer a number of amenities and services. 🐾 *97 rms, 3-4 story, 48 suites. July-Aug: S, D $135-$238; suites $218-$265; each addl $25; lower rates May-June, Sept-Oct. Closed rest of yr. TV; cable (premium), VCR avail. 2 heated pools, 1 indoor; whirlpool. Complimentary coffee in rms. Restaurant 7-11 am, 5:30-9:30 pm. Rm serv. Bar 4-11 pm. Ck-out 11 am. Coin lndry. Meeting rm. Business servs avail. Bellhops. Gift shop. Tennis privileges, pro. 18-hole golf privileges. Exercise equipt; weight machine, bicycles. Refrigerators; many fireplaces, bathrm phones. Balconies. Ocean view. Cr cds: MC, V*

Kennebunkport

★★★★☆
CAPTAIN LORD MANSION
Pleasant & Green Sts, Kennebunkport ME 04046
☎ *207/967-3141*
FAX *207/967-3172*

This Federal-style building (1812) was the former residence of a shipbuilder and is decorated with antique furnishings. A cupola overlooks the river. 🐾 *16 rms, 3 story. May-Dec: D $159-$249; each addl $25; 2-night min wkends, 3-night min hol wkends; lower rates rest of yr. Children over 5 yrs only. Playground. Complimentary full bkfst, afternoon tea. Restaurant nearby. Ck-out 11 am, ck-in after 3 pm. Meeting rms.*

Business servs avail. Gift shop. Many fireplaces. Some refrigerators. Totally nonsmoking. Cr cds: DS, MC, V

★★★★
INN AT HARBOR HEAD
41 Pier Rd, Kennebunkport ME 04046
☎ *207/967–5564*
FAX *207/967–1294*

A restored farmhouse, this inn has antiques, hand-painted murals, a deck overlooking the harbor, a private wharf and ocean swimming. 🐾 *5 rms, 2 story, 2 suites. Rm phones avail. Memorial Day–mid-Oct: S, D $170–$195; suites $215–$250; lower rates rest of yr. Children over 12 yrs only. Complimentary full bkfst, coffee, tea/sherry. Ck-out 11 am, ck-in 3 pm. Balconies. Private beach. Totally nonsmoking. Cr cds: MC, V*

WHITE BARN
37 Beach St, Kennebunk ME 04046
☎ *207/967–2321*

In a Maine coastal resort, lobster is expected, but not haute cuisine this imaginative. The prix-fixe dinner menu includes the best seafood, fowl and meat of the season in generous portions. The restored stable features original timber, art and antiques with a view of the flower garden. 🐾 *Hrs: 6–9 pm. Closed Jan–mid-Feb. Res accepted. Bar. Complete meals: dinner (4-course) $45–$52. Specializes in fresh Maine seafood, seasonal game. Pianist. Parking. Cr cds: A, MC, V*

Portland

★★★★
INN BY THE SEA
40 Bowery Beach Rd, Cape Elizabeth ME 04107
☎ *207/799–3134 or 800/888–4287*
FAX *207/799–4779*

The Inn by the Sea affords breathtaking views of the Atlantic from Cape Elizabeth's headlands. Rooms in the Main House are furnished in Chippendale cherry furniture

MAINE

and feature fully functional kitchens; Cottage Suites, situated away from the Main House, are furnished in wicker and light pine and are ideal for longer stays.  *43 kit. suites, 3 story. No A/C. July–Aug: S, D $160–$390; package plans off-season; lower rates rest of yr. Pet accepted. TV; cable (premium), VCR (movies). Heated pool; whirlpool, poolside serv. Full bkfst off-season. Coffee in rms. Restaurant 7:30 am–9:30 pm. Rm serv. Ck-out noon. Meeting rms. Business servs avail. In-rm modem link. Bellhops. Concierge. Lighted tennis. Lawn games. Bicycle rental. Bathrm phones. Balconies, decks. Picnic tables. On ocean; access to swimming beach. Totally nonsmoking. Cr cds: A, DS, MC, V*

Maryland

Baltimore

★★★★ MR MOLE BED & BREAKFAST
1601 Bolton St, Baltimore MD 21217
☎ *410/728-1179*
FAX *410/728-3379*

This restored 1870 redbrick row house with oriel windows still possesses many original details, including 14-foot ceilings, plaster moldings, marble fireplaces and gilt mirrors and cornices. The large guest rooms are furnished with 18th- and 19th-century antiques and stocked with vintage books. *5 rms, 5 story, 2 suites. S $87; D $97–$125; each addl $15; suites $100–$145; 2-day min wkends Mar-Dec. Children over 12 yrs only. Complimentary bkfst. Restaurant nearby. Ck-out 11 am, ck-in 4–6 pm. Business servs avail. In-rm modem link. Totally nonsmoking. Cr cds: A, C, D, DS, MC, V*

★★★★ HAMPTON'S
In the Harbor Court
550 Light St, Baltimore MD 21202
☎ *410/234-0550*

This hotel dining room setting is similar to an 18th-century mansion. *Hrs: 5:30–11 pm; Sun to 10 pm; Sun brunch 10:30 am–3 pm. Closed Mon. Res required. Serv bar. Wine list. A la carte entrees: dinner $23–$36. Vegetarian prix fixe dinner: $36–$49. Sun brunch $19.95–$27.95. Specializes in seafood, regional dishes. Own pastries. Valet parking. Jacket. Totally nonsmoking. Cr cds: A, C, D, DS, ER, JCB, MC, V*

MARYLAND

Ocean City

★★★★
LIGHTHOUSE CLUB
56th St In The Bay, Ocean City MD 21842
☎ *410/524-5400 or 800/767-6060*
FAX *410/524-9327*

Rooms are wedge-shaped with spectacular views of the bay in this luxuriously appointed hotel, which was designed to resemble an archetypal Chesapeake Bay lighthouse. 🚭 *23 rms, 2 story. Memorial Day-Labor Day: S, D $139-$249; each addl $15; package plan; lower rates rest of yr. TV; cable (premium), VCR avail (movies). Pool privileges. Complimentary continental bkfst. Complimentary coffee in rms. Restaurant adj 11 am-11 pm. Ck-out noon. Meeting rm. Business servs avail. In-rm modem link. Concierge. Airport transportation. Health club privileges. Bathrm phones, in-rm whirlpools, refrigerators, wet bars; some fireplaces. Balconies. Footbridge over marsh provides access to adj recreational and dining facilities. Cr cds: A, C, D, MC, V*

St Michaels

★★★★
INN AT PERRY CABIN
308 Watkins Ln, St Michaels MD 21663
☎ *410/745-2200 or 800/722-2949*
FAX *410/745-3348*

This white dormered farmhouse, built on the banks of the Miles River in the late 18th century, was refurbished by Sir Bernard Ashley to showcase the designs of his late wife, Laura Ashley, and has the ambiance of an English country house. 🚭 *41 rms, 3 story, 6 suites. S, D $195-$575; suites $475-$575. Children over 10 yrs only. TV; cable (premium), VCR avail (movies). Pool; whirlpool. Complimentary full bkfst. Dining rm 8-10:30 am, 12:30-2:30 pm, 6-10 pm. Rm serv. Ck-out noon, ck-in 3 pm. Business center. In-rm modem link. Bellhops. Valet serv. Concierge. Exercise equipt; weights, bicycles, sauna, steam rm. Massage. Lawn games. Dockage. Cr cds: A, D, MC, V*

Massachusetts

Bedford

★★★★
RENAISSANCE BEDFORD
44 Middlesex Tpke, Bedford MA 01730
☎ 617/275-5500
FAX 617/275-8956

In this contemporary hotel on 24 wooded acres a skylight illuminates the lobby, and guest rooms are modern with overstuffed armchairs. 285 rms, 2-3 story. S, D $159-$179; suites $180-$225; wkend rates; under 18 free. Crib free. Pet accepted with prior approval. TV; cable (premium), VCR avail. Indoor pool; poolside serv. Restaurant 6:30 am-11 pm. Rm serv 24 hrs. Complimentary coffee and newspaper delivered to rms. Bar 11:30-1 am; entertainment. Ck-out 1 pm. Meeting rms. Business center. In-rm modem link. Concierge. Indoor & outdoor tennis, pro. Exercise equipt; weight machine, bicycles, whirlpool, sauna. Refrigerators, minibars. Cr cds: A, C, D, DS, ER, JCB, MC, V

Boston

★★★★
BOSTON HARBOR
70 Rowes Wharf, Boston MA 02110
☎ 617/439-7000 or 800/752-7077
FAX 617/330-9450

Located on Boston's waterfront within walking distance of major sights, this property has a copper-domed observatory with views of Boston. Numerous objets d'art embellish the public areas. 230 rms, 16 story, 26 suites. S $195-$330; D $225-$375; each addl $50; suites $425; under 18 free; wkend packages. Crib free. Pet accepted, some restrictions; kennel facilities also available. Garage parking, valet $23 or self-park. TV; cable (premium), VCR avail. Indoor pool; poolside serv. Restaurant 6 am-11 pm. Rm serv 24 hrs. Bar 11:30-2 am; entertainment. Ck-out 1 pm. Meeting rms. Business center. In-rm modem link. Concierge. Complimentary transportation throughout the greater Boston area. Exercise

MASSACHUSETTS

rm; instructor, weight machines, bicycles, whirlpool, sauna, steam rm. Masseuse. European-style spa. Bathrm phones, minibars. Balconies. Water shuttle service to and from Logan airport. Cr cds: A, C, D, DS, JCB, MC, V

THE ELIOT

370 Commonwealth Ave, Boston MA 02215
☎ *617/267–1607 or 800/44-ELIOT*
FAX *617/536–9114*

The Eliot exudes the atmosphere of an elegant European hotel. Suites have marble baths and period furnishings. 91 kit. suites, 9 story. S $205–$245; D $245–$265. Crib free. Pet accepted, some restrictions. Valet parking $18. TV; cable (premium), VCR avail (movies). Complimentary coffee in rms. Bkfst rm 6:30–10:30 am; Sat & Sun 7–11 am. Restaurants nearby. Bar 3:30 pm–midnight. Ck-out noon. Meeting rms. Business center. In-rm modem link. Concierge. Health club privileges. Minibars. Some balconies. Cr cds: A, D, MC, V

FOUR SEASONS

200 Boylston St, Boston MA 02116
☎ *617/338–4400*
FAX *617/423–0154*

The Four Seasons hotel is elegant, has a highly attentive staff and is eminently comfortable for leisure or work. Rooms are large and tastefully furnished, and most face the Boston Public Garden or an attactively landscaped business area behind it. 288 rms, 15 story. S $295–$455; D $350–$490; each addl $40; suites $455–$3,000; under 18 free; wkend rates. Crib free. Pet accepted, some restrictions. Valet, garage parking $28. TV; cable (premium), VCR avail (movies). Indoor pool; poolside serv. Complimentary continental bkfst in lobby. Restaurant 7 am–11 pm (also see AUJOUR-D'HUI). Rm serv 24 hrs. Bar 11–2 am; entertainment. Ck-out 1 pm. Convention facilities. Business center. In-rm modem link. Concierge. Gift shop. Exercise equipt; weights, bicycles, whirlpool, sauna. Bathrm phones, refrigerators. Cr cds: A, C, D, ER, JCB, MC, V

BOSTON

MERIDIEN
★★★★

250 Franklin St, Boston MA 02110
☎ 617/451–1900
FAX 617/423–2844

The respected French chain refurbished the old Federal Reserve Building downtown, a landmark Renaissance Revival building erected in 1922. Some rooms have cleverly designed skylighted lofts. 326 rms, 9 story. S, D $225–$245; each addl $25; suites $400–$790; under 12 free; wkend plans. Crib free. Pet accepted, some restrictions. Valet parking $25. TV; cable (premium), VCR avail. Pool. Restaurant 7 am–10 pm. Rm serv 24 hrs. Bar 11–2 am; pianist. Ck-out 1 pm. Meeting rms. Business center. In-rm modem link. Concierge. Exercise rm; instructor, weights, treadmill, sauna. Massage. Bathrm phones, minibars, refrigerators. Cr cds: A, C, D, DS, ER, JCB, MC, V

THE RITZ-CARLTON, BOSTON
★★★★

15 Arlington St, Boston MA 02117
☎ 617/536–5700 or 800/241–3333
FAX 617/536–1335

This Boston institution is famous for its service and overall exellence. Rooms are traditionally furnished, and public spaces tasteful and elegant. 278 rms, 17 story. S $245–$345; D $285–$385; each addl $20; 1–2 bedrm suites $325–$1,495; under 12 free; wkend rates. Crib free. Pet accepted, some restrictions. Garage $22. TV; cable (premium), VCR avail (movies). Restaurant 6:30 am–midnight. Rm serv 24 hrs. Bar 11:30–1 am. Ck-out noon. Convention facilities. Business servs avail. In-rm modem link. Concierge. Barber. Airport transportation. Exercise equipt; weights, bicycles, sauna. Masseuse. Health club privileges. Bathrm phones, refrigerators. Fireplace in suites. Overlooks Public Garden. Luxury level. Cr cds: A, C, D, DS, ER, JCB, MC, V

MASSACHUSETTS

 ★★★★

AUJOURD'HUI
In the Four Seasons
200 Boylston St, Boston MA 02116
☎ *617/338-4400*

If you're lucky enough to get a table near the broad windows, you can dine on regional specialties while gazing out on the Boston Public Garden. 🍴 *Hrs: 6:30 am–2:30 pm, 5:30–10:30 pm; Sat 7 am-noon, 5:30–10:30 pm; Sun 7–11 am, 6–10:30 pm; Sun brunch 11:30 am–2:30 pm. Res accepted. Bar. Wine cellar. A la carte entrees: bkfst $10–$18, lunch $16.50–$27, dinner $31–$70. Sun brunch $39. Child's meals. Menu changes seasonally. Own baking. Valet parking. Jacket (dinner). Cr cds: A, C, D, DS, ER, JCB, MC, V*

D ✈

 ★★★★

BIBA
272 Boylston St, Boston MA 02116
☎ *617/426-7878*

This is a popular people-watching spot—both inside and out—from the huge windows in the downstairs bar. Striking art and vivid murals deck the dining room. The seasonal menu showcases fresh and innovative meals for affordable prices. 🍴 *Hrs: 11:30 am–2:30 pm, 5:30–10 pm; Fri to 11 pm; Sat 5:30–11 pm; Sun 11:30 am–3 pm, 5:30–10 pm. Closed some major hols. Res accepted. Bar. A la carte entrees: lunch $8–$16, dinner $16–$36. Specialties: ham hock ravioli with toasted Parmesan and peas, sweet ginger rice wrapped in spring brook trout. Valet parking. Cr cds: A, C, D, DS, MC, V*

D ✈

✗ ★★★★

HAMERSLEY'S BISTRO
553 Tremont St, Boston MA 02116
☎ *617/423-2700*

Hamersley's includes a full bar and cafe area as well as a large dining room that's a bit more formal. The menu changes daily; the wine list is replete with offerings from France, Spain, Italy and California. 🍴 *Hrs: 6–10 pm; Sat, Sun from 5:30 pm. Closed major hols. French, Amer menu. Bar. A la carte entrees: dinner $18.50–$28. Specialties: mush-*

room sandwich, roast chicken, lemon custard. Valet parking. Outdoor dining. Totally nonsmoking. Cr cds: A, D, DS, MC, V

L'ESPALIER ★★★★

30 Gloucester St, Boston MA 02115
☎ *617/262-3023*

Elegance prevails in the three small dining rooms of this 19th-century Back Bay townhouse. 🦋 *Hrs: 6–10 pm. Closed Sun; most major hols. Res accepted. Contemporary French menu. Bar. Wine cellar. Prix fixe: dinner $62. Menu dégustation (Mon–Fri): dinner $78/person. Specialties: grilled beef short ribs with black bean mango salsa, ragout of dayboat wolffish, pan-roasted free-range chicken in tamarind orange glaze with radishes. Own baking. Valet parking. Daily menu. Totally nonsmoking. Cr cds: A, C, D, DS, MC, V*

Brewster (Cape Cod)

CHILLINGSWORTH ★★★★

1 mi E of jct MA 6A & MA 124, Brewster (Cape Cod) MA 02631
☎ *508/896-3640*

Classical music accompanies meals at this 300-year-old property decorated in 18th-century style. 🦋 *Hrs: mid-June-mid-Sept, 2 dinner sittings: 6–6:30 pm & 9–9:30 pm; mid-May–mid-June & mid-Sept–Nov, wkends only; casual greenhouse lunches and dinners Tues–Sat, 11:30 am–2:30 pm & 6–9:30 pm, Sun brunch 11:30 am–2:30 pm. Off season dinner, 1 sitting: 7–8 pm. Closed Mon; also Dec–mid-May. Res accepted. Modern French menu. Bar. Wine list. Table d'hôte: 7-course dinner from $40. A la carte entrees: lunch from $7.50, dinner from $9.50, Sun brunch from $7.50. Daily changing menu emphasizing fresh native seafood, veal, pheasant. Own baking, pasta. Grows own herbs. Parking. Outdoor dining. Guest rms (3) avail. Cr cds: A, C, D, MC, V*

MASSACHUSETTS

Chatham (Cape Cod)

★★★★
WEQUASSETT INN
Pleasant Bay Rd, Chatham (Cape Cod) MA 02633
☎ *508/432-5400 or 800/225-7125*
FAX *508/432-5032*

On 23 acres with gardens, the Wequassett Inn overlooks the bay. 🌸 *104 rms, 1-2 story. May-Oct: S, D $210-$350; suite $400-$500. Closed rest of yr. Crib free. TV; cable (premium), VCR. Heated pool; poolside serv. Supervised child's activities (in season); ages infant-12 yrs. Coffee in rms. Dining rm 7 am-10 pm. Rm serv. Ck-out 11 am, ck-in 3 pm. Business center. Valet serv. Gift shop. Airport, bus depot, National Seashore transportation. Tennis, pro. Golf privileges. Exercise equipt; bicycles, treadmill. Refrigerators. Many private patios, balconies. Private beach. Sailboats, windsurfing, deep-sea fishing charters, whale-watching cruises. Boat shuttle to National Seashore beach. Cr cds: A, C, D, DS, MC, V*

Lenox

★★★★
BLANTYRE
16 Blantyre Rd, Lenox MA 01240
☎ *413/637-3556*
FAX *413/637-4282*

The facade of this 1902 mansion combines Norman and Tudor elements; the opulent interior is decorated in Regency style with ornamental plasterwork, oak paneling and antiques. The grounds are extensive and landscaped, punctuated with formal gardens and crossed by many walking trails. 🌸 *23 rms in main house, carriage house & cottages, 2 story, 6 suites. Mid-May-Oct: S, D $230-$475; each addl $40; suites $300-$650. Closed rest of yr. Children over 12 yrs only. TV; cable, VCR avail. Heated pool; whirlpool, sauna, poolside serv. Complimentary continental bkfst, mineral water & cheese, before-dinner sherry. Dining rm (see BLANTYRE). Rm serv 7 am-10 pm. Ck-out noon, ck-in 3 pm. Meeting rms. Business servs avail. In-rm modem link. Luggage handling. Valet serv. Airport, bus depot transportation. Tennis, pro. Masseuse. Competition croquet courts, pro. Some fire-*

LENOX

places. In Berkshires, near Tanglewood. Cr cds: A, C, D, DS, MC, V

★★★★
WHEATLEIGH
Hawthorne Rd, Lenox MA 01240
☎ *413/637-0610*
FAX *413/637-4507*

This elegant country house was built in 1893 on 22 landscaped acres near Tanglewood. Antiques and abstract sculptures complement the stately columns, carved mantels and magnificent Tiffany windows. Many rooms have fireplaces, balconies and wonderful mountain views. ✈ *17 rms, 2 story. S, D $155-$385; 2-day min wkends. Children over 12 yrs only. TV; cable, VCR. Pool. Complimentary tea and sherry. Dining rm (see WHEATLEIGH). Rm serv. Ck-out noon, ck-in 3 pm. Business servs avail. Luggage handling. Concierge serv. Tennis. Downhill ski 9 mi. Cr cds: A, C, D, MC, V*

✗ ★★★★
BLANTYRE
16 Blantyre Rd, Lenox MA 01240
☎ *413/637-3556*

This unique, castlelike Tudor mansion is set on 85 acres of meticulously sculpted ground. You choose from formal dining in the paneled dining room; a moire-walled Regency sitting room or the less-formal garden conservatory. Baking is done on the premises, and many entrees are prepared with fresh local New England ingredients. ✈ *Hrs: 6-9 pm; July-Aug also 12:30-1:45 pm. Closed Mon; also Nov-Apr. Res required. Contemporary French menu. Serv bar. Wine cellar. A la carte entrees: lunch (July-Aug) $7-$25. Prix fixe: dinner $68. Serv charge 18%. Specializes in fresh game and seafood. Own baking, ice cream. Pianist, harpist at dinner. Parking. Outdoor dining at lunch. Jacket, tie. Cr cds: A, C, D, MC, V*

135

MASSACHUSETTS

✕ ★★★★★
WHEATLEIGH
Hawthorne Rd, Lenox MA 01240
☎ 413/637-0610

An antique buffet, chandeliers and an ornate fireplace with candelabras highlight the elegant, formal atmosphere here. 🕊 *Hrs: 6-9 pm. Res required. French menu. Bar. Tasting menu: $68. Menu changes daily. Totally nonsmoking. Cr cds: A, C, D, MC, V*

Martha's Vineyard

🏠 ★★★★★
THORNCROFT
278 Main St, Vineyard Haven MA 02568
☎ 508/693-3333 or 800/332-1236
FAX 508/693-5419

Set on 3½ acres of woods a mile from the ferry, this property is rather formal, with antique and reproduction furnishings, despite its setting in a 1918 bungalow. 🕊 *14 rms in 2 buildings, 2 story. Mid-June-Labor Day: D $200-$450; lower rates rest of yr. TV; cable. Complimentary full bkfst, coffee, afternoon tea. Ck-out 10 am, ck-in 2-9 pm. Business servs avail. In-rm modem link. Luggage handling. Fireplace in 10 rms. Whirlpool in 3 rms, hot tub in 2 rms. Some balconies. Ocean 1 blk; swimming beach. Residential area. Totally nonsmoking. Cr cds: A, C, D, DS, ER, MC, V*

Nantucket Island

🏠 ★★★★★
THE WAUWINET
Wauwinet Rd, Nantucket Island MA 02584
☎ 508/228-0145 or 800/426-8718
FAX 508/228-6712

Guest rooms in this 1870 inn are done in a country style with pine antiques. 🕊 *36 rms, 1-3 story, 4 suites. Mid-June-late Sept: S, D $320-$710; each addl $55; suites $610-$1,400; lower rates early May-mid-June, late Sept-Oct. Closed rest of yr. Crib free. TV; VCR (movies). Complimen-*

tary full bkfst; refreshments in afternoon. Dining rm 8 am–11 pm; closed Nov–early May. Rm serv to 9 pm. Ck-out 11 am, ck-in 4 pm. Business servs avail. In-rm modem link. Tennis, pro, shop. Rowboats & sailboats. Bicycles. Lawn games. Refrigerators avail. Some patios. Library. All recreational facilities are complimentary. On ocean; swimming beach; complimentary harbor cruises. Totally nonsmoking. Cr cds: A, C, D, MC, V

Sandwich (Cape Cod)

DAN'L WEBSTER INN

149 Main St, Sandwich (Cape Cod) MA 02563
☎ *508/888–3622 or 800/444–3566*
FAX *508/888–5156*

Guest rooms in this traditional inn, modeled on an 18th-century house, are furnished with fine reproductions, including some canopy beds. 46 rms, 1–3 story. Late May–Oct: S, D $120–$165; each addl $10; suites $195–$325; under 12 free; also MAP, addl $44/person; lower rates rest of yr. Crib free. TV; cable (premium). Pool. Dining rm 8 am–10 pm. Rm serv. Bar noon–1 am; entertainment. Ck-out 11 am, ck-in 3 pm. Meeting rms. Business center. In-rm modem link. Luggage handling. Airport transportation. Health club privileges. Some fireplaces. Whirlpool in suites. Cr cds: A, C, D, DS, MC, V

Williamstown

ORCHARDS

222 Adams Rd, Williamstown MA 01267
☎ *413/458–9611 or 800/225–1517*
FAX *413/458–3273*

Guest rooms are furnished with reproductions of antiques and four-poster beds. 49 rms, 3 story. Mid-May–mid-Nov: S, D $155–$225; each addl $30; MAP packages; lower rates rest of yr. Crib $10. TV; cable (premium), VCR (movies). Pool. Dining rm 7–10 am, noon–2 pm, 5:30–9 pm. Afternoon tea 4–5 pm. Rm serv. Bar noon–11:30 pm. Ck-out noon, ck-

MASSACHUSETTS

in 4 pm. Business servs avail. Luggage handling. Concierge serv. Tennis privileges. 18-hole golf privileges, pro, greens fee $55–$75. Downhill/x-country ski 6 mi. Exercise equipt; bicycles, rowing machines, whirlpool, sauna, steam rm. Bathrm phones; many refrigerators; some fireplaces. Library. Dessert & cordials in living rm 7:30–10 pm (seasonal). Courtyard has fountain pond with exotic fish. Herb garden, blueberry bushes, wild strawberries. Cr cds: A, C, D, MC, V

Michigan

Birmingham

🏨
TOWNSEND
100 Townsend St, Birmingham MI 48009
☎ *810/642–7900 or 800/548–4172*
FAX *810/645–9061*

French furniture, a wood-burning fireplace and a mahogany bookshelf full of antique books lend intimacy to the lobby here. 🕊 *87 rms, 4 story, 51 suites. S from $199; D from $209; each addl $20; suites $225–$505; under 12 free. Crib free. TV; cable (premium), VCR (movies). Restaurant 7 am–midnight. Afternoon tea Wed–Sun by res; pianist. Rm serv 24 hrs. Bar to 2 am. Ck-out 1 pm. Meeting rms. Business servs avail. In-rm modem link. Concierge. Gift shop. Covered parking. Exercise bicycle brought to rm upon request. Tennis privileges. Downhill ski 20 mi; x-country ski 5 mi. Health club privileges. Bathrm phones; many minibars. Balconies. Located opp park. Cr cds: A, C, D, MC, V*

🅳 ⛷ 🏃 🚭 🔥

Bloomfield Hills

🍽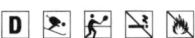
THE LARK
6430 Farmington Rd, West Bloomfield MI
☎ *810/661–4466*

This restaurant overlooks a walled garden filled with potted flowers and herbs, a grape arbor and a stone fountain decorated with a spouting lion's head and tile frogs. 🕊 *Hrs: 6–10:30 pm (last sitting 8:30 pm); Fri & Sat to 9 pm (last sitting). Closed Sun, Mon; major hols; also 1st wk Jan & 1st wk Aug. Res required. French menu. Bar. Wine cellar. Complete meals: dinner $50–$60. Specializes in rack of lamb, monthly theme dinners. Parking. Outdoor dining. Own herb garden. Cr cds: A, D, MC, V*

MICHIGAN

Dearborn

★★★★ THE RITZ-CARLTON, DEARBORN

300 Town Center Dr, Dearborn MI 48126
☎ *313/441–2000*
FAX *313/441–2051*

At this hotel, the service is polished and the public rooms sumptuously decorated with chandeliers, marble, art and antiques. Guest rooms are spacious and have marble bathrooms. 🏊 *308 rms, 11 story. S, D $135–$195; suites $375–$900; under 12 free; wkend rates. Crib free. Valet/garage parking $12. TV; cable (premium), VCR avail. Indoor pool; poolside serv. Restaurant 6:30 am–2:30 pm, 6–10 pm. Rm serv 24 hrs. Bar 11–1 am; entertainment. Ck-out noon. Convention facilities. Business servs avail. In-rm modem link. Concierge. Gift shop. Tennis & golf privileges. Exercise equipt; weight machine, bicycles, whirlpool, sauna. Bathrm phones, minibars; some wet bars. Ballroom. Luxury level. Cr cds: A, C, D, DS, ER, JCB, MC, V*

Grand Rapids

★★★★ AMWAY GRAND PLAZA

Pearl St at Monroe Ave, Grand Rapids MI 49503
☎ *616/774–2000 or 800/253–3590*
FAX *616/776–6496*

In this renovated 1913 hotel, chandeliers, period furnishings and many antiques set a grandiose mood. 🏊 *682 rms, 29 story. S $107–$185; D $106–$170; each addl $15; suites $215–$1,100; under 12 free; wkend packages. Crib free. TV; cable (premium), VCR avail. Indoor pool; poolside serv. 7 restaurants. Rm serv 24 hrs. Bars 11:30–2 am, Sun from noon; entertainment exc Sun. Ck-out noon. Meeting rms. Business center. Concierge. Shopping arcade. Barber, beauty shop. Airport transportation. Lighted tennis. Downhill ski 15 mi; x-country ski 10 mi. Exercise rm; instructor, weights, bicycles, whirlpool, sauna. Massage. Bathrm phone, refrigerator in suites. Some balconies. On the Grand River. Luxury level. Cr cds: A, C, D, DS, JCB, MC, V*

Minnesota

St Paul

THE SAINT PAUL
350 Market St, St Paul MN 55102
☎ *612/292–9292 or 800/292–9292*
FAX *612/228–9506*

This stately, stone hotel overlooks Rice Park and the center of St. Paul. Rooms are done in an eclectic, traditional decor. Business services and health club privileges are available; exercise equipment will be delivered to your room on request. ✈ *254 rms, 12 story. S, D $139–$154; each addl $15; suites $425–$650; under 19 free; wkend rates; package plans. Crib free. Garage $10.95. TV; cable, VCR avail. Restaurant 11:30 am–midnight. Bar 11–1 am. Ck-out noon. Meeting rms. Business center. In-rm modem link. Concierge. Downhill ski 15 mi; x-country ski 4 mi. Exercise equipt; bicycles, stair machine; equipt delivered to rms on request. Health club privileges. Connected to downtown skyway system. Cr cds: A, C, D, DS, MC, V*

Stillwater

LOWELL
102 N 2nd St, Stillwater MN 55082
☎ *612/439–1100*
FAX *612/439–4686*

A colonial motif predominates, punctuated with distinctive antique furnishings. ✈ *21 rms (some with shower only), 3 story. D $69–$159; higher rates Fri & Sat (MAP). TV. Bkfst 8–10:30 am. Restaurant 8 am–10 pm. Bar 11:30 am–2:30 pm, 5:30 pm–1 am; Sun, hols noon–11 pm. Ck-out noon. Business servs avail. Downhill ski 15 mi; x-country ski 9 mi. Cr cds: MC, V*

Missouri

Kansas City

★★★★ THE RITZ-CARLTON, KANSAS CITY
401 Ward Pkwy, Kansas City MO 64112
☎ *816/756-1500 or 800/241-3333*
FAX *816/756-1635*

Crystal chandeliers, imported marble and original art create an air of luxury. Some guest rooms have balconies with views of Country Club Plaza. 🐾 *373 rms, 12 story. S, D $154-$184; suites $235-$1,200; under 17 free; wkend rates; higher rates Thanksgiving. Crib free. Garage: free self-park, valet $9. TV; cable (premium), VCR avail. Heated pool; wading pool, poolside serv. Restaurant 6:30 am-2:30 pm, 5:30-10 pm. Rm serv 24 hrs. Bar 5 pm-midnight; entertainment. Ck-out noon. Convention facilities. Business center. In-rm modem link. Concierge. Airport transportation. Exercise equipt; weights, bicycles, sauna, steam rm. Massage. Bathrm phones, refrigerators, minibars. Private patios, balconies. Luxury level. Cr cds: A, C, D, DS, ER, JCB, MC, V*

★★★★ SOUTHMORELAND
116 E 46th St, Kansas City MO 64112
☎ *816/531-7979*
FAX *816/531-2407*

Accommodations in this 1913 Colonial revival-style mansion honor notable Kansas citizens. The Thomas Hart Benton Room has the Mission oak furniture favored by the artist, while the Satchel Paige Room resembles a sportsman's lodge. 🐾 *12 rms, 3 story. S $100-$150; D $115-$165. Adults preferred. TV in sitting rm; cable (premium), VCR avail. Complimentary full bkfst; afternoon wine & cheese. Restaurants nearby. Ck-out 11 am, ck-in 4:30 pm. Business servs avail. In-rm modem link. Airport transportation. Solarium. Totally nonsmoking. Cr cds: A, MC, V*

THE AMERICAN RESTAURANT

25th & Grand Ave, Kansas City MO
☎ *816/426–1133*

Designer pastries are a specialty here. Intricate wood ceilings, a white grand piano and rich burgundy carpeting accent the dining area, which offers broad views of the Kansas City skyline. ✈ *Hrs: 11:15 am–2 pm, 6–10 pm; Fri & Sat 6–11 pm. Closed Sun; major hols. Res accepted. Bar. Wine cellar. A la carte entrees: lunch $8–$14, dinner $18–$32. Dinner tasting menu avail. Specializes in contemporary American cuisine with ethnic influences and traditional American cuisine. Own baking, ice cream. Pianist. Valet parking. Jacket. Cr cds: A, C, D, DS, MC, V*

St Louis

THE RITZ-CARLTON, ST LOUIS

100 Carondelet Plaza, Clayton MO 63105
☎ *314/863–6300 or 800/241–3333*
FAX *314/863–3524*

Fine oil paintings and 18th- and 19th-century antiques decorate public areas throughout the hotel. Some guest rooms on the top floors offer views of the skyline. ✈ *301 rms, 18 story, 34 suites. S, D $165–$325; suites $295–$1,500; under 12 free; wkend, package plans. Crib free. Garage, valet parking in/out $10/day. TV; cable (premium), VCR avail. Indoor pool; poolside serv. Restaurant 5–11 pm. Rm serv 24 hrs. Bar 11–1 am; entertainment. Ck-out noon. Convention facilities. Business center. In-rm modem link. Concierge. Gift shop. Exercise rm; instructor (by appt), weight machine, bicycles, whirlpool, sauna, steam rm. Massage. Bathrm phones, refrigerators, minibars. Complimentary newspaper. Luxury level. Cr cds: A, C, D, DS, JCB, MC, V*

MISSOURI

✗
TONY'S
410 Market St, St Louis MO 63102
☏ 314/231–7007

A St Louis favorite ornamented by classical statues, this restaurant has been operated by the Bommarito family for three generations. *✱ Hrs: 5–11 pm; Fri & Sat to 11:30 pm. Closed Sun; major hols; also 1st wk Jan, 1st wk July. Res accepted. Italian menu. Bar. Wine cellar. Semi-a la carte: dinner $18.75–$29.75. Child's meals. Specializes in prime veal and beef, fresh seafood, homemade pasta. Own baking. Valet parking. Family-owned. Jacket. Cr cds: A, C, D, DS, ER, MC, V*

Montana

Bigfork

⌂ ★★★★

FLATHEAD LAKE LODGE
½ mi SW of MT 35, Bigfork MT 59911
☎ 406/837-4391
FAX 406/837-6977

The 2,000 acres of this rustic lakeside ranch with a huge stone fireplace is redolent of the feel for Big Sky country. 🐟 19 rms in 2-story lodge, 22 cottages. No A/C. AP (inclusive), mid-June-Sept, wkly: S, D $1,650; 13-19 yrs $1,225; 6-12 yrs $1,040; 3-5 yrs $775; under 3, $96. Closed rest of yr. Crib free. Heated pool. Free supervised child's activities (June-Sept); ages 6-teens. Dining rm 8 am-6:30 pm. Patio barbecues. Ck-out 11 am, ck-in 1 pm. Grocery, package store 1 mi. Coin lndry. Business servs avail. Valet serv. Gift shop. Airport, RR station transportation. Tennis. Private beach; boats, motors, canoes, sailboats, raft trips, waterskiing, instruction. Lake cruises. Fly-fishing instruction. Whitewater rafting. Soc dir. Indoor, outdoor games. Rec rm. Many private patios, balconies. Picnic tables, grills. Cr cds: A, MC, V

Nevada

Incline Village

★★★★ HYATT REGENCY LAKE TAHOE

111 Country Club Dr, Incline Village NV 89450
☎ *702/832-1234*
FAX *702/831-7508*

Large, attractive rooms have warm color schemes and lake views. The casino has a forest theme. ✈ *458 rms, 12 story. May-Sept, wkends, hols: S, D $170-$260; each addl $25; suites $365-$625; cottages $475-$705; under 18 free; ski packages; lower rates rest of yr. Crib free. TV; cable (premium), VCR avail (movies). Heated pool; whirlpool, poolside serv. Supervised child's activities (daily in season; Fri, Sat evenings off-season); ages 3-12. Restaurant open 24 hrs. Rm serv 24 hrs. Bar. Ck-out 11 am. Convention facilities. Business servs avail. In-rm modem link. Concierge. Shopping arcade. Free valet parking. Tennis. Downhill ski 1½ mi; x-country ski 6 mi. Exercise rm; instructor, weights, bicycles, sauna, steam rm. Massage. Private beach. Game rm. Rec rm. Lawn games. Bicycles avail. Minibars; some refrigerators, fireplaces. Some balconies. Wet bar in suites. Casino. Luxury level. Cr cds: A, C, D, DS, ER, JCB, MC, V*

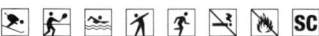

Las Vegas

★★★★ CAESARS PALACE

3570 Las Vegas Blvd S, Las Vegas NV 89109
☎ *702/731-7110 or 800/634-6001*
FAX *702/731-6636*

This opulent casino-hotel with an Ancient Rome accent offers a variety of luxurious accommodations. It often hosts world-class sporting and entertainment events and screens movies in its Omnimax theater. ✈ *1,509 rms, 14-22 story. S, D $100-$299; each addl $15; suites $225-$930; under 13 free. TV; cable (premium), VCR avail (movies). Heated pool; whirlpool, lifeguard. Restaurant open 24 hrs. Bars. Circus Maximus, star entertainment; dancing. Ck-out noon. Convention*

LAS VEGAS

facilities. Business center. In-rm modem link. Concierge. Shopping arcade. Barber, beauty shop. Parking free. Exercise rm; instructor, weight machines, bicycles, sauna, steam rm. Massage. Solarium. Racquetball. Handball. Game rm. Casino. Bathrm phones; many whirlpools; some refrigerators. Many bi-level suites with wet bar. Cr cds: A, C, D, DS, JCB, MC, V

GOLDEN NUGGET
129 E Fremont St, Las Vegas NV 89125
702/385-7111 or 800/634-3454
FAX *702/386-8362*

Behind the palm-tree-shaded exterior is a lobby filled with gold, white marble and greenery. Guest rooms reflect the same elegance. 1,907 rms, 18-22 story. S, D $59-$129; each addl $20; suites $275-$750. Crib free. TV; cable, VCR avail. Heated pool; whirlpool, poolside serv, lifeguard. Restaurant open 24 hrs. Bar; entertainment. Ck-out noon. Meeting rms. Business center. In-rm modem link. Gift shop. Barber, beauty shop. Exercise rm; instructor, weight machines, bicycles, sauna, steam rm. Massage. Casino. Some bathrm phones. Cr cds: A, C, D, DS, JCB, MC, V

MGM GRAND
3799 Las Vegas Blvd S, Las Vegas NV 89109
702/891-1111 or 800/929-1111
FAX *702/891-1030*

This movieland-styled mega-resort is the largest in the world. Outstanding features include a 33-acre theme park, 7-story replica of The Emerald City complete with Yellow Brick Road, and two showrooms with headline entertainment. 5,005 rms, 30 story, 740 suites. S, D $89-$169; suites $119-$269; under 12 free; higher rates hols. Crib free. TV; cable (premium). Heated pool; wading pool, poolside serv, lifeguard. Supervised child's activities; ages 3-12. Restaurants open 24 hrs. Rm serv. Bars; entertainment. Ck-out 11 am. Convention facilities. Business center. In-rm modem link. Concierge. Shopping arcade. Barber, beauty shop. Lighted tennis; pro. Exercise rm; instructor, weight machines, treadmill, steam rm. Complete spa service with masseur, facials,

NEVADA

body treatments. Game rm. Refrigerators, minibars. Cr cds: A, C, D, DS, ER, JCB, MC, V

LE MONTRACHET
★★★★

In the Hilton
3000 Paradise Rd, Las Vegas NV 89114
☎ 702/732–5111

Here's a quiet place away from the chatter of the slot machine. Pastoral scenes of the French countryside on the walls and elaborate table settings mark the luxurious decor. ✈ *Hrs: 6–10 pm. Closed Tues. Res accepted. French menu. Bar. Wine cellar. A la carte entrees: dinner $23.50–$35. Specialties: salmon medallions, sauteed lobster tails, roasted breast of Muscovy duck. Parking. Cr cds: A, C, D, DS, JCB, MC, V*

Stateline

HARRAH'S HOTEL CASINO
★★★★

US 50, Stateline NV 89449
☎ 702/588–6611 or 800/648–3773
FAX 702/586–6607

Top-name entertainment and extensive gaming opportunities are available at this property. The guest rooms offer lake and mountain views. ✈ *534 rms, 18 story. Mid-June–mid-Sept: S, D $149–$209; each addl $20; suites $199–$950; under 15 free; ski package plans; higher rates wkends & hols; lower rates rest of yr. Crib free. TV; cable, VCR avail. Indoor pool; whirlpool, poolside serv. 7 restaurants. Bars open 24 hrs; theater-restaurant; entertainment. Ck-out noon. Convention facilities. Business servs avail. In-rm modem link. Concierge. Shopping arcade. Barber, beauty shop. Free covered valet parking. Exercise equipt; weights, bicycles, sauna, steam rm. Game rm. Casino. Wedding chapel. Youth center. Each rm has 2 bathrms with phone & TV. Butler serv in suites. Cr cds: A, C, D, DS, ER, JCB, MC, V*

★★★★
HARVEY'S RESORT
US 50, Stateline NV 89449
☎ *702/588-2411 or 800/427-8397*
FAX *702/588-6643*

Established in 1944, this casino-hotel was Tahoe's first gaming establishment. Today it stands out for its variety of amenities and facilities. 🐾 *740 rms, 19 story. July–Aug: S, D $115–$175; each addl $20; suites $275–$725; package plans; higher rates wkends & hols; lower rates rest of yr. Crib free. TV; cable. Pool; whirlpool. Complimentary continental bkfst. 8 restaurants. Rm serv 24 hrs. 6 bars open 24 hrs; entertainment. Ck-out noon. Convention facilities. Business servs avail. Concierge. Shopping arcade. Barber, beauty shop. Covered parking; free valet and self-park. Airport, recreation area transportation. Exercise equipt; weights, bicycles, sauna. Massage. Game rm. Rec rm. Casino. Bathrm phones; many minibars; wet bar in suites. Cr cds: A, C, D, DS, MC, V*

New Hampshire

Dixville Notch

★★★★
THE BALSAMS
On NH 26, Dixville Notch NH 03576
☎ 603/255-3400 or 800/255-0600
FAX 603/255-4221

This lavish turn-of-the-century resort occupies a 15,000-acre estate amid mountains and meadows. 🅿 *212 rms, 3-6 story. No A/C. AP, July-Labor Day: S $200-$225; D $315-$600; suites avail; family rates; late Dec-late Mar, MAP, ski plans. 15% serv charge (late May-June, Sept-mid-Oct). Closed rest of yr. Crib avail. TV rm; cable, VCR avail (movies). Heated pool; attendant. Free supervised child's activities (July-Aug); ages 5-12. Dining rm 8-9:30 am, 12:30-2 pm, 6:30-8 pm. Ski area cafeteria open in winter 8:30 am-4 pm; also coffee shop, golf club house 11:30 am-3:30 pm. Box lunches; snacks. Rm serv. Bars 11:30-12:45 am. Ck-out noon, ck-in 4 pm. Business servs avail. In-rm modem link. Bellhops. Shopping arcade. 6 tennis courts, pro. 27-hole golf, pro, 2 putting greens. Private lake, boats, paddleboats, canoes. Alpine & x-country ski on site. Snowmobile trails, ice-skating. Mountain bikes. Horse-drawn hay rides. Hiking trails. Lawn games. Game rm. Rec rm. Library. Soc dirs; dancing, entertainment, lectures, movies; theater. Stocked trout pond, no license required. Natural history program; naturalist on site. Cr cds: A, DS, MC, V*

New Jersey

Atlantic City

BALLY'S PARK PLACE CASINO
Park Place at Boardwalk, Atlantic City NJ 08401
☎ 609/340-2000 or 800/225-5977
FAX 609/340-4713

The two buildings composing this hotel are emblematic of Atlantic City present and past—there is the new hexagonal tower with a glitzy 93-foot escalator at its core, and the old Denis Hotel, built of stone, with a mansard roof and guest rooms decorated in art deco style. *1,265 rms, 49 story. Mid-June-Sept: S, D $125-$215; each addl $15; under 13 free; lower rates rest of yr. Crib free. TV; cable (premium), VCR avail. 2 pools, 1 indoor; poolside serv, lifeguard. Restaurants open 24 hrs. Bars. Ck-out noon. Convention facilities. Business servs avail. In-rm modem link. Barber, beauty shop. Valet parking; self-park garage. Exercise rm; instructor, weight machines, bicycles, whirlpool, sauna, steam rm. Massage. Bathrm phones; refrigerators avail. On beach. Cr cds: A, C, D, DS, MC, V*

TRUMP PLAZA HOTEL & CASINO
Mississippi & Boardwalk, Atlantic City NJ 08401
☎ 609/441-6000 or 800/677-7378
FAX 609/441-7881

In keeping with its casino's reputation as the place for serious gamblers, the hotel has guest rooms that are ultramodern; suites are extravagantly rococo. *902 rms, 38 story. June-Sept: S, D $185-$230; each addl $10; under 16 free; lower rates rest of yr. Crib avail. TV; cable (premium), VCR avail. Indoor pool; lifeguard. Restaurants open 24 hrs. Bar; entertainment. Ck-out noon. Business servs avail. In-rm modem link. Concierge. Shopping arcade. Garage parking. Tennis. Golf privileges. Exercise rm; instructor, weights, bicycles, whirlpool, sauna, steam rm. Massage. Game rm. Bathrm phones. On ocean. Cr cds: A, C, D, DS, MC, V*

NEW JERSEY

★★★★ TRUMP TAJ MAHAL CASINO RESORT

1000 Boardwalk, Atlantic City NJ 08401
☎ 609/449–1000 or 800/825–8786
FAX 609/449–6818

As the tallest building in New Jersey, with the largest casino and most convention space of any Atlantic City hotel, this property fulfills its grand intentions. Its glittering turrets, domes and belvederes are prominent features of the local skyline. *1,250 rms, 51 story, 246 suites.* July-Labor Day: S, D $165–$225; each addl $25; suites $275–$800; lower rates rest of yr. Crib free. TV; cable (premium). Indoor pool; poolside serv, lifeguard. Restaurant open 24 hrs, dining rm 6 pm–midnight. Rm serv 24 hrs. Bar open 24 hrs; entertainment. Ck-out noon. Convention facilities. Business center. Concierge. Shopping arcade. Barber, beauty shop. Valet parking. Exercise rm; instructor, weights, bicycles, whirlpool, sauna, steam rm. Massage. Casino. Game rm. Bicycles avail. Refrigerators avail. On Boardwalk facing ocean. Cr cds: A, C, D, DS, MC, V

★★★★ TRUMP'S CASTLE CASINO RESORT

1 Castle Blvd, Atlantic City NJ 08401
☎ 609/441–2000 or 800/777–8477
FAX 609/441–8541

With its helicopter service and the state's largest marina, this hotel caters to a sophisticated clientele. Decorated with fanciful medieval motifs, it hosts major sports and entertainment events. *728 rms, 27 story.* July–mid-Sept: S, D $110–$160; each addl $15; suites $150–$265; under 12 free; package plans; lower rates rest of yr. Crib free. TV; cable (premium), VCR avail. Pool; wading pool, whirlpool, poolside serv, lifeguard. Restaurants open 24 hrs. Bars; entertainment. Ck-out noon. Convention facilities. Business servs avail. In-rm modem link. Shopping arcade. Barber, beauty shop. Garage parking. Lighted tennis. Exercise rm; instructor, weights, bicycles, sauna, steam rm. Massage. Miniature golf. Basketball. Lawn games. Game rm. On ocean inlet. Cr cds: A, C, D, DS, JCB, MC, V

Bernardsville

THE BERNARDS INN
27 Mine Brook Rd, Bernardsville NJ 07924
☎ *908/766-0002 or 800/766-0002*
FAX *908/766-4604*

This completely renovated inn, built in 1907, offers plush accommodations and gracious hospitality. ✱ *21 rms (1 with shower only), 5 story, 3 suites. S, D $99–$155; suites $165–$185. Crib $20. TV; cable (premium). Complimentary continental bkfst. Restaurant 11:30 am–3 pm, 5:30–10 pm. Rm serv Mon-Fri. Bar. Ck-out 11 am, ck-in 2 pm. Business servs avail. In-rm modem link. Luggage handling. Concierge serv. Cr cds: A, C, D, MC, V*

Millburn

HILTON AT SHORT HILLS
41 John F Kennedy Pkwy, Short Hills NJ 07078
☎ *201/379-0100*
FAX *201/379-6870*

Less than an hour's drive from mid-Manhattan, this elegant suburban hotel offers many facilities of a fine resort. The hotel is located across from the Mall at Short Hills with branches of many of the nation's top stores. ✱ *300 rms, 7 story, 37 suites. S $225–$255; D $250–$280; each addl $20; suites $255–$900; family rates; wkend rates. Crib free. TV; cable (premium), VCR avail. 2 pools, 1 indoor; lifeguard. Restaurant 6:30 am–10:30 pm. Rm serv 24 hrs. Bar 11:30–1:30 am; entertainment. Ck-out 1 pm. Convention facilities. Business center. In-rm modem link. Concierge. Gift shop. Beauty shop. Valet parking avail. Exercise rm; instructor, weight machines, bicycles, whirlpool, sauna, steam rm. Massage. Refrigerator in suites. Luxury level. Cr cds: A, C, D, DS, ER, JCB, MC, V*

Somerville

RYLAND INN
US 22W, Whitehouse NJ 08888
☎ *908/534-4011*

Dine in one of five dining rooms of this 200-yr-old Victorian manor house set on 55 sweeping acres complete with a six-acre vegetable garden. *Hrs: 11:30 am–2 pm, 5:30–9 pm; Fri to 10 pm; Sat 5:30–10 pm; Sun 4–9 pm. Closed 1st wk in Jan. Res accepted. Contemporary French menu. Bar. Wine cellar. A la carte entrees: lunch $11–$15, dinner $24–$35. Eight-course tasting menu: $80. Child's meals. Specialties: veal chop with asparagus and morels, warm lobster tarte, grilled foie gras with banyuls sauce. Valet parking. Jacket. Cr cds: A, D, DS, MC, V*

New Mexico

Santa Fe

★★★★ ELDORADO

309 W San Francisco, Santa Fe NM 87501
☎ *505/988-4455 or 800/955-4455*
FAX *505/988-5376*

In this Pueblo revival-style hotel in the town's historic district, all the chic Southwestern guest rooms have views of the Santa Fe mountains. 🐾 *219 rms, 5 story. S, D $169-$309; suites $280-$750; under 18 free. Crib free. Garage parking $6.95. Pet accepted. TV; cable (premium), VCR avail (movies). Rooftop heated pool; poolside serv. Restaurant 7 am-9:30 pm. Bar 11:30-2 am; entertainment. Ck-out 11:30 am. Convention facilities. Business center. In-rm modem link. Concierge. Butler service avail in 68 upscale rms. Shopping arcade. Barber, beauty shop. Downhill ski 12 mi; x-country ski 7 mi. Exercise equipt; weight machine, treadmill, whirlpool, sauna. Refrigerators, minibars. Balconies. Cr cds: A, C, D, DS, MC, V*

★★★★ INN OF THE ANASAZI

113 Washington Ave, Santa Fe NM 87501
☎ *505/988-3030 or 800/688-8100*
FAX *505/988-3277*

This sophisticated adobe hotel one block from the Plaza embodies Santa Fe style. Contained within are native and Southwestern art and artifacts, four-poster beds and kiva fireplaces in the guest rooms. 🐾 *59 units, 3 story, 8 suites. Apr-Oct: S, D $235-$395; each addl $20; under 12 free; lower rates rest of yr. Crib free. Valet parking $10/night. Pet accepted, some restrictions; $30 nonrefundable. TV; cable (premium), VCR (movies $5). Complimentary coffee in rms. Restaurant (see THE ANASAZI). Ck-out noon, ck-in 3 pm. Business servs avail. Concierge. Tennis privileges. 18-hole golf privileges, putting green, driving range. Downhill ski 13 mi; x-country ski 7 mi. Health club privileges. Cr cds: A, C, D, DS, MC, V*

NEW MEXICO

✗ ★★★★
THE ANASAZI

In the Inn of the Anasazi
113 Washington Ave, Santa Fe NM 87501
☎ *505/988–3236*

Stone walls, a beamed ceiling, artwork and antiques set the scene for innovative takes on local and regional cuisine. ✈ Hrs: 7–10:30 am, 11:30 am–2:30 pm, 5:30–10 pm; Sun brunch 7 am–2:30 pm. Res accepted. Southwestern menu. Bar 11 am–midnight. Wine cellar. A la carte entrees: bkfst $5.25–$9.50, lunch $4–$12.75, dinner $6.50–$29. Sun brunch $6–$12.75. Child's meals. Specialties: tortilla soup, fresh fish, cinnamon chile with mango salsa, organically grown foods. Menu changes seasonally. Classical guitarist (brunch). Cr cds: A, C, D, DS, MC, V

New York

Fishkill

✕ ★★★★☆
HARRALDS
3110 Rt 52, Stormville NY 12582
☎ *914/878–6595*

This pleasant, rural, ma-and-pa gourmet restaurant occupies an attractive, timbered country cottage decorated with period furnishings, wooden beams, and a fireplace. The extensive wine list covers many modestly priced choices. 🕊 *Hrs: 6 pm–midnight. Closed Sun–Tues; Dec 24–25; also Jan. Res required. Traditional international menu. Bar. Wine cellar. Prix fixe: dinner $65. Specialties: truite au bleu, Zürcher rahm schnitzel, poached fresh North Atlantic salmon. Own baking, desserts. Parking. Blackboard menu. Trout tank. Chef-owned. Jacket. No cr cds accepted.*

Garden City, L. I.

🏠 ★★★★☆
THE GARDEN CITY HOTEL
45 Seventh St, Garden City, L. I. NY 11530
☎ *516/747–3000 or 800/547–0400*
FAX *516/747–1414*

This sophisticated, world-class hotel is the most opulent on Long Island. 🕊 *273 rms, 16 kits. S $195–$310; D $220–$340; each addl $20; suites $400–$1,200; under 12 free; wkly, wkend rates. Crib free. TV; VCR avail. Indoor pool; lifeguard. Restaurant 6:30 am–11 pm. Rm serv 24 hrs. Bar 11:30–2 am; entertainment. Ck-out 1 pm. Convention facilities. Business servs avail. In-rm modem link. Concierge. Shopping arcade. Beauty shop. Free parking. Free airport transportation. 18-hole golf privileges. Exercise rm; instructor, weights, bicycles, sauna. Masseuse. Bathrm phones; some refrigerators. Balconies. Cr cds: A, C, D, DS, JCB, MC, V*

Garrison

XAVIAR'S
NY 9D, at Highland Country Club, Garrison NY 10524
☎ 914/424-4228

Extensive floral arrangements give a romantic touch to this elegant dining room. Outdoor dining on a large terrace affords a view of a golf course. Hrs: 6-9:30 pm; Sun brunch 11:30 am-3 pm. Closed Mon-Thurs; some major hols; also mid-Jan-mid-Feb. Res required. Continental menu. Serv bar. Wine cellar. Prix fixe: dinner $72. Sun brunch $32. Child's meals. Specializes in contemporary cuisine. Entertainment Fri, Sat. Parking. No cr cds accepted.

Hillsdale

AUBERGINE
Jct NY 22 & 23, Hillsdale NY 12529
☎ 518/325-3412

This comfortable restaurant has a country French atmosphere. Hrs: 5:30 pm-closing. Closed Mon & Tues. Res accepted. French, Amer menu. Bar. Wine cellar. A la carte entrees: dinner $16.50-$23. Specialties: hot soufflés, Maine scallop cakes, pave of Atlantic salmon. Own baking. Parking. Fireplaces; antiques. 18th-century inn. Garden. Chef-owned. Cr cds: MC, V

Ithaca

ROSE INN
813 Aubrun Rd, Groton NY 13073
☎ 607/533-7905
FAX 607/533-7908

Guest rooms in this 19th-century Italianate mansion are individually decorated with period furnishings. The 20 landscaped acres include a pond and a garden. 15 rms, 2 story, 5 suites. S $100-$150; suites $175-$250. Children over 10 yrs only (or with advance arrangements). TV in public rm and in 2 suites. Complimentary full bkfst. Dining rm: 1 sit-

ting (res required) Tues–Sat 7 pm. Rm serv on request. Bar. Wine cellar. Ck-out 11 am, ck-in 3 pm. Meeting rm (1850s carriage house). Business servs avail. In-rm whirlpool, fireplace in suites. Totally nonsmoking. Cr cds: MC, V

New York City

★★★★★
CARLYLE
Madison Ave at E 76th St, Manhattan NY 10021
☎ *212/744–1600 or 800/227–5737*
FAX *212/717–4682*

The fabled Carlyle has hosted world leaders and the very, very rich for years and continues to be a symbol of European graciousness. Yet the formality is matched by friendly service. The lobby has Gobelin tapestries and a striking black marble floor, while the charming Bemelman's Bar contains murals created by the illustrator of the beloved children's book character Madeliene. At the Café Carlyle, entertainers such as Bobby Short perform. And on top of all this, the tony boutiques of Madison Avenue are just steps away. *196 rms, 35 story. S $295–$400; D $325–$430; suites (1–2 bedrm) $500–$2,000. Pet accepted, some restrictions. Garage $37. TV; cable (premium), VCR (movies); stereo cassette and CD player. Restaurant 7–10:30 am, noon–2:30 pm, 6 pm–1 am. Rm serv 24 hrs. Bar from noon; Cafe Carlyle from 6 pm; entertainment: Bobby Short and other stars (cover charge). Ck-out 1 pm. Meeting rms. Business center. In-rm modem link. Concierge. Exercise rm; instructor, weights, bicycles, sauna, steam rm. Massages. Large rms, most with serv pantry. Bathrm phones, refrigerators, wet bars, minibars. Many in-rm whirlpools. Grand piano in many suites. Each rm individually decorated; many antiques. Some terraces. Cr cds: A, C, D, JCB, MC, V*

★★★★★
FOUR SEASONS
57 E 57th St, Manhattan NY 10022
☎ *212/758–5700*
FAX *212/758–5711*

This 52-story hotel, New York's tallest, was designed by I.M. Pei, and the huge, multilevel marble lobby seems more like an Egyptian monument. You quickly learn, however, that this is a place to live it up, providing you can afford the steep tariffs. Guest rooms are large and elegantly furnished in contemporary style. Details are meticulous, such as draperies and curtains that can be opened and closed by flicking a switch from bed. Service is abundant and thoughtful, with such special touches as complimentary overnight shoe shines. An excellent fitness center, complimentary to hotel guests, has a television at every treadmill and help-yourself fruit and cold bottled mineral water always available. 370 rms, 52 story, 61 suites. S $420–$560; D $470–$610; each addl $50; suites $795–$6,000; under 12 free; wkend rates. Crib free. Pet accepted, some restrictions. Garage, valet parking $33. TV; cable (premium), VCR. Restaurant 7 am–10:30 pm (also see FIFTY SEVEN FIFTY SEVEN). Rm serv 24 hrs. Bar 11:30–1 am. Ck-out noon. Convention facilities. Business center. In-rm modem link. Concierge. Exercise rm; instructor, weight machine, bicycles, whirlpool, sauna. Masseuse. Spa & fitness center. Bathrm phones, minibars. Some terraces. Cr cds: A, C, D, ER, MC, V

★★★★★
THE ST REGIS HOTEL

2 E 55th St, Manhattan NY 10022
212/753–4500 or 800/759–7550
FAX *212/787–3447*

I.T.T. Sheraton has marvelously restored this landmark Italianate building to present the ultimate luxury in lodging, feeding and generally pampering guests. After a complete recent renovation, the 1904 building is perhaps more glorious than ever before, containing a striking marbled lobby, an acclaimed restaurant (Lespinasse) and a famous Maxfield Parrish mural over the King Cole Bar. Guest rooms are furnished elegantly but not ostentatiously, and have state-of-the-art technology. A butler on each floor provides superb 24-hour service. The St. Regis isn't cheap, but if you can afford it, you'll probably agree that your money is well spent. 313 rms, 20 story, 92 suites. S, D $455–$565; suites $695–$4,500; under 12 free; wkend packages. Crib free. Garage parking, valet, in/out $36. TV; cable (premium), VCR avail. Restaurant (see LESPINASSE). Afternoon tea 2:30–5:30 pm, harpist. Rm serv 24 hrs. Bar 11–1 am; Fri, Sat 11:30–2 am; Sun noon-midnight. Ck-out 1 pm. Meeting rms. Business center. In-rm modem link. Concierge. Gift shop. Barber, beauty shop. Florist. Men's & ladies' designer apparel shops. Chocolatier. Exercise equipt; weight machine, bicycles, sauna. Fitness center; massage by appt. Bathrm phones. Private butler (24 hrs) each floor. Cr cds: A, C, D, DS, ER, JCB, MC, V

★★★★ ESSEX HOUSE HOTEL NIKKO NEW YORK

160 Central Park South, Manhattan NY 10019
☎ *212/247–0300*
FAX *212/315–1839*

This New York landmark (1931) overlooks Central Park and exemplifies classic art deco style. The spacious guest rooms are traditional with marble baths. Many have park views. 597 units, 40 story, 80 suites. S $295–$325; D $375–$360; each addl $25; suites $395–$2,500; under 18 free; wkend rates. Crib free. Garage parking, valet $33. TV; cable (premium), VCR. Restaurant 7 am–11 pm (also see LES CÉLÉBRITÉS). Rm serv 24 hrs. Bar noon–1 am. Ck-out noon. Convention facilities. Business center. In-rm modem link. Concierge. Gift shop. Exercise equipt; weight machine, bicycles, saunas, steam rms. Health spa with massage, herbal wraps, mud packs. Minibars. Cr cds: A, C, D, DS, ER, JCB, MC, V

★★★★ LOWELL

28 E 63rd St, Manhattan NY 10021
☎ *212/838–1400 or 800/221–4444*
FAX *212/319–4230*

Accommodations are elegant, decorated with French and Oriental period furnishings, in this New York institution. 65 rms, 17 story, 56 kit. suites. S, D $295–$385; each addl $20; kit. suites $485–$1,550; under 12 free; wkend rates. Crib free. Valet parking $35. TV; cable (premium), VCR (movies). Restaurants 7 am–11 pm. Tea rm (exc July–Aug) 3:30–6:30 pm. Bar noon–midnight. Ck-out 1 pm. Meeting rm. Business servs avail. In-rm modem link. Concierge. Exercise equipt; bicycles, treadmills. Bathrm phones, refrigerators, minibars. Many wood-burning fireplaces. Some balconies. Complimentary newspaper, shoeshine. Cr cds: A, C, D, DS, ER, JCB, MC, V

NEW YORK

MAYFAIR ★★★★

610 Park Ave, Manhattan NY 10021
☎ *212/288-0800 or 800/223-0542*
FAX *212/737-0538*

Less glitzy and more low-key than other expensive Manhattan hotels, the Mayfair is gracious, friendly and always lively. Service is superefficient. ✈ *201 rms, 16 story, 105 suites. S $295; D $315; suites (most with pantries) $395–$1,800; wkend plan. Crib free. Valet parking $34. TV; cable (premium), VCR avail (movies). Restaurant 7–11 am, light lunch 11 am–2:30 pm; high tea 3–5:30 pm; also dining adj. Rm serv 24 hrs. Bar 11–1 am. Ck-out 1 pm. Meeting rms. Business servs avail. In-rm modem link. Concierge. Exercise equipt; weights, rowing machine. Complete fitness center (including putting green). Exercise bicycle avail in rm on request. Bathrm phones; some refrigerators & wet bars. Wood-burning fireplace in some rms. Complimentary shoeshine, newspaper. Cr cds: A, C, D, JCB, MC, V*

MILLENIUM HILTON ★★★★

55 Church St, Manhattan NY 10007
☎ *212/693-2001*
FAX *212/571-2316*

A new high-rise hotel with a high-tech look, this property caters primarily to business travelers. ✈ *561 units, 55 story. S $255–$325; D $285–$350; each addl $25; suites $450–$1,500; under 16 free; wkend rates; package plans. Crib free. Garage; valet parking $35. TV; cable (premium), VCR avail. Indoor pool; poolside serv, lifeguard, sauna. Supervised child's activities. Restaurants 6:30 am–midnight. Rm serv 24 hrs. Bar 11:30–1:30 am. Ck-out noon. Meeting rms. Business center. In-rm modem link. Concierge. Gift shop. Exercise rm; instructor, weight machine, bicycles. Massage. Bathrm phones; minibars. Cr cds: A, D, DS, ER, JCB, MC, V*

NEW YORK CITY

★★★★ THE PENINSULA NEW YORK

700 Fifth Ave, Manhattan NY 10019
☎ *212/247-2200 or 800/262-9467*
FAX *212/903-3949*

The lobby of this 1905 Beaux Arts building features a vast marble staircase and a lavish carved ceiling. Guest rooms are done in Art Nouveau style.  *200 rms, 23 story, 42 suites. S, D $365-$475; each addl $20; suites $700-$3,500; under 12 free. Crib free. Parking $31. TV; cable (premium), VCR avail (movies). Indoor pool; poolside serv, lifeguard. Restaurant 7 am-midnight. Rm serv 24 hrs. Tea served in Gotham Lounge (2:30-5:30 pm). Rooftop bar noon-midnight, closed Sun. Ck-out noon. Meeting rms. Business servs avail. In-rm modem link. Concierge. Exercise rm; instructor, weight machines, bicycles, whirlpool, sauna, steam rm. Trilevel health & fitness spa. Bathrm phones, minibars. Cr cds: A, C, D, DS, ER, JCB, MC, V*

★★★★ THE PIERRE

2 E 61st St, Manhattan NY 10021
☎ *212/838-8000 or 800/743-7734*
FAX *212/940-8109*

Personal service and traditional style are hallmarks of this landmark at Central Park.  *202 rms, 42 story. S $355-$500; D $395-$545; suites $610-$2,600. Crib free. Garage $33. TV; cable (premium), VCR avail. Restaurant 7-1 am. Rm serv 24 hrs. Bar from 11 am; entertainment from 8 pm. Ck-out noon. Meeting rms. Business servs avail. In-rm modem link. Concierge. Barber, beauty shop. Many boutiques. Exercise equipt; bicycles, treadmill. Masseuse. Minibars. Serv pantry in suites. Cr cds: A, C, D, ER, JCB, MC, V*

★★★★ PLAZA ATHÉNÉE

37 E 64th St, Manhattan NY 10021
☎ *212/734-9100 or 800/447-8800*
FAX *212/772-0958*

Marble, reproductions of fine antiques and Oriental rugs add style to this tastefully decorated hotel in the mode of the Paris original; the property is grand, but on an intimate scale. 153 rms, 17 story. S, D $320–$475; each addl $35; suites $690–$2,900. Crib free. Parking $38/24 hrs. TV; cable (premium), VCR avail. Restaurant 7 am–9:30 pm. Rm serv 24 hrs. Bar 11 am–midnight. Ck-out 1 pm. Meeting rm. Business servs avail. In-rm modem link. Concierge. Exercise equipt; weights, bicycles. Refrigerators. Deluxe toiletry amenities. Some suites with private dining rm. Some private patios, glassed-in balconies. Cr cds: A, C, D, ER, JCB, MC, V

THE PLAZA HOTEL
Fifth Ave at 59th St & Central Park South, Manhattan NY 10019
212/759-3000 or 800/759-3000
FAX 212/759-3167

Set on the southwest corner of Central Park West and 5th Avenue, the world-renowned Plaza occupies one of the most valuable pieces of real estate in Manhattan. Spacious guest rooms are furnished in fine period details, including marble fireplaces and crystal chandeliers. A drink at the Oak Bar or brunch at Palm Court are New York experiences that should not be missed. 808 rms, 18 story. S, D $235–$625; each addl $35; suites $650–$1,950; under 18 free. Crib free. Garage $35. TV; cable (premium), VCR avail. Restaurant 6:30 am–midnight. Rm serv 24 hrs. Bar 11–2 am. Ck-out noon. Business center. In-rm modem link. Concierge. Gift shop. Barber, beauty shop. Boutiques. Exercise equipt; bicycles, treadmill. Health club privileges. Refrigerators, minibars. Cr cds: A, C, D, DS, ER, JCB, MC, V

THE REGENCY HOTEL
540 Park Ave, Manhattan NY 10021
212/759-4100 or 800/233-2356
FAX 212/826-5674

The graceful guest rooms here are decorated with period furniture, and suites have marble foyers. 365 rms, 21 story, 185 kit. suites. S, D $275–$325; suites $350–$1,500 under 18 free; wkend & shopping packages. Crib free. Garage $30. TV; cable (premium), VCR. Restaurant 7 am–10 pm. Rm serv 24 hrs. Ck-out 1 pm. Meeting rms. Business center. In-rm modem link. Concierge. Barber, beauty shop. Exercise rm;

instructor, weights, bicycles, sauna. Refrigerators, bathrm TVs. Cr cds: A, C, D, DS, MC, V

★★★★
THE RITZ-CARLTON
112 Central Park South, Manhattan NY 10019
☎ *212/757–1900*
FAX *212/757–9620*

The Manhattan branch of this chain, which overlooks Central Park, has the look of an English club.  *214 rms, 25 story. S, D $275–$475; each addl $30; suites $495–$4,000; under 16 free. Crib free. Garage $35. TV; cable (premium), VCR avail. Restaurant 7–10:30 am, noon–2 pm, 5:30–11 pm. Rm serv 24 hrs. Bar 4 pm–1 am. Ck-out noon. Business center. In-rm modem link. Exercise equipt; bicycles, treadmill, sauna. Some refrigerators. Cr cds: A, C, D, DS, ER, JCB, MC, V*

★★★★
THE STANHOPE
995 Fifth Ave, Manhattan NY 10028
☎ *212/288–5800 or 800/828–1123*
FAX *212/517–0088*

This stylish 1926 landmark hotel is across the street from Central Park.  *140 units, 17 story, 70 suites, some with kits. S, D $325; suites $450–$1,325; under 12 free; wkend rates; package plans. Crib free. Garage $35. TV; cable (premium), VCR (movies). Restaurant 7 am–11 pm; also outdoor cafe and tea room. Rm serv 24 hrs. Bar noon–1 am. Ck-out 1 pm. Meeting rms. Business center. In-rm modem link. Concierge. Exercise equipt; weight machine, bicycles, sauna. Massage. Bathrm phones, minibars; some wet bars. Fine antiques and paintings; library lounge. Many rms with views of Central Park and the Manhattan skyline. Cr cds: A, C, D, DS, JCB, MC, V*

NEW YORK

★★★★ U.N. PLAZA-PARK HYATT

1 UN Plaza, Manhattan NY 10017
☎ *212/758-1234*
FAX *212/702-5051*

Guest rooms in this modern chrome-and-glass tower offer fine views of UN Headquarters and the surrounding area. *427 rms on floors 28-38. S, D $280; each addl $25; suites $500-$1,100; under 18 free; wkend rates; wkend package plan. Crib free. Garage; valet parking $26/day. TV; cable (premium), VCR. Indoor pool; lifeguard. Restaurant 7 am-2:30 pm, 6-10:30 pm. Bar noon-1 am. Ck-out noon. Meeting rms. Business center. In-rm modem link. Indoor tennis $60/hr. Exercise rm; instructor, weights, bicycles, sauna, steam rm. Masseuse (fee). Minibars. Some bathrm phones, refrigerators. View from all rms. Complimentary newspaper, shoe shine. Cr cds: A, C, D, DS, ER, JCB, MC, V*

★★★★ WALDORF-ASTORIA

301 Park Ave, Manhattan NY 10022
☎ *212/355-3000 or 800/HILTONS*
FAX *212/872-7272*

This Art Deco masterpiece personifies New York at its most lavish and powerful. The richly tinted, hushed lobby serves as an interior centerpoint of city life. *1,219 rms, 42 story. S $260-$370, D $300-$410; each addl $40; suites $400-$1,000; children free; wkend rates. Crib free. Garage $34/24 hrs. TV; cable (premium), VCR avail (movies). Restaurant 7 am-11:45 pm (also see PEACOCK ALLEY). Rm serv 24 hrs. Bars 10:30-2:30 am; Sun noon-1 am. Ck-out noon. Convention facilities. Business center. In-rm modem link. Concierge. Barber, beauty shop. Great variety of shops and services. Exercise rm; instructors, weight machines, bicycles, steam rm. Massage. Complete physical fitness training center. Refrigerators, minibars. Luxury level. Cr cds: A, C, D, DS, ER, JCB, MC, V*

NEW YORK CITY

✕ ★★★★★
CHANTERELLE
2 Harrison St, in Mercantile Exchange Bldg,
Manhattan NY 10013
☎ 212/966-6960

The menu changes monthly at this bright, inviting restaurant on the ground floor of a restored loft building in Manhattan's recently gentrified Tribeca. The marvelous contemporary French cuisine of chef/owner David Waltuck is matched by the beautiful welcome of his wife, Karen. There are two prix-fixe dinner menus: a three-course version and a six-course chef's menu, but all of Waltuck's masterpieces are imaginatively conceived, carefully prepared, beautifully presented and graciously served with laudable consistency.  *Hrs: noon-2:30 pm, 5:30-11 pm; Mon from 5:30 pm. Closed Sun; major hols; also 2 wks Aug. Res required. French menu. Bar. Wine cellar. A la carte entrees: lunch $18.50-$25. Prix fixe: lunch $35, dinner $73 & $89. Specialty: grilled seafood sausage. Chef-owned. Cr cds: A, C, D, DS, MC, V*

[D]

✕ ★★★★★
DANIEL
20 E 76th St, Manhattan NY 10021
☎ 212/288-0033

Meals at this refined restaurant are served in a French country setting with a changing display of paintings from local galleries. Exotic floral displays punctuate the subdued beige and pale-green hues of the dining room. Beautifully appointed tables—complete with votive candles, Scott Zwiesel crystal and custom Bernaud china—are the perfect showplace for the exquisite creations of chef Daniel Boulud. The menu, which changes frequently, lists more than 20 entrees, several prix fixe menus and wonderful dessert lists. *Hrs: noon-3:30 pm, 5:45-11:30 pm; Mon from 5:45 pm. Closed Sun; most major hols. Res required. French menu. Bar. Wine cellar. A la carte entrees: lunch $28-$34, dinner $31-$36. Table d'hôte: lunch $33, dinner $66, $76 & $96. Specialties: black sea bass in a crispy potato shell with red wine sauce, salad of Maine crab with mango, coriander and lime dressing, seasonal cuisine. Outdoor sidewalk terrace dining offers casual, bistro-style atmosphere. Chef-owned. Jacket. Cr cds: A, D, MC, V*

[D]

NEW YORK

✕ ★★★★★
LES CÉLÉBRITÉS

In the Essex House Hotel Nikko New York
160 Central Park South, Manhattan NY 10019
☎ 212/484–5113

The name, the menu, the chefs and some of the attentive and informative wait staff give Les Célébrités a traditional French cast, but the cuisine is innovative, sometimes experimental. In the rear of the Essex House Hotel, this jewel box of a restaurant has developed into one of the best in the country. Entrées feature a range of seafood, fish, fowl and meat, and two degustation menus, one five-course and one six, are offered. All this is served in polished surroundings, where paintings by Hollywood celebrities adorn the walls. ✈ *Hrs: 6–10 pm; Sat to 10:30 pm. Closed Sun & Mon; also mid-Aug-mid-Sept. Res required. French menu. Bar. Wine cellar. A la carte entrees: dinner $30–$42. Table d'hôte: $75 & $95. Specialties: burger of fresh duck foie gras, squab with artichokes, honey- & orange-lacquered duck. Valet parking. Jacket. Cr cds: A, C, D, DS, ER, JCB, MC, V*

D

✕ ★★★★★
LESPINASSE

In the St Regis Hotel
2 E 55th St, Manhattan NY 10022
☎ 212/339–6719

Inside the landmark St. Regis Hotel on Manhattan's Fifth Avenue, this restaurant is undeniably sumptuous, with silk brocade paneling, lavish floral displays, ivory Louis XV furnishings and fine crystal chandeliers. The star, however, is the cuisine of chef Gray Kunz, who combines Asian and western ingredients using the techniques of classic French cookery. Flavors and presentations are both stunning. A la carte offerings, a four-course seasonal menu, vegetarian tasting menu and chef's degustation menu are all available. ✈ *Hrs: 7–10:30 am, noon–2 pm, 6–10 pm; Sat 5:30–10 pm; Sun 7 am–11:30 am. Res required. French menu. Bar 11:30–1 am; Fri, Sat to 2 am. Extensive wine list. A la carte entrees: bkfst $11.50–$17.50, dinner $36–$43. Complete meals: lunch $48, dinner $74–$105. Specialties: turbotin with herb broth, roast lamb chop, braised rib of beef. Valet parking. Jacket, tie. Cr cds: A, C, D, DS, ER, JCB, MC, V*

NEW YORK CITY

AQUAVIT
13 W 54th St, Manhattan NY 10019
☏ *212/307-7311*

A towering glass-walled atrium and indoor waterfall accent this cooly elegant restaurant set in a townhouse once owned by Nelson Rockefeller. The extensive wine list is accompanied by New York's largest selection of aquavits. 🏃 *Hrs: noon-3 pm, 5:30-10:30 pm; Sat from 5:30 pm; Sun brunch noon-4 pm. Closed major hols. Res accepted. Scandinavian menu. Bar. Wine cellar. A la carte entrees: lunch $12-$20, dinner $15-$22. Prix fixe: lunch $29, dinner $48-$62. Pretheater menu (5:30-6:30 pm): 2-course dinner $25, 3-course dinner $39. Specialties: Scandinavian shrimp, game, salmon. Two dining rms; informal cafe; casual cafe & dining rm. Near Museum of Modern Art. Cr cds: A, C, D, MC, V*

AUREOLE
34 E 61st St, Manhattan NY
☏ *212/319-1660*

Charles Palmer's fashionable restaurant is one of the toughest reservations in town. The elegant townhouse location with lovely outdoor garden offers a lush, romantic setting. 🏃 *Hrs: noon-2:30 pm, 5:30-11 pm; Sat 5:30-11 pm. Closed Sun; some major hols. Res required. French, Amer menu. Bar. A la carte entrees: lunch $16-$24. Prix fixe: lunch $32, dinner $63. Tasting menu $85. Specializes in fish, game. Own baking. Jacket, tie. Cr cds: A, C, D, JCB, MC, V*

BARBETTA
321 W 46th St, Manhattan NY 10036
☏ *212/246-9171*

An 18th-century Venetian harpsichord sets the mood in this venerable establishment, known for classic northern Italian cooking. The property comprises two elegant antique-furnished townhouses and an enchanting garden with century-old trees, perfumed in season with magnolia, wisteria, jasmine and gardenia. 🏃 *Hrs: noon-2 pm, 5 pm-midnight. Closed Sun. Res accepted. Italian menu. A la carte* *entrees: lunch $14–$21, dinner (after 8 pm) $25–$30. Pre-theater dinner $39. Cr cds: A, C, D, DS, JCB, MC, V*

✕ ★★★★
FELIDIA
243 E 58th St, Manhattan NY 10022
☎ *212/758-1479*

Manhattanites love this place as much for the enthusiasm of owner Lidia Bastianich as for the food. Guests can dine in an attractive front room with a wooden bar, in the rustic room beyond or in a skylit balcony with terra-cotta floor, hanging tapestry and lovely plants. ✈ *Hrs: noon–3 pm, 5–11 pm; Sat from 5 pm. Closed Sun; major hols. Res accepted. Italian menu. Bar. Wine cellar. A la carte entrees: lunch $18–$26, dinner $18–$29. Specializes in homemade pasta, veal, seafood. Own baking. Menu changes daily. Garden rm. Jacket. Cr cds: A, C, D, DS, MC, V*

✕ ★★★★
FIFTY SEVEN FIFTY SEVEN
In the Four Seasons
57 E 57th St, Manhattan NY 10022
☎ *212/758-5700*

Housed in the Four Seasons Hotel, designed by I.M. Pei, this is a spectacular, open, airy variation on a brasserie, with 22-foot coffered ceilings, bare maple floors with walnut inlays, bronze chandeliers and art deco touches. Dining is sophisticated, luxurious and comfortable. ✈ *Hrs: 7 am–2 pm, 6–10:30 pm; early-bird dinner 6–7 pm. Bar to 1 am; Fri & Sat to 2 am; Sun to midnight. Contemporary American menu. A la carte entrees: bkfst $8.50–$18.50, lunch $18–$28, dinner $19–$30. Pre-theater menu (6–7 pm) $42. Child's meals. Specialties: Maryland crab cakes, thyme-seared Atlantic salmon, herb-roasted rack of lamb. Pianist Mon-Thurs, jazz Fri & Sat to 1 am. Valet parking. Art deco, contemporary decor. Jacket. Cr cds: A, C, D, ER, MC, V*

✕ ★★★★
THE FOUR SEASONS
Seagram Bldg, Manhattan NY 10022
☎ *212/754-9494*

Designed by Philip Johnson, this New York favorite is now a designated local landmark. ✈ *Hrs: Pool Dining Room:*

noon–2:30 pm, 5–9:30 pm; Sat to 11:15 pm; pretheater dinner 5–6:15 pm, Sat also 10–11:15 pm. Grill Room: noon–2 pm, 5:30–9 pm; Sat 5–10 pm. Closed Sun; major hols. Res accepted. Bar. Wine cellar. A la carte entrees: Pool Dining Room, lunch $29.50–$48, dinner $32.50–$45. Pretheater dinner $41.50. Grill Room: A la carte entrees: lunch $25–$38.50. Prix fixe: dinner $29.50–$41.50. Unusual dishes. Own baking. Grow own herbs. Menu changes with the season. Jacket. Cr cds: A, C, D, DS, JCB, MC, V

GOTHAM BAR AND GRILL
12 E 12th St, Manhattan NY 10003
☎ *212/620–4020*

Chef Alfred Portale originated the vertical style of food presentation here—each plate is an artful edible tower. Multi-leveled and post-modern in design, the Gotham was the prototype of the new-style New York restaurant. 🕭 *Hrs: noon–2 pm, 5:30–10 pm; Fri to 11 pm; Sat 5:30–11 pm; Sun from 5:30. Closed most major hols. Res required. Bar. A la carte entrees: lunch $9.25–$18, dinner $26–$31. Prix fixe: lunch $19.97. Specializes in game, seafood, lamb, quail. Own pastries. Menu changes seasonally. In converted auction warehouse. Cr cds: A, C, D, MC, V*

✕ ★★★★
GRAMERCY TAVERN
42 E 20th St, Manhattan NY 10003
☎ *212/477–0777*

A 91-foot-long mural of fruit and vegetables wraps around the bar of this cozy colonial-decor tavern. Elegant dining is available in three rooms; furnishings include a blend of antiques, quilts and modern art. 🕭 *Hrs: 5:30–10 pm; Fri & Sat to 11 pm. Closed major hols. Res required. Bar to midnight. Wine cellar. A la carte entrees: lunch $15–$21. Complete meal: lunch $33, dinner $56. Specialties: seared tuna with white beans, roast rabbit with black olives and sherry vinegar, lobster and artichoke salad. Elegant dining in three rms with blend of antiques, quilts and modern art. Totally nonsmoking. Cr cds: A, D, MC, V*

HUDSON RIVER CLUB ★★★★

In Building 4 of World Financial Center, Manhattan NY 10281
☎ 212/786-1500

As its name suggests, this spacious and clubby dining room has river views of New York Harbor and the Statue of Liberty. Rotating art displayed on walls. Hudson River Valley produce is showcased, and the towering desserts are like edible sculptures. *Hrs: 11:30 am-2:30 pm, 5-9:30 pm; Sat 5:30-10 pm; Sun brunch 11:30 am-3:30 pm; pretheater dinner Mon-Fri 5-6 pm. Closed Sun (July-Aug); Dec 25. Res required. Bar. Wine cellar. A la carte entrees: lunch $24-$28, dinner $28-$34. Complete meals: pretheater dinner $42. Menu dégustation: 6-course dinner $60. Sun brunch $32. Child's meals. Specialties: roasted oysters with leeks, salmon in woven potatoes, Hudson River Valley dishes, seasonal dishes. Own pastries. Jacket. Cr cds: A, C, D, DS, MC, V*

D

LA CÔTE BASQUE ★★★★

60 W 55th St, Manhattan NY
☎ 212/688-6525

Murals of the Basque coast, dark wooden cross beams and faux windows are just some of the elements that have followed this restaurant to its new home. Dramatic presentation—such as the signature roast duckling carved at tableside, or the glazed pumpkin custard served with a flaming candle inside a pumpkin lantern—adds to the dining experience here. *Hrs: noon-2:30 pm, 5:30-10:30 pm; Fri to 11:30 pm; Sat 5:30-11 pm; Sun 5-10 pm. Closed major hols. Res required. French menu. Bar. Prix fixe: lunch $30, dinner $56. Own pastries. Chef-owned. Jacket, tie. Cr cds: A, C, D, JCB, MC, V*

D

LA CARAVELLE ★★★★

33 W 55th St, Manhattan NY
☎ 212/586-4252

Murals of Parisian scenes decorate the walls, and light peach banquettes provide seating in this spacious and comfortable dining room. *Hrs: noon-2:30 pm, 5:30-10 *pm. Closed Sun; major hols; also 1 wk prior to Labor Day. Res required. Classic and contemporary French menu. Bar. Wine cellar. A la carte entrees avail: lunch from $25, dinner from $40. Prix fixe: 3-course lunch $36, 3-course dinner $62, 5-course tasting menu $75, 7-course tasting menu $95. Pretheater menu 5:30–6:30 pm, $39. Child's meals. Specialties: truffeled pike quenelles in lobster sauce, grilled smoked salmon, crispy duck with cranberries, souffles. Own baking. Cr cds: A, C, D, JCB, MC, V*

D

LE BERNARDIN
155 W 51st St, Manhattan NY 10019
☏ *212/489–1515*

Huge seascapes fill the paneled walls of this polished, high-ceilinged restaurant, where fish and seafood dinners are as delicious and well prepared as you can get anywhere. 🕊 *Hrs: noon–2:15 pm, 6–10:30 pm; Fri & Sat 5:30–11 pm. Closed Sun; major hols. Res accepted. French, seafood menu. Bar. Prix fixe: lunch $42, dinner $68. Specialties: monkfish with cabbage, thyme and pepper rare-seared yellowfin tuna, crispy Chinese-spiced red snapper. Own pastries. Jacket. Cr cds: A, C, D, JCB, MC, V*

D

LE CHANTILLY
106 E 57th St, Manhattan NY 10022
☏ *212/751–2931*

Murals of the château of Chantilly, fresh flowers and comfortable banquettes set a French mood at this New York institution. 🕊 *Hrs: noon–3 pm, 5:30–10:30 pm; Sun 4:30–10 pm. Closed major hols. Res required. French menu. Bar. Wine list. A la carte entrees: lunch $18–$24. Prix fixe: dinner $53. Pretheater dinner (5:30–6:30 pm) $29.50. 7-course tasting menu $75. Specialties: crispy salmon and artichokes, peppered spring lamb loin, roasted pigeon with green lentils. Daily specials. Own baking. Cr cds: A, C, D, DS, JCB, MC, V*

NEW YORK

LUTÈCE ✕ ★★★★★
249 E 50th St, Manhattan NY 10017
☎ *212/752–2225*

Dining at this New York City culinary favorite is in four different rooms: an airy, high-ceilinged main room in a covered garden, a quiet room decorated with stenciled foliage and two upstairs rooms subtly lighted by crystal chandeliers and hung with original oil paintings. 🍽 *Hrs: noon–2 pm, 5:30–10 pm; Sat & Mon from 5:30 pm. Closed Sun; also mid-Aug–Labor Day. Res required. French haute cuisine. Bar. Wine cellar. Table d'hôte: lunch $38. Prix fixe: dinner $60. Specialties: snails and wild mushroom in phyllo, sauteed turbotin on a black truffle vinaigrette, grilled squab, roast rack of lamb with a mustard honey glaze. Cr cds: A, C, D, MC, V*

MARCH ✕ ★★★★★
405 E 58th St, Manhattan NY 10022
☎ *212/838–9393*

Elegantly understated, the three dining rooms in this romantic townhouse are filled with antiques, a travertine floor and burled wood wainscoting. Service is polished, and there are hints of Asian influences in the cuisine. 🍽 *Hrs: 6–10:30 pm; Sun 5–9 pm. Closed Jan 1, Thanksgiving, Dec 25. Res required. Contemporary Amer menu. Bar. Complete meals: dinner $39–$59. Tasting menu $70 & $85. Specialties: five-spice salmon, grilled Long Island duck, roast rack of lamb with herbed crust. Outdoor dining. Jacket. Cr cds: A, C, D, JCB, MC, V*

MONKEY BAR ✕ ★★★★★
60 E 54th St, Manhattan NY 10022
☎ *212/838–2600*

Art deco accents, vivid colors and eclectic decor come together here for a unique and exciting atmosphere. Monkeys hang from overhead lighting, while celebrity pix fill the walls and whimsical monkey murals decorate the bar. Among the signature entrees is a perfectly roasted cod with luscious mashed potatoes, carrots and celery-root chips. 🍽 *Hrs: noon–2:30 pm, 6–11 pm; Fri to 11:30 pm; Sat 5:30–11:30 pm. Closed Sun Memorial Day–Labor Day. Res accepted. Bar to 2 am; Fri, Sat to 3 am. A la carte entrees: lunch $16–$21, dinner $19–$34. Specialties: roasted Amish*

NEW YORK CITY

chicken breast, mustard-crusted rack of lamb, roasted cod. Pianist Tues-Sat. Jacket. Smoking in bar area only. Cr cds: A, D, MC, V

NOBU

105 Hudson St, Manhattan NY 10013
212/219-0500

A curved wall of river-worn black pebbles, bare-wood tables, birch trees and a hand-painted beech floor create a dramatic setting that invites conversation. Sake is the drink of choice; the clientele is as interesting as the menu, which features such tours de force as rock-shrimp tempura and black cod with miso. *Hrs: 11:45 am-2:15 pm; 5:45-10:15 pm. Sat, Sun from 5:45 pm. Closed some major hols. Res accepted. Japanese menu. Serv bar. A la carte entrees: lunch $12-$30, dinner $20-$52. Sushi bar. Cr cds: A, D, MC, V*

OTABE

68 E 56th St, Manhattan NY 10022
212/223-7575

Complete dinners, which change monthly to reflect the seasons, are served in the traditional Japanese dining room. In the Teppan Grill Room, personal chefs prepare steak, fish and other seafood on steel griddles built onto a large semi-circular counter and into tables in secluded alcoves. *Hrs: noon-2:30 pm, 5:30-10:30 pm; Sat from 5:30 pm; Sun 5-9 pm. Res accepted. Japanese menu. A la carte entrees: lunch, dinner $15-$20. Complete meal: dinner $50-$70. Specialties: tuna steak, swordfish teriyaki, eel teriyaki, traditional kaiseki tasting menu including shashimi & tempura. Cr cds: A, C, D, JCB, MC, V*

PALIO

151 W 51st St, Manhattan NY 10019
212/245-4850

Upstairs in this elegant duplex restaurant is a spacious and colorful dining room, but the first-floor bar is even more spectacular. Its four walls are painted with a Chia mural that transports you to Sienna. *Hrs: noon-2:30 pm, 5:30-11* pm; Sat from 5:30 pm. Closed Sun; major hols. Res accepted. Italian menu. Bar 11:30 am–midnight; Sat from 4:30 pm. Wine cellar. A la carte entrees: lunch $22–$32, dinner $22–$32. Prix fixe: lunch $35, pretheater dinner $42.50. Bar lunch $20. Menu changes daily. Own baking. Cr cds: A, C, D, DS, JCB, MC, V

|D|

PARIOLI ROMANISSIMO
24 E 81st St, Manhattan NY 10028
☎ *212/288–2391*

At this townhouse restaurant with neo-Renaissance architecture, seating is inside in an elegant dining room or outside in the striking garden. The clientele is of the money-is-no-object genre. 🕊 Hrs: 6–11 pm; Fri & Sat to 11:30 pm. Closed Sun; major hols; also Aug. Res required. Northern Italian menu. Bar. Wine cellar. A la carte entrees: dinner $28–$35.50. Specialties: fettuccine with white truffles, venison, roasted rack of lamb. Own baking. Jacket, tie. Cr cds: A, D, MC, V

PATRIA
250 Park Ave S, Manhattan NY 10003
☎ *212/777–6211*

This trendy tri-level Caribbean cafe is painted in striking earth tones and decorated in colorful mosaics and Latin American art. The signature dessert is a chocolate-filled cigar with edible matches. 🕊 Hrs: noon–2:45 pm, 6–11 pm; Fri to midnight; Sat 5:30 pm–midnight; Sun 5:30–9:30 pm. Closed most major hols. Res accepted. Latin American menu. Bar to 1 am. A la carte entrees: lunch $9–$16, dinner $17–$26. Specialties: Ecuadorian ceviche, Nicaraguan skirt steak, sugarcane tuna with malanga puree. Multilevel dining with Latin American art. Cr cds: A, D, MC, V

PEACOCK ALLEY

In the Waldorf-Astoria
301 Park Ave, Manhattan NY 10022
☎ *212/872–4895*

This very luxurious Waldorf-Astoria salon has always offered professional service, fine china, a comprehensive wine cellar, soothing lighting and cushy seating. Recently, however, it's added an updated classical decor and such interesting culinary offerings as theme dinners, showcasing famous chefs and cuisines from around the world. *Hrs: 7–10:30 am, noon–2:30 pm, 5:30–10:30 pm; Sat 7:30–10:30 am, 5:30–10:30 pm; Sun brunch 11 am–2:30 pm. Res accepted. Continental menu. Bar. Wine cellar. A la carte entrees: bkfst $14–$23, lunch $18–$29.50, dinner $23–$39.50. Complete meal: dinner $44, $55, $64. Sun brunch $45. Specialties: baby rack of lamb, fried wild bass. Entertainment Fri, Sat. Own baking. Cr cds: A, D, MC, V*

PETROSSIAN

182 W 58th St, Manhattan NY 10019
☎ *212/245–2214*

Near Carnegie Hall, this art-deco dining room is decorated with Erté murals and Lalique crystal panels. *Hrs: 11:30–1 am; Sat & Sun brunch to 3 pm. Res accepted. French, Amer menu. Bar. A la carte entrees: lunch $19, dinner $22–$34. Prix fixe: lunch $29, dinner $35. Sat & Sun brunch $22. Specialties: caviar, smoked salmon, foie gras. Own pastries. Menu changes quarterly. Jacket. Cr cds: A, C, D, MC, V*

RAINBOW ROOM

30 Rockefeller Plaza, Manhattan NY 10112
☎ *212/632–5000*

At the top of a restored landmark skyscraper (1934) is this famous restaurant with a revolving dance floor under a domed ceiling and views of midtown Manhattan through two-story, floor-to-ceiling windows. Rotating exhibit on display. *Hrs: 5:30 pm–1 am; Sun to midnight; Sun brunch noon–2:30 pm. Closed Mon. Res required. Continental menu. Bar. Wine cellar. A la carte entrees: dinner $26–$42. Prix fixe: pretheater dinner $38.50. Sun brunch $12–$16. Cover* *charge $20/person (exc pretheater & brunch). Specialties: seafood extravaganza, lobster Thermidor, baked Alaska. Own baking. Entertainment. Parking. Jacket, tie. Cr cds: A, C, D, MC, V*

SAN DOMENICO
240 Central Park South, Manhattan NY 10019
☎ *212/265-5959*

The setting overlooking Central Park is like a private villa, with terra-cotta and Italian marble floors, Florentine stucco walls, sumptuous leather chairs and lots of warm, earthy hues. *Hrs: noon-2:30 pm, 5:30-11 pm; Sat from 5:30 pm; Sun 5:30-10 pm. Closed Jan 1, Dec 25. Res accepted. Italian menu. Bar. Wine cellar. A la carte entrees: lunch $15.50-$32, dinner $16.50-$42.50. Prix fixe pretheater dinner $29.50, tasting menu $65. Specialities: ravioli with truffle butter, Alaska prawns with beans, breast of duck with olive sauce. Jacket. Cr cds: A, C, D, MC, V*

SIGN OF THE DOVE
1110 Third Ave, Manhattan NY 10021
☎ *212/861-8080*

Skylights, stunning floral arrangements, well-spaced tables, brick arches and 19th-century antiques distinguish the dining rooms here, some of the prettiest in town. There's also outdoor dining, enhancing the garden atmosphere. *Hrs: noon-2:30 pm, 6-11 pm; Mon, Sat from 5:30 pm; Sun 6-10 pm; Sat & Sun brunch 11:30 am-2:30 pm. Res accepted. Bar. Wine cellar. A la carte entrees: lunch $12-$20. Prix fixe: lunch $20 & $25, dinner $30-$45. Sat, Sun brunch $12-$20. Specialties: filet mignon with morel flan, crispy sea bass with polenta gnocchi, seared duck with fennel and leek napolean. Own baking. Jazz combo and vocalist. Cr cds: A, C, D, DS, JCB, MC, V*

Saranac Lake

THE POINT
HCR 1, Box 65, Saranac Lake NY 12983
☎ *518/891–5674 or 800/255–3530*
FAX *518/891–1152*

This exclusive hideaway resort is located on a 10-acre wooded peninsula on Upper Saranac Lake. Built during the 1930s for William Avery Rockefeller, the buildings are made of local stone and wood. 🍽 *10 units in 3 bldgs. Reservations & advance payment required. AP: D $800–$1,050; each addl $150; 2-day min wkends, 3-day min hols. Adults only. 15% serv charge. TV rm; VCR. Dining rm with gourmet meals, jacket & tie requested for dinner. Bar. Tennis. Golf privileges. X-country ski on site; snowshoes avail. Bicycles. Lawn games. Game rm. Massages avail. Cr cds: A, MC, V*

White Plains

LA PANETIERE
530 Milton Rd, Rye NY 10580
☎ *914/967–8140*

This Westchester County restaurant has a formal atmosphere with many French object d'art and antiques. The private dining room on the second floor features a greenhouse. 🍽 *Hrs: noon–2:30 pm, 6–9:30 pm; Sat from 6 pm; Sun 1–8:30 pm. Res required. French menu. Bar. Wine list. A la carte entrees: lunch $16.50–$19.50, dinner $22–$31. Complete meals: dinner $70. Child's meals. Specialties: Dover sole, roast breast of duckling, chessboard of dark and white chocolate mousse. Own baking. Valet parking. Jacket. Cr cds: A, C, D, MC, V*

North Carolina

Asheville

★★★★
GROVE PARK INN RESORT
290 Macon Ave, Asheville NC 28804
☎ *704/252-2711 or 800/438-5800*
FAX *704/253-7053*

The renovation of this inn overlooking the Blue Ridge Mountains preserves the original 1913 decor, including the fireplaces in the lobby and the terraced guest rooms. The roster of distinguished guests includes Henry Ford and F. Scott Fitzgerald. *510 rms, 5-10 story. Apr-Dec: S, D $125-$215; each addl $25; suites $450; under 16 free; golf, honeymoon packages; lower rates rest of yr. Crib free. TV; cable (premium), VCR avail. 2 heated pools, 1 indoor; lifeguard. Supervised child's activities (May-Dec); ages 3-16. Dining rms (public) 6:30 am-midnight. Rm serv. Bar from 11 am; entertainment. Ck-out noon, ck-in 4 pm. Convention facilities. Business center. In-rm modem link. Bellhops. Valet serv. Shopping arcade. 9 lighted tennis courts, 3 indoor. Golf, greens fee $60 incl cart (cart required before 3 pm), nine holes $30, putting green. Rec rm. Exercise rm; instructor, weights, bicycles, whirlpool, sauna. Raquetball & squash courts. Massage. Luxury level. Cr cds: A, C, D, DS, JCB, MC, V*

Blowing Rock

★★★★
HOUND EARS LODGE & CLUB
½ mi off NC 105, Blowing Rock NC 28605
☎ *704/963-4321*
FAX *704/963-8030*

This alpine resort, tucked into a valley of the Blue Ridge Mountains, is named for the 4,000-ft rock outcropping that looms above it. *27 rms in lodge & club house, 2 story. MAP, mid-June-Oct: S $150; D $244; each addl $48; suites $290; under 11, $22; lower rates rest of yr. Serv charge 17%. TV; cable (premium), VCR avail. Heated pool; poolside serv, lifeguard. Free supervised child's activities (June-Sept);*

ages 8–16. Dining rm 7–10 am, noon–2:30 pm, 6:30–9:30 pm (res required; jacket, tie at dinner). Rm serv. Setups; entertainment. Ck-out noon, ck-in 1:30 pm. Meeting rms. Business servs avail. Bellhops. Valet serv. 6 tennis courts, pro. 18-hole golf, greens fee $25, pro. Sleigh rides in winter. Exercise equipt; weight machines, bicycle, sauna. Cr cds: A, MC, V

Chapel Hill

★★★★
FEARRINGTON HOUSE

2000 Fearrington Village Center, Pittsboro NC 27312
☎ *919/542–2121*
FAX *919/542–4202*

This French-style country inn on an old farm is decorated with chintz, original art and pinewood antiques. A courtyard and fountain welcome visitors at the entrance. *28 rms, 2 story. S, D $165–$200; suites $225–$275. TV; cable (premium), VCR avail. Pool; whirlpool. Complimentary full bkfst, refreshments. Dining rm 6–9 pm. Rm serv 24 hrs. Beer, wine. Ck-out noon, ck-in 3 pm. Meeting rms. Business servs avail. In-rm modem link. Tennis. Lawn games. Totally nonsmoking. Cr cds: A, MC, V*

Charlotte

★★★★
THE PARK HOTEL

2200 Rexford Rd, Charlotte NC 28211
☎ *704/364–8220 or 800/334–0331*
FAX *704/365–4712*

Marble, brass and traditional patterns, cast in rich colors, are used throughout the public areas and in the well-appointed guest rooms. *194 rms, 6 story. S $119–$160; D $134–$175; each addl $15; suites $325–$625; under 18 free; wkend rates. Crib free. TV; cable (premium), VCR avail. Heated pool; poolside serv. Restaurant 6:30 am–11 pm. Rm serv 24 hrs. Bars 11–2 am; entertainment. Ck-out noon. Meeting rms. Business servs avail. In-rm modem link. Concierge. Free valet parking. Airport, RR station, bus depot transportation. Tennis & golf privileges. Exercise equipt; weight machines, bicycles,* *whirlpool, steam rm. Some refrigerators. Cr cds: A, C, D, DS, JCB, MC, V*

Durham

★★★★
WASHINGTON DUKE INN & GOLF CLUB
3001 Cameron Blvd, Durham NC 27706
☎ *919/490-0999 or 800/443-3853*
FAX *919/688-0105*

On the campus of Duke University, this luxurious hotel overlooks the Robert Trent Jones golf course. Memorabilia belonging to the Duke family, for whom the hotel and university are named, is on display in the public rooms. The bar is called the Bull Durham. ✈ *171 rms, 5 story. S, D $150-$215; each addl $10; suites $400-$550; under 17 free; golf plans. Crib free. TV; cable (premium), VCR avail. Heated pool. Complimentary coffee in lobby. Restaurant 7 am-10 pm. Bar 11:30 am-midnight; Sun from 1 pm. Ck-out noon. Meeting rms. Business center. In-rm modem link. Concierge. Gift shop. Airport transportation. Lighted tennis, pro. 18-hole golf, greens fee $55-$70, pro, putting green, driving range. Health club privileges. Refrigerators avail. Cr cds: A, C, D, DS, MC, V*

Linville

★★★★
ESEEOLA LODGE
US 221 & NC 105, Linville NC 28646
☎ *704/733-4311 or 800/742-6717*
FAX *704/733-3227*

This rustic lakeside lodge, built in the late 1880s, is the focal point of the village. Its interiors are richly detailed with chestnut paneling and stonework. ✈ *29 rms, 2 story. MAP, mid-May-mid-Oct: S $160-$220; D $225-$260; each addl $50. Closed rest of yr. Crib free. TV; cable (premium). Pool; lifeguard. Supervised child's activities (mid-June-mid Aug). Coffee in rms. Dining rm (public by res) 7:30-9:30 am, 11:30 am-2:30 pm, 7-9 pm (jacket, tie at dinner). Rm serv. Box* *lunches. Bar. Ck-out noon. Business servs avail. Grocery 2 blks. Tennis $10/day. 18-hole golf, greens fee $38, pro, putting green. Croquet court. Rec rm. Soc dir. Free morning newspaper. Boating, trout fishing. Cr cds: MC, V*

Waynesville

★★★★
THE SWAG

N on US 276, W on Hemphill Rd for 4 mi,
Waynesville NC 28786
☎ *704/926-0430 or 800/789-7672*
FAX *704/926-2036*

This mountaintop inn, decorated with early American crafts and furniture, was constructed out of six authentic log structures, including an old church, which were transported from their sites to their present setting on 250 wooded acres. 14 rms, 1-2 story, 3 cabins. AP, late May-Oct: S $150-$390; D $200-$440; each addl $80; higher rates: 2-night wkends, hols (3-night min), fall foliage. Closed rest of yr. Children over 7 yrs only. Coffee & tea in rms. Dining rm (public by res), 2 sittings: 12:30 & 7 pm. Ck-out 11 am, ck-in 3 pm. Business servs avail. Gift shop. Underground raquetball court. Badminton, croquet court. Sauna, whirlpool. Fireplaces. Balconies. Library, video collection. Swimming pond with swinging bridge. Walking trails. Cr cds: DS, MC, V

Ohio

Cincinnati

✕ ★★★★★
MAISONETTE
114 E 6th St, Cincinnati OH
☎ *513/721-2260*

This downtown restaurant has been a Cincinnati landmark for nearly half a century, but its traditional French cuisine has been tempered by the contemporary innovations of chef Jean-Robert de Cavel. A degustation menu provides an opportunity to sample his culinary artistry. The extensive wine list has maps showing the origin of each label, and though the setting is formal, service is meticulous, friendly and exceptionally attentive. *Hrs: 11:30 am–2:30 pm, 6–10:30 pm; Mon from 6 pm; Sat 5:15–11 pm. Closed Sun; major hols. Res accepted. French cuisine. Bar. Wine cellar. A la carte entrees: lunch $13.75–$15.75, dinner $25–$34. Specialties: escalopes de foie gras, fresh, imported French fish dishes, seasonal offerings. Own pastries. Valet parking (dinner). Jacket. Cr cds: A, C, D, DS, MC, V*

D

✕ ★★★★
ORCHID'S
In the Omni Netherland
35 W 5th St, Cincinnati OH 45202
☎ *513/421-1772*

Located in the Carew Tower's grand Omni Netherland Plaza, this restaurant in the Palm Court echoes the elegant, art-deco atmosphere of the hotel. The menu features creative American cuisine. *Hrs: 11 am–2 pm, 6–10 pm; Sat 6–11 pm; Sun 6–10 pm; Sun brunch 10 am–2 pm. Res accepted. Bar to 2 am; Sun 1 pm–midnight. Wine list. Semi-a la carte: lunch $12.95–$18.95. A la carte entrees: dinner $24.95–$54. Sun brunch $21.95. Specializes in fresh seafood, veal, beef. Pianist; Jazz Fri, Sat evenings. Valet parking. Cr cds: A, C, D, DS, ER, JCB, MC, V*

Cleveland

★★★★ THE RITZ-CARLTON, CLEVELAND
1515 W Third St, Cleveland OH 44113
☏ *216/623-1300*
FAX *216/623-0515*

China cabinets in the halls and guest rooms with easy chairs add Victorian flourish to the modern elegance of this hotel. ✈ *208 rms, 7 story, 21 suites. S, D $149-$215; suites $350-$650; under 12 free; wknd rates. Valet parking (fee). TV; cable, VCR avail (movies). Indoor pool; poolside serv. Restaurant 6:30 am-11 pm. Rm serv 24 hrs. Bar 11:30-1 am; pianist. Afternoon tea. Ck-out noon. Meeting rms. Business servs avail. In-rm modem link. Concierge. Gift shop. Exercise equipt; weight machine, bicycles, whirlpool, sauna. Masseuse. Bathrm phones, minibars. Overlooks Lake Erie. Luxury level. Cr cds: A, C, D, DS, ER, JCB, MC, V*

★★★★ PARKER'S
2801 Bridge Ave, Cleveland OH 44113
☏ *216/771-7130*

This pleasant, unpretentious country French oasis is in the reviving Ohio City neighborhood, about a five-minute ride from downtown. Chef Parker Bosley's limited menu offers a variety of seafood, beef, lamb, pork and poultry entrees for a la carte lunches and five-course prix-fixe dinners. ✈ *Hrs: 11:30 am-2:30 pm; 5:30-9:15 pm. Closed Sun; major hols. Res accepted. French, Amer menu. Bar. Wine cellar. A la carte entrees: lunch $8-$14. Complete meals: dinner $41. Valet parking. Country French atmosphere. Jacket. Totally nonsmoking. Cr cds: A, DS, MC, V*

Oregon

Bend

MEADOWS
In the Sunriver Resort
15 mi S of Bend, 2 mi W of US 97,
Sunriver OR 97707
☎ 541/593−1221

True to its name, this restaurant has tables with meadow views, as well as views of Mount Bachelor. Handwoven hangings and pine walls lend warmth to an otherwise formal dining room. *Hrs: 5:30−10 pm. Res accepted. Northwest High Desert menu. Bar noon−2 am. Extensive wine list. A la carte entrees: dinner $12−$25. Own pastries, desserts. Totally nonsmoking. Cr cds: A, C, D, DS, MC, V*

| D |

Eugene

VALLEY RIVER INN
1000 Valley River Way, Eugene OR 97440
☎ 541/687−0123 or 800/543−8266
FAX 541/683−5121

A massive brick-and-copper fireplace and logging memorabilia create a pioneer feeling at this modern resort. A number of guest rooms have views of the Willamette River. *257 rms, 2−3 story. S, D $115−$170; suites $195−$300; under 12 free. Crib free. Pet accepted, some restrictions. TV; cable, VCR avail. Heated pool; wading pool, poolside serv. Restaurant 6:30 am−2 pm, 5:30−9:30 pm. Rm serv. Bar 11:30 am−midnight, Sun 9 am−11 pm; entertainment. Ck-out 11 am. Meeting rms. Business servs avail. Bellhops. Valet serv. Concierge. Gift shop. Free airport, RR station, bus depot transportation. Exercise equipt; bicycles, stair machine, weight machine, whirlpool, sauna. Private patios, balconies. Cr cds: A, C, D, DS, MC, V*

Gold Beach

TU TU' TUN LODGE
★★★★
96550 N Bank Rogue, Gold Beach OR 97444
☎ *541/247-6664*
FAX *541/247-0672*

This richly appointed fishing lodge—the name is pronounced "Too Tootin'"—sits on the clear-blue Rogue River. Private decks of individually decorated rooms look out on the water and surrounding old-growth forest. *16 rms, 2 suites, 1 garden house. S, D $130-$310; each addl $10; suites $175-$185; garden house $200. 2 River Suites and Garden House avail all yr. Pool. Complimentary hors d'oeuvres. Dining rm open May-Oct (public by res): bkfst 7:30-9:30 am, lunch sitting (registered guests only) 1 pm; dinner sitting May-Oct 7 pm. Dining rm closed Nov-Apr. Bar. Ck-out 11 am, ck-in 3 pm. Business center. In-rm modem link. Free airport transportation. Dock; guides, whitewater boat trips. 4-hole pitch & putt golf; horseshoes. Rec rm. Library. Complimentary daily newspaper. Private patios, balconies. Cr cds: DS, MC, V*

Lincoln City

THE DINING ROOM AT SALISHAN
★★★★
In the Salishan Lodge
1 blk E of US 101, Gleneden Beach OR 97388
☎ *541/764-2371*

Carved teak panels and natural Oregon woods complement the sparkling crystal and silver at this three-tiered, candlelit dining room, which has a panoramic view of Siletz Bay. *Hrs: 5:30-10 pm; Fri & Sat to 11 pm; Sun brunch 9:30 am-1:30 pm. Res accepted. Northwest menu. Serv bar. Wine cellar. Table d'hôte: dinner $14-$28. Sun champagne brunch $17.50. Child's meals. Specializes in Oregon lamb, fresh seafood, regional cuisine. Own baking. Valet parking. Cr cds: A, C, D, DS, MC, V*

Portland

5TH AVENUE SUITES
★★★★

506 SW Washington, Portland OR 97205
☎ *503/222-0001 or 800/711-2971*
FAX *503/222-0004*

Built in 1912, this former department store has been completely renovated and redecorated in turn-of-the-century, American country-home style. Rooms are comfortable, light and airy. There are on-site business and fitness centers and the Red Star Tavern is open daily for breakfast, lunch and dinner. *221 rms, 10 story, 139 suites. S $150–$165; D $165–$180; each addl $15; suites $160–$225; under 18 free; wkend, hol rates. Crib free. Pet accepted, some restrictions. Garage/valet parking $13. TV; cable (premium), VCR avail (movies). Pool privileges. Complimentary continental bkfst. Restaurant 7 am–10:30 pm. Rm serv 24 hrs. Bar 11–1 am. Ck-out noon. Meeting rms. Business center. In-rm modem link. Concierge. Health club facilities. Sauna. Refrigerators. Cr cds: A, C, D, DS, JCB, MC, V*

RIVERPLACE
★★★★

1510 SW Harbor Way, Portland OR 97201
☎ *503/228-3233 or 800/227-1333*
FAX *503/295-6161*

This intimate hotel has large, airy rooms furnished with teak tables and comfortable chairs; many offer sweeping views of the skyline as well as of the river and the marina. *84 rms, 4 story. S, D $185–$245; condos $375–$475; suites $205–$700; under 18 free. Valet, garage parking in/out $15. Crib free. Pet accepted, some restrictions; $100. TV; cable (premium), VCR avail. Complimentary continental bkfst, newspaper. Restaurant 6:30 am–2 pm, 5–10 pm. Rm serv 24 hrs. Bar 11–1 am; entertainment Wed–Sun evenings. Ck-out 1 pm. Meeting rms. Business servs avail. In-rm modem link. Concierge. Shopping arcade. Whirlpool, sauna. Health club privileges. Minibars. Some bathrm phones. Some refrigerator, fireplace in suites. Balconies. On river. Cr cds: A, C, D, DS, ER, JCB, MC, V*

VINTAGE PLAZA

422 SW Broadway, Portland OR 97205
☎ *503/228–1212 or 800/243–0555*
FAX *503/228–3598*

This historic building's dramatic decor was inspired by Oregon vineyards; there's a winery theme throughout. 107 rms, 10 story, 23 suites. S $160–$175; D $175–$190; each addl $15; suites $195–$250; under 18 free; wkend packages. Crib free. Valet parking $13. TV; cable, VCR avail. Restaurant 7 am–10 pm. Rm serv 24 hrs. Bar 11–1 am. Ck-out noon. Meeting rms. Business center. In-rm modem link. Concierge. Gift shop. Exercise equipt; bicycles, rowers. Minibars. Cr cds: A, C, D, DS, JCB, MC, V

WILDWOOD

1221 NW 21st Ave, Portland OR 97209
☎ *503/248–9663*

Chef Cory Schreiber celebrates the local bounty in his simple, yet sumptuous, creations. The dining room is decidedly Art Deco, done in blond wood, with lofty ceilings and wraparound windows. The open-counter kitchen adds warmth and familiarity. Hrs: 11:30 am–2:30 pm, 5:30–10 pm; Fri, Sat to 10:30 pm; Sun 10 am–2 pm (brunch), 5–8:30 pm. Closed Jan 1, Thanksgiving, Dec 25. Res accepted. Pacific Northwest menu. Bar. Wine cellar. Semi-a la carte: lunch $8–$13, dinner $16–$24. Sun brunch $5.50–$12. Specializes in mussels, breast of duck, salmon. Parking. Outdoor dining. Cr cds: A, MC, V

Pennsylvania

Philadelphia

BELLEVUE ★★★★

Broad & Walnut Sts, Philadelphia PA 19102
☎ *215/893–1776 or 800/221–0833*
FAX *215/893–9868*

This classic hotel, located on the Avenue of Arts, occupies the top 7 stories of a landmark building. It has lavish public rooms, including the 7-story Conservatory atrium and the stained-glass-domed Barrymore Room in which high tea is served. Guest rooms are spacious and pleasant. ✈ *170 rms, 7 story. S $210–$290; D $240–$320; suites $395–$1,850; under 18 free; special packages. Crib free. Pet accepted. Garage $14, valet $21. TV; cable (premium), VCR. Indoor pool privileges; whirlpool, sauna, lifeguard. Restaurants 7 am–11 pm. Dinner/dancing Wed, Fri & Sat. Rm serv 24 hrs. Bar 11–1 am. Ck-out 1 pm. Meeting rms. Business center. In-rm modem link. Concierge. Shopping arcade. Barber, beauty shop. Health club privileges. Bathrm phones, mini-bars. Some balconies. State-of-the-art athletic club is connected by skywalk. Cr cds: A, C, D, DS, ER, JCB, MC, V*

FOUR SEASONS HOTEL PHILADELPHIA ★★★★

1 Logan Square, Philadelphia PA 19103
☎ *215/963–1500*
FAX *215/963–9506*

This elegant 8-story hotel has a magnificent setting on Logan Circle, reminiscent of the Place de la Concorde in Paris. Guest rooms are large and uncluttered, and the spacious marble lobby has an indoor garden with a fountain that makes it easy to forget that this is the heart of a large city. ✈ *371 rms, 8 story. S $250–$325; D $280–$355; each addl $30; suites $540–$1,290; under 18 free; wkend rates. Garage $12–$24. Pet accepted. TV; cable (premium), VCR avail. Indoor pool; poolside serv, lifeguard. Restaurant 6:30–1 am; Sat, Sun from 7 am (also see FOUNTAIN). Rm serv 24 hrs.*

Bar 11–2 am; pianist. Ck-out 1 pm. Convention facilities. Business center. In-rm modem link. Concierge. Beauty salon. Exercise rm; instructor, weights, bicycles, whirlpool, sauna. Massage. Minibars. Some balconies. Cr cds: A, C, D, ER, JCB, MC, V

OMNI HOTEL AT INDEPENDENCE PARK

4th & Chestnut Sts, Philadelphia PA 19106
☎ *215/925–0000*
FAX *215/925–1263*

Imported marble floors, fine fabrics and classical music greet you in the lobby of this elegant Philadelphia establishment. The thoughtfully detailed rooms offer soothing views of Independence Park, a peaceful oasis in the heart of the city. The pool, spa and health club have been recently renovated for luxury and comfort. 🕊 *150 rms, 14 story. S $189; D $209; each addl $20; suites from $300; under 18 free; wkend rates. Crib free. Garage (fee). TV; cable (premium), VCR avail. Indoor pool. Restaurant 7 am–2:30 pm, 5:30–10 pm. Rm serv 24 hrs. Bar 3–11 pm; entertainment Tues–Sat. Ck-out noon. Meeting rms. Business center. In-rm modem link. Concierge. Exercise equipt; weight machine, bicycles, whirlpool, sauna. Bathrm phones, minibars. Complimentary newspaper. Cr cds: A, C, D, DS, ER, JCB, MC, V*

THE RITTENHOUSE

210 W Rittenhouse Square, Philadelphia PA 19103
☎ *215/546–9000 or 800/635–1042*
FAX *215/732–3364*

Subdued elegance and superior, intimate service are the hallmarks of the lower floors of a residential building on fashionable Rittenhouse Square, a verdant park in central Philadelphia. The hotel is suitable for business travelers, family vacationers and honeymooners. 🕊 *133 rms, 9 story. S $250–$270; D $275–$295; suites $400–$1,200; wkend rates. Crib free. Pet accepted. Garage; valet parking $21. TV; cable (premium), VCR (movies avail). Indoor pool; poolside serv. Restaurant 6:30 am–10:30 pm. Rm serv 24 hrs. Bar; entertainment. Ck-out 1 pm. Meeting rms. Business center. In-rm modem link. Concierge. Shopping arcade. Bar-*

PENNSYLVANIA

ber, beauty shop. Exercise rm; instructor, weight machine, bicycles, sauna, steam rm. Massage. Health club privileges. Bathrm phones, minibars. Complimentary newspaper. Cr cds: A, C, D, DS, MC, V

THE RITZ-CARLTON, PHILADELPHIA
17th and Chestnut Sts, Philadelphia PA 19103
☎ *215/563–1600*
FAX *215/567–2822*

The opulent decor of this contemporary hotel includes Italian mantelpieces, silk wallpaper and an art collection worth one million dollars. The fully appointed guest rooms are furnished in refined colonial style. *290 rms, 15 story. S, D $205–$265; suites $350–$1,250; wkend rates. Crib free. Garage (fee). TV; cable (premium), VCR avail. Restaurant 6:30 am–11 pm. Rm serv 24 hrs. Bar 11–1 am; pianist. Ck-out noon. Meeting rms. Business center. In-rm modem link. Concierge. Gift shop. Airport, RR station transportation. Town car transportation within city. Exercise rm; instructor, bicycles, sauna. Masseuse. Bathrm phones, minibars. Luxury level. Cr cds: A, C, D, DS, ER, JCB, MC, V*

LE BEC-FIN
1523 Walnut St, Philadelphia PA 19102
☎ *215/567–1000*

Dinner here is long to be remembered—for the superb French cuisine, the regal surroundings, the impeccable service and, stunningly to some, the size of the check. Course after course emerges tantalizingly from the kitchen, each a gastronomical delight demonstrating the unique talents of Georges Perrier, the owner/chef. It's hard to choose among the appetizers (cold, warm and hot), fish or seafood courses and meats. There are about 10 options for each. Following is salad, cheeses or both. Choosing among roughly 24 desserts is no easier, and these are followed by petits fours. Don't be surpised if the tab surpasses $300 for two with the addition of aperitifs, wine, tax, tip and the prix-fixe $10 per car valet charge. *Sittings: lunch 11:30 am & 1:30 pm; dinner 6 pm & 9 pm, Fri & Sat 9:30 pm. Closed Sun; major hols. Res required. French menu. Bar to 1 am. Wine cellar. Prix fixe: lunch $36, dinner $102. Specializes* in seasonal dishes. Own baking. Valet parking dinner. Chef-owned. Jacket. Cr cds: A, C, D, DS, MC, V

FOUNTAIN
In the Four Seasons Hotel Philadelphia
1 Logan Square, Philadelphia PA 19103
☏ *215/963–1500*

This quiet, luxurious restaurant, nestled in the lavish yet dignified lobby of the Four Seasons, maintains the atmosphere of a private club. Breads and pastries are made on site; entrees are predominantly local and American. 🐦 *Hrs: 6:30 am–2:30 pm, 6–10:30 pm; Sun brunch 11 am–2:30 pm. Res accepted. Continental menu. Bar to 2 am. Wine cellar. A la carte entrees: bkfst $12–$17, lunch $22–$27.50, dinner $32–$38. Prix fixe: dinner $67. Sun brunch $31–$39. Child's meals. Specialties: rack of lamb, sautéed snapper, sautéed venison medallion. Own baking, desserts. Entertainment exc Sun. Valet parking. Overlooks Logan Square and fountain. Jacket (dinner). Cr cds: A, C, D, DS, MC, V*

STRIPED BASS
1500 Walnut St, Philadelphia PA 19102
☏ *215/732–4444*

This stylish, highly popular, fish-and-seafood-only restaurant is in a striking former bank building with marble columns. The creative menu is accompanied by a broad international selection of wines by the bottle and glass. 🐦 *Hrs: 11:30 am–2:30 pm, 5–11 pm; Fri to 11:30 pm; Sat 5–11:30 pm; Sun 11:30 am–2:30 pm, 5–10 pm. Closed major hols. Res accepted. Bar. Wine cellar. A la carte entrees: lunch $14–$22, dinner $23–$65. Specializes in fresh seafood, shellfish. Menu changes daily. Valet parking. Smoking at bar only. Cr cds: A, D, MC, V*

PENNSYLVANIA

Sharon

TARA-A COUNTRY INN ★★★★
3665 Valley View Rd, Clark PA 16113
☎ *412/962–3535 or 800/782–2803*
FAX *412/962–3250*

This antebellum mansion, dating from 1854, contains a library and in-room whirlpools. Its rooms are furnished with antiques and works of art. The formal gardens containing 10 Remington sculptures overlook picturesque Lake Schenago. *27 rms, 2 story. MAP: S, D $180–$355; wkly rates; package plans; higher rates Sat. Adults preferred. TV; cable. 3 pools, 2 indoor. Dining: Stonewall's Tavern 11 am–3 pm, 5–8 pm; wkend hrs vary. Ashley's Gourmet Dining 6–8 pm. Ck-out noon, ck-in 3 pm. Meeting rm. Business servs avail. In-rm modem link. Exercise equipt; ski machine, treadmill, whirlpool. Croquet court. Cr cds: A, DS, MC, V*

South Carolina

Beaufort

★★★★
RHETT HOUSE
1009 Craven St, Beaufort SC 29902
☎ *803/524–9030*
FAX *803/524–1310*

Reminiscent of a grand plantation house, this Greek-revival townhouse, replete with galleries and gardens, is furnished with antiques and Oriental rugs. *10 rms, 3 story. D $125–$200; each addl $25. Children over 5 yrs only. TV; VCR avail. Swimming privileges. Complimentary full bkfst; continental bkfst avail in rms. Dining rm (public by res) Tues–Sun evenings, 6–9 pm. Afternoon tea & cookies, evening refreshments. Ck-out 11 am, ck-in 3 pm. Business servs avail. Gift shop. Tennis privileges, pro. 18-hole golf privileges. Some fireplaces. Bicycles. Cr cds: A, MC, V*

Charleston

★★★★
CHARLESTON PLACE
130 Market St, Charleston SC 29401
☎ *803/722–4900 or 800/611–5545*
FAX *803/722–0728*

This graceful structure is in the city's historic district near a fashionable shopping area. The lobby contains antiques, a magnificent hand-blown Venetian chandelier and Italian marble floors. *440 rms, 8 story. S $295; D $315; each addl $20; suites $350–$2,000; under 17 free. Crib free. Garage $8, valet parking $12. TV; cable (premium). Indoor/outdoor pool; poolside serv. Supervised child's activities June–Aug. Restaurant 6:30 am–10 pm. Rm serv 24 hrs. Bar 11:30–1 am; entertainment. Ck-out noon. Convention facilities. Business servs avail. In-rm modem link. Concierge. Shopping arcade. Tennis & golf privileges. Exercise rm; instructor, weights, bicycles, whirlpool, sauna. Massage. Some balconies.*

SOUTH CAROLINA

Pool area has retractable roof for fair weather. Luxury level. Cr cds: A, C, D, DS, MC, V

★★★★ JOHN RUTLEDGE HOUSE
116 Broad St, Charleston SC 29401
☎ *803/723–7999 or 800/476–9741*
FAX *803/720–2615*

This historic inn comprises the revolutionary-era main house, built by a signer of the Constitution, and two carriage houses (each with four rooms). The guest rooms have high ceilings, wood floors, antique furnishings and four-poster beds.  *19 rms, 2–3 story, 3 suites. Mid-Mar–mid-June, mid-Sept–Oct: S $180–$240; D $200–$260; each addl $20; suites $310; under 12 free; lower rates rest of yr. Crib free. TV; cable (premium). Complimentary continental bkfst, afternoon tea, wine. Restaurant nearby. Ck-out noon, ck-in 3 pm. Business servs avail. In-rm modem link. Luggage handling. Valet serv. Concierge serv. Stocked refrigerators. Fireplaces. Cr cds: A, D, DS, MC, V*

★★★★ MILLS HOUSE
115 Meeting St, Charleston SC 29401
☎ *803/577–2400 or 800/874–9600*
FAX *803/722–2112*

This luxurious hotel is a reconstruction of the 19th-century inn that once stood on the site. Reproductions of period furnishings and an extensive collection of antiques create an atmosphere of great charm. A carriage conducts sightseers around the area. *214 rms, 7 story. Mid-Mar–mid-June, mid-Sept–mid-Nov: S, D $195; each addl $20; under 19 free; lower rates rest of yr. Crib free. Garage $9. TV; cable (premium). Elevated pool. Restaurant 6:30 am–2 pm, 5:30–10 pm. Bar 11–2 am. Ck-out 11 am. Meeting rms. Business servs avail. In-rm modem link. Concierge. Cr cds: A, C, D, DS, MC, V*

Tennessee

Maryville

★★★★
INN AT BLACKBERRY FARM
1471 W Millers Cove Rd, Walland TN 37886
☎ *423/984–8166 or 800/862–7610*
FAX *423/983–5708*

This English country house (1940) sits on 1,100 acres. 29 rms, 2 story. No rm phones. AP: S, D $395–$475; each addl $125; wkend plan (2-day min). Children over 10 yrs only. TV in sitting rms; cable. Heated pool. Complimentary full bkfst. Dining rm 8 am–8:30 pm. Ck-out 1 pm, ck-in 4 pm. Business servs avail. Valet serv. Concierge serv. Tennis. Game rm. Picnic tables. Antiques. Cr cds: A, MC, V

Memphis

★★★★
PEABODY
149 Union Ave, Memphis TN 38103
☎ *901/529–4000 or 800/732–2639*
FAX *901/529–9600*

This Italian Renaissance hostelry opened in 1869 and was rebuilt and restored to its former opulence in 1925. An ornate travertine marble fountain is home to famed resident ducks, who waddle down from their penthouse apartment each morning and return each evening. 468 rms, 13 story. S $130–$285; D $150–$290; each addl $35; suites $380–$1,475; under 18 free. Crib free. TV; cable (premium), VCR avail. Heated pool. Restaurants 6:30 am–midnight (also see CHEZ PHILLIPE). Rm serv 24 hrs. Bar 11–2 am; entertainment daily; dancing Thurs–Sat. Ck-out 11 am. Meeting rms. Business center. In-rm modem link. Concierge. Shopping arcade. Barber, beauty shop. Airport transportation. Exercise rm; instructor, weights, bicycles, whirlpool, sauna, steam rm. Extensive exercise facilities. Cr cds: A, C, D, DS, ER, JCB, MC, V

TENNESSEE

CHEZ PHILIPPE
In the Peabody
149 Union Ave, Memphis TN 38103
901/529-4188

Chef Jose Gutierrez serves up some of Memphis' most innovative and sophisticated cuisine here. Dishes range from delicate terrines to hot souffles, all served in a lavish dining room marked by high ceilings, silk drapes and huge murals. Hrs: 6-10 pm. Closed Sun; most major hols. Res accepted. Continental menu. Serv bar. Wine list. A la carte entrees: dinner $18-$30. Specialties: hushpuppies stuffed with shrimp provençale, roasted lamb rack. Jacket. Cr cds: A, C, D, DS, ER, JCB, MC, V

D

RAJI
712 W Brookhaven Circle, Memphis TN
901/685-8723

Chef-owner Raji Jallepalli blends nouvelle styles and Indian seasonings for a subtle yet distinct taste. Several intimate dining rooms in a former residence have elegant and refined decor. Hrs: 5-9 pm. Closed Sun, Mon; most major hols. Res required. French, Indian menu. Bar. Wine list. Semi-a la carte: dinner $25-$36. Specialties: tandoori game hens with corn and cumin tomato sauce, grilled scallops and lobster in lentil pastry with ginger-flavored beurre blanc. Cr cds: A, MC, V

Texas

Austin

★★★★
BARTON CREEK RESORT
8212 Barton Club Dr, Austin TX 78735
512/329–4000 or 800/336–6158
FAX *512/329–4597*

Recreational facilities are top-notch at this deluxe conference resort, with its gently rolling grounds and appealing restaurants and watering holes. 🦅 *147 rms, 5 story. Mar-Nov: S $185; D $200; suites $350–$750; under 17 free; golf & spa plans; AP avail; lower rates rest of yr. Crib free. TV; cable (premium), VCR avail. 2 pools, 1 indoor; poolside serv, lifeguard (summer). Supervised child's activities; ages 6 months–8 yrs. Dining rm 7 am–10 pm. Snack bar. Grill rm. Rm serv to midnight. Bar 11–1 am. Ck-out noon, ck-in 4 pm. Valet serv. Barber, beauty shop. Gift shop. Convention facilities. Business center. In-rm modem link. Airport transportation. Limo service avail. Sports dir. Lighted tennis, pro. 54-hole golf, greens fee $85–$125, pro, putting green, driving range. Golf school. Exercise rm; instructor, weight machines, bicycles, whirlpool, sauna, steam rm. Massage. Lawn games. Soc dir. Game rm. Refrigerators, minibars; fireplace in suites. Some balconies. Cr cds: A, C, D, MC, V*

★★★★
FOUR SEASONS
98 San Jacinto Blvd, Austin TX 78701
512/478–4500
FAX *512/478–3117*

Queen Elizabeth II has stayed at this property. Facilities combine European tone with Texas Hill Country comfort; many rooms have lovely Town Lake views. 🦅 *292 units, 9 story. S $175–$220; D $195–$240; each addl $20; suites $245–$1,200; under 18 free; wkend rates. Crib free. Covered parking $7; valet parking $12. Pet accepted, some restrictions. TV; cable (premium), VCR avail. Heated pool; poolside serv. Restaurant 6:30 am–11 pm. Rm serv 24 hrs. Bar 11–2 am. Ck-out 1 pm. Convention facilities. Business center. In-rm modem link. Concierge. Gift shop. Exercise rm; instructor,* *weights, bicycles, whirlpool, sauna. Massage. Bathrm phones; some refrigerators. Balconies. Complimentary newspaper. Cr cds: A, C, D, ER, JCB, MC, V*

Dallas

★★★★★
MANSION ON TURTLE CREEK
2821 Turtle Creek Blvd, Dallas TX 75219
☎ *214/559-2100 or 800/527-5432*
FAX *214/528-4187*

This well-known hotel was converted from the 1926 home of a cotton baron and retains an atmosphere of privilege and calm. Guests are pampered as soon as they enter the turret-shaped, white-marble lobby, which has huge flower arrangements, European antiques, a fireplace and a glass-domed roof. Leading off the lobby is the glass-walled setting for Dallas's #1 power breakfast, which in turn leads into the clubby bar and the award-winning eponymous restaurant. Deep-carpeted guest rooms feature mirrored alcoves and mahogany armoires, Hollywood dressing room lights over vanity tables, white-marble bathrooms and French windows that open onto balconies. A dish of dried fruits and nuts and a glass of iced tea are served on arrival. Exercise instructors in the well-equipped gymnasium offer personal guidance, and drinks and snacks are served around the small outdoor pool. 🐿 *140 rms, 9 story. S $290-$370; D $320-$400; each addl $40; suites, kit. units $495-$1,350; wkend packages. Crib free. Valet parking $10. TV; cable (premium), VCR. Heated pool; poolside serv. Restaurant 7 am-10:30 pm (also see RESTAURANT AT THE MANSION ON TURTLE CREEK). Rm serv 24 hrs. Bar 11-2 am; entertainment. Ck-out 2 pm. Meeting rms. Business center. In-rm modem link. Concierge. Beauty salon. Airport, downtown transportation. Lighted tennis privileges. Golf privileges. Health club. Bathrm phones; wet bar in suites. Private patios, balconies. Cr cds: A, C, D, DS, ER, JCB, MC, V*

DALLAS

THE ADOLPHUS
★★★★

1321 Commerce St, Dallas TX 75202
☎ *214/742-8200 or 800/221-9083*
FAX *214/651-3588*

17th-century Flemish tapestries grace the lobby of this Beaux Arts hotel created by beer baron Adolphus Busch in 1912. Guest rooms, unusually soundproof, are furnished in Queen Anne and Chippendale styles. *426 rms, 22 story. S, D $200–$300; each addl $25; suites $400–$2,000; under 12 free; wkend rates. Crib free. Valet parking $10. TV; cable (premium), VCR avail. Restaurant 6:30 am–10:30 pm (also see FRENCH ROOM). Rm serv 24 hrs. Bar 11–2 am. Ck-out 1 pm. Convention facilities. Business servs avail. In-rm modem link. Concierge. Shopping arcade. Barber, beauty shop. Complimentary downtown transportation. Tennis & golf privileges. Exercise equipt; weight machine, bicycles. Health club privileges. Bathrm phones, refrigerators, minibars. Some private patios. Grand Lobby is the setting for afternoon tea; pianist signals evening cocktails. Cr cds: A, C, D, DS, MC, V*

CRESCENT COURT
★★★★

400 Crescent Court, Dallas TX 75201
☎ *214/871-3200 or 800/654-6541*
FAX *214/871-3272*

Modeled after the Royal Crescent spa in Bath, England, this hotel is part of a castle-like complex that includes a posh retail gallery. Furnishings are reminiscent of those in an English manor house; all the suites have hardwood floors and some have lofts. *216 rms, 7 story. S $270–$350; D $270–$380; each addl $30; suites $550–$1,550; under 12 free; wkend rates. Crib free. Pet accepted, some restrictions; $25. Garage $5.50; valet $12. TV; cable (premium), VCR avail. Pool; poolside serv. Restaurant 6:30 am–midnight. Afternoon tea 3–5 pm. Rm serv 24 hrs. Bar 11:30–2 am. Ck-out 1 pm. Meeting rms. Business center. In-rm modem link. Concierge. Shopping arcade. Free Love Field airport transportation. Exercise rm; instructor, weights, bicycles, whirlpool, sauna, steam rm. Massage. Fully equipped spa. Bathrm phones; refrigerators. Cr cds: A, C, D, DS, ER, JCB, MC, V*

TEXAS

HOTEL ST GERMAIN
2516 Maple Ave, Dallas TX 75201
☎ *214/871–2516 or 800/683–2516*
FAX *214/871–0740*

Combining Old World character with modern amenities, this restored 1906 Victorian house features elegant French antiques and wood-burning fireplaces. The dining room opens onto a New Orleans-style walled courtyard. *7 suites, 3 story. EP: S, D $200–$600. TV; cable (premium), VCR (free movies). Complimentary refreshments. Dining rm: bkfst hrs flexible for inn guests; dinner res required; public by res (wkends only, dinner). Rm serv 24 hrs. Ck-out noon, ck-in 4 pm. Business servs avail. Luggage handling. Valet serv. Concierge serv. Wraparound balcony; library/sitting rm. Cr cds: A, C, MC, V*

OMNI MANDALAY AT LAS COLINAS
221 E Las Colinas Blvd, Irving TX 75039
☎ *214/556–0800*
FAX *214/556–0729*

Located on five elaborately landscaped acres, this luxury property is conveniently located on the Mandalay Canal as well as Lake Carolyn. An extensive art collection gives the public areas a special touch. *410 rms, 28 story. S, D $180–$200; each addl $10; suites $200–$250; under 18 free; wkend, honeymoon rates. Crib free. Valet parking $8 overnight. TV; cable (premium), VCR avail. Heated pool; whirlpool, poolside serv (seasonal). Supervised child's activities (Memorial Day–Labor Day). Restaurant 6:30–10 pm. Rm serv 24 hrs. Bar 11:30–1:30 am. Ck-out noon. Convention facilities. Business center. In-rm modem link. Concierge. Gift shop. Free airport transportation. Golf privileges. Exercise rm; instructor, weights, bicycles, sauna. Masseur. Bathrm phones. Some private patios, balconies. Cr cds: A, C, D, DS, ER, JCB, MC, V*

RESTAURANT AT THE MANSION ON TURTLE CREEK

2821 Turtle Creek Blvd, Dallas TX 75219
☎ 214/559-2100

Dean Fearing is a nationally known chef, thanks partly to his cookbooks and awards, but also to the exuberant cuisine served at this famous hotel's gorgeous dining rooms. A fantastical circular black-and-white marble-floored lobby leads to the buzzy salon, featuring art on the walls, banquette seating and crisp white napery, all enhanced by service that's friendly, not haughty. Fearing invented tortilla soup—one of his signature dishes that has been much copied. Another appetizer typical of his complex style might be a bacon-wrapped scallop on barbequed duck with sweet corn sauce and jalapeño potato. Entrees, too, borrow from all the world's kitchens. ✈ *Hrs: noon–2:30 pm, 6–10:30 pm; Fri & Sat to 11 pm. Sun brunch 11 am–2:30 pm. Res accepted; required Fri & Sat. Amer Southwest menu. Bar 11–2 am. Wine cellar. A la carte entrees: lunch from $15, dinner from $30. Sun brunch $29.50. Specialties: tortilla soup, lobster taco, crème brulée, rack of lamb. Own baking. Valet parking. Private dining areas. Jacket, tie. Cr cds: A, C, D, DS, ER, JCB, MC, V*

D

FRENCH ROOM

In the Adolphus
1321 Commerce St, Dallas TX 75202
☎ 214/742-8200

Exceptionally detailed presentations—such as veal that arrives looking like a delicately wrought hummingbird—match the ornate Louis XIV style and service of this gorgeous restaurant. ✈ *Hrs: 6–10:30 pm. Closed Sun. Res accepted. Neoclassic cuisine. Bar 5 pm–1:30 am. Wine list. A la carte entrees: dinner $26–$45. Specialties: Dover sole, foie gras, roast rack of lamb, sautéed Norwegian salmon. Menu changes with season. Valet parking. Jacket. Cr cds: A, C, D, DS, MC, V*

D

TEXAS

Dallas/Fort Worth Airport Area

🏨 ★★★★
FOUR SEASONS RESORT & CLUB
4150 N MacArthur Blvd, Irving TX 75038
☎ *214/717–0700*
FAX *214/717–2550*

This property combines top-notch resort amenities—including a superb health center and spa—and state-of-the-art conference facilities with the comforts of an elegant hotel. 🐦 *357 rms, 9 story. S, D $260–$300; suites $350–$1,000; under 18 free; golf, spa, wkend plans. Valet parking $5. TV; cable (premium), VCR avail. 4 pools, 2 heated, 1 indoor & 1 child's; poolside serv, lifeguard (wkends in season). Supervised child's activities; ages 6 months–8 yrs. Restaurant 6:30 am–11 pm. Rm serv 24 hrs. Bar 11–2 am. Ck-out noon. Convention facilities. Business center. In-rm modem link. Concierge. Gift shop. Barber, beauty shop. 12 tennis courts, 4 indoor, pro. 18-hole TPC golf, greens fee $110, pro, 2 putting greens, driving range. Exercise rm; instructor, weight machines, bicycles, whirlpool, sauna, steam rm. Massage. Lawn games. Minibars. Private patios, balconies. Cr cds: A, C, D, JCB, MC, V*

Fort Worth

🏨 ★★★★
WORTHINGTON
200 Main St, Fort Worth TX 76102
☎ *817/870–1000 or 800/433–5677*
FAX *817/882–1755*

This ultra-modern high-rise stretches along two city blocks, forming a dramatic glassed-in bridge over Houston Street. Fresh flowers in every room are among the many luxurious touches. 🐦 *504 rms, 12 story. S $165–$185; D $185–$205; each addl $10; suites $330–$1,000; under 18 free; wkend, honeymoon rates. Crib free. Covered parking $6, valet parking $9. TV; cable (premium), VCR avail. Indoor pool; poolside serv. Restaurant 6 am–11 pm. Rm serv 24 hrs. Bar 11–1:30 am; Sun from noon. Ck-out noon. Convention facilities. Business center. In-rm modem link. Concierge. Shopping arcade. Tennis. Golf privileges. Exercise rm; instructor, weights,* bicycles, whirlpool, sauna. Some refrigerators. Private patios, balconies. Cr cds: A, C, D, DS, MC, V

Galveston

★★★★
TREMONT HOUSE
2300 Ship's Mechanic Row, Galveston TX 77550
☎ *409/763-0300 or 800/874-2300*
FAX *409/763-1539*

A hand-carved mahogany bar is but one of the magnificent details of the public spaces in this grand 1879 building. Guest rooms feature Italian tile, soaring ceilings and 11-foot windows. *117 rms, 4 story. S, D $135-$185; each addl $15; suites $250-$350; under 18 free. Crib free. TV; cable (premium), VCR avail (movies). Restaurant 6:30 am-10:30 pm. Rm serv 24 hrs. Bar 11-2 am; pianist. Ck-out noon. Meeting rms. Business servs avail. Concierge. Shopping arcade. Free downtown transportation. Cr cds: A, C, D, MC, V*

Houston

★★★★
FOUR SEASONS HOTEL HOUSTON CENTER
1300 Lamar St, Houston TX 77010
☎ *713/650-1300*
FAX *713/650-1203*

This tony high-rise with etched-glass doors and thick carpeting is all marble, fresh flowers and antiques. Ten of the 30 stories are occupied by apartments that are home to well-to-do Houstonians.  *399 rms, 30 story. S $195-$235; D $225-$265; each addl $25; suites $550-$1,200; under 18 free; wkend rates. Crib free. Pet accepted. Valet & covered parking $13/day. TV; cable (premium), VCR avail (movies). Heated pool; poolside serv. Restaurant 6:30 am-1:30 pm, 6-10 pm. Rm serv 24 hrs. Bar 11-1 am; entertainment. Ck-out 1 pm. Meeting rms. Business center. In-rm modem link. Concierge. Shopping arcade. Beauty shop. Free transportation to downtown area. Exercise rm; instructor, bicycles, rowing machine, whirlpool, sauna. Massage. Health* *club privileges. Bathrm phones, minibars; some refrigerators. Cr cds: A, C, D, ER, JCB, MC, V*

HOUSTONIAN

111 N Post Oak Lane, Houston TX 77024
☎ *713/680–2626 or 800/231–2759*
FAX *713/680–2992*

In true Texas form, the Houstonian sprawls over 18 acres of heavily wooded land. But don't be put off by its size—the atmosphere is warm and inviting. The real draw is the renowned fitness center, which includes everything from free weights and cardio machines to private TVs and an indoor jogging track. 291 rms, 4 story. S $164–$195; D $174–$205; suites $249–$975; under 18 free; wknd, hol rates, packages. Crib free. TV; cable (premium). 3 heated pools. Supervised child's activities; ages 3–11. Restaurant 6:30 am–10 pm. Rm serv 24 hrs. Bar 3 pm–2 am; Sat & Sun from noon. Ck-out noon. Convention facilities. Business center. In-rm modem link. Concierge. Gift shop. Free garage parking; valet $10. Lighted tennis, pro. Exercise rm; instructor, weights, bicycles, whirlpool, sauna. Game rm. Lawn games. Minibars. Luxury level. Cr cds: A, C, D, DS, MC, V

LA COLOMBE D'OR

3410 Montrose Blvd, Houston TX 77006
☎ *713/524–7999*
FAX *713/524–8923*

Walter Fondren, founder of Humble Oil (now Exxon), built this huge 21-room Prairie-style mansion in 1923. Guest quarters are stunning, with private dining rooms, marble baths and artwork from local and well-known artists. 6 suites, 3 story. Suites $195–$575. TV; cable (premium), VCR avail. Restaurant 11:30 am–2 pm, 6–10 pm. Rm serv. Bar. Concierge. Ck-out noon, ck-in 3 pm. Whirlpool. Fruit furnished daily. Cr cds: A, C, D, DS, MC, V

HOUSTON

LANCASTER
701 Texas Ave, Houston TX 77002
☎ *713/228-9500*
FAX *713/223-4528*

In this beautifully refurbished theater-district hotel dating from the 1920s, rich hunter green and Chinese red draperies provide a backdrop for gleaming antiques. 93 rms, 12 story. S $180–$220; D $190–$240; each addl $25; suites $325–$825; under 16 free; wkend rates. Crib free. Valet parking $12. TV; cable, VCR (movies). Restaurant 6:30 am–11 pm. Rm serv 24 hrs. Bars 11 am–midnight. Ck-out 1 pm. Meeting rms. Business center. In-rm modem link. Concierge. Downtown transportation 7 am–11 pm. Exercise equipt; bicycles, weights. Bathrm phones, refrigerators, minibars. Complimentary newspaper, shoe shine. Cr cds: A, C, D, DS, JCB, MC, V

OMNI HOUSTON HOTEL
4 Riverway, Houston TX 77056
☎ *713/871-8181 or 800/843-6664*
FAX *713/871-0719*

This striking, curvilinear, resort-style high-rise has an especially large pool, a dramatic modern lobby and bar with fountains and sculpture. Guest rooms have sitting areas, marble and dark-wood furniture and floor-to-ceiling windows. 381 rms, 11 story. S $145–$205; D $170–$220; each addl $25; suites $225–$650; under 17 free; wkend rates. Crib free. Garage: valet parking $13, self-park $4. TV; cable (premium), VCR avail. 2 pools, 1 heated; poolside serv. Restaurant (see LA RESERVE). Rm serv 24 hrs. Bar 11:30–2 am; entertainment. Ck-out 1 pm. Meeting rms. Business center. In-rm modem link. Concierge. Transportation to Galleria area. Tennis. Exercise rm; instructor, weights, bicycles, whirlpool, sauna. Massage therapy. Minibars. Cr cds: A, C, D, DS, ER, JCB, MC, V

TEXAS

THE RITZ-CARLTON, HOUSTON
1919 Briar Oaks Lane, Houston TX 77027
☎ *713/840−7600 or 800/241−3333*
FAX *713/840−8036*

Margaret Thatcher and Adnan Khashoggi patronize this elegant property, convenient to the Galleria shops and to many museums. Exotic flowers perfume the hallways; some rooms afford views of the Houston skyline. *232 rms, 12 story. S, D $175−$250; each addl $30; suites $275−$400; kit. units $1,500−$2,000; under 18 free; wkend rates. Valet parking $13.50. Crib free. TV; cable (premium). Heated pool; poolside serv. Restaurants 6:30 am−2:30 pm, 6−10:30 pm (also see THE BAR AND GRILL). Bar; entertainment. Harpist at afternoon tea (3−5 pm). Ck-out noon. Meeting rms. Business center. Concierge. Gift shop. Free transportation within 3 mi radius. Exercise equipt; treadmill, bicycle. Health club privileges. Bathrm phones; whirlpool in suites. Luxury level. Cr cds: A, C, D, DS, ER, JCB, MC, V*

WOODLANDS
2301 N Millbend St, Houston TX 77380
☎ *713/367−1100 or 800/433−2624*
FAX *713/364−6345*

This executive conference center and resort offers everything from championship golf and hiking trails to tennis courts and an outdoor sculpture garden. There are magnificent views of tall pine forests and peaceful waters, and it's conveniently located near shopping and cultural centers. *268 rms, 2 story. S $125−$160; D $140−$180; each addl $15; suites $145−$350; kit. units $145−$225; under 12 free; AP avail; wkend rates (seasonal), golf, tennis, package plans. TV; cable (premium). 2 pools; wading pool, poolside serv. Restaurants 6 am−11 pm. Rm serv. 3 bars 11−2 am; Sun from noon. Ck-out noon, ck-in after 3 pm. Meeting rms. Business center. In-rm modem link. Valet serv. Gift shop. Airport transportation. Indoor & outdoor lighted tennis, pro. 36-hole golf, greens fee $50−$95, 3 putting greens, 3 driving ranges, pro shop. Hiking, bicycle trails. Bicycle rentals. Game rm. Exercise rm; instructor, weights, bicycles, whirlpool, steam rm, sauna. Health spa. Lawn games. Refrigerators. Private patios, balconies. Some lake views. Cr cds: A, C, D, DS, MC, V*

🍴 ★★★★
THE BAR AND GRILL
In the Ritz-Carlton, Houston
1919 Briar Oaks Lane, Houston TX 77027
☎ *713/840–7600*

There's a masculine, clubby atmosphere to this restaurant in the Ritz-Carlton hotel. Dinners feature fresh seafood, grilled meats and farm-raised poultry. 🕊 *Hrs: dinner 6–10:30 pm; lite menu 3–6 pm & 10:30 pm–1:30 am. Res accepted. Bar. Wine cellar. Semi-a la carte: dinner $21–$26; lite menu $5.95–$14. Child's meals. Specialties: chili-roasted filet, grilled salmon, Felix's mixed grill. Entertainment exc Sun. Valet parking. Jacket. Cr cds: A, C, D, DS, ER, JCB, MC, V*

D

🍴 ★★★★
LA RESERVE
In the Omni Houston Hotel
4 Riverway, Houston TX 77056
☎ *713/871–8181*

In this dusty-rose dining room, the many beveled mirrors seem to multiply the eye-catching central flower arrangement. Candlelight and antique accent pieces add intimacy to large contemporary space. 🕊 *Hrs: 6:30–10:30 pm. Closed Sun. Res accepted. Continental menu. Bar 5 pm–midnight. A la carte entrees: dinner $19–$32. Table d'hôte: dinner $50–$70 (with wine). Specialties: pomegranate-glazed venison, charred citrus-pepper tuna, grilled double lamb chops, porcini-crusted monkfish. Also dietary menu. Own baking. Menu changes daily; fresh food only. Valet parking. Jacket (dinner). Cr cds: A, C, D, DS, ER, JCB, MC, V*

San Antonio

🏨 ★★★★
HYATT REGENCY HILL COUNTRY
9800 Hyatt Resort Dr, San Antonio TX 78251
☎ *210/647–1234*
FAX *210/681–9681*

A 56-foot-long wood-and-copper bar, the world's largest antler chandelier and a man-made river for tubing are on this cushy, Texas ranch-style property, spread out over 200

TEXAS

beautifully landscaped acres. 500 units, 4 story. Mid-Mar–Nov: S, D $220–$325; each addl $25; suites $425–$2,250; under 18 free; holiday, golf plans; lower rates rest of yr. Parking; valet $8. TV; cable (premium). 2 heated pools; poolside serv. Supervised child's activities; ages 3–12. Restaurants 5:30–10 pm. Rm serv 6 am–midnight. Bar 4 pm–1 am; entertainment. Ck-out noon. Coin lndry. Convention facilities. Business center. In-rm modem link. Bellhops. Valet serv. Concierge. Sundries. Shopping arcade. Beauty shop. Lighted tennis, pro. 18-hole golf, pro, greens fee $80–$90. Bicycle rentals. Exercise rm; instructor, weights, treadmill, whirlpool, sauna. Masseuse. Lawn games. Rec rm. Game rm. Refrigerators. Balconies. Luxury level. Cr cds: A, C, D, DS, JCB, MC, V

★★★★
LA MANSION DEL RIO
112 College St, San Antonio TX 78205
☎ *210/225–2581 or 800/323–7500*
FAX *210/226–0389*

Beamed ceilings highlight rooms that overlook a courtyard or the San Antonio River. The property was built around a restored historic 19th-century law school building. 337 rms, 7 story. S $120–$245; D $145–$270; each addl $25; suites $375–$1,500; under 18 free; wkend rates; Sea World packages. Crib free. Pet accepted. Valet parking $12. TV; cable, VCR avail. Pool; poolside serv. Restaurants 7 am–11 pm. Rm serv 24 hrs. Bar 11–2 am; entertainment. Ck-out noon. Convention facilities. Business servs avail. In-rm modem link. Concierge. Gift shop. Airport transportation. Minibars. Private patios, balconies. Cr cds: A, C, D, DS, JCB, MC, V

Utah

Park City

STEIN ERIKSEN LODGE ★★★★

7700 Stein Way, Park City UT 84060
☎ *801/649–3700 or 800/453–1302*
FAX *801/649–5825*

A dramatic 5-story stone fireplace dominates the lobby of this spectacular high-mountain resort with extensive grounds. 127 rms, 13 rms in main lodge, 2 story, 40 kit. suites. Early Dec–early Apr: S, D $350–$450; each addl $25; kit. suites $600–$1,850; under 12 free; summer rates; ski rates; higher rates hol season; lower rates rest of yr. Crib free. TV; cable (premium), VCR (movies). Heated pool; poolside serv. Complimentary full bkfst (in season). 2 dining rms 7 am–10 pm. 2nd dining rm open winter only (wild game menu). Rm serv 6:30 am–9:30 pm. Box lunches. Bar; pianist in winter. Ck-out 11 am, ck-in 4 pm. Grocery 4 mi. Meeting rms. Business servs avail. Concierge. Sundries. Boutique. Underground parking. Complimentary transportation to Park City. Tennis. Downhill ski on site; x-country ski 3 mi. Sleighing. Snowmobiles. Hot-air balloons; mountain bikes avail. Lawn games. Exercise equipt; weight machines, bicycle, whirlpool, sauna. Masseuse. Bathrm phone, whirlpool, washer, dryer in most rms. Some refrigerators, fireplaces. Many balconies. Cr cds: A, D, DS, MC, V

Salt Lake City

BRIGHAM STREET
1135 E South Temple St, Salt Lake City UT 84102
☎ *801/364-4461*
FAX *801/521-3201*

Rooms are individually decorated in this restored Victorian mansion. 🐾 *9 rms, 3 story. S, D $75-$175; each addl $10. Crib free. TV; VCR avail. Complimentary continental bkfst. Setups. Ck-out noon, ck-in 3 pm. Business servs avail. X-country ski 15 mi. Fireplace in 5 rms. Cr cds: A, D, DS, MC, V*

Vermont

Killington

✕ ★★★★
HEMINGWAY'S
On US 4, Killington VT 05751
☎ *802/422–3886*

Antique mixes with modern in these three dining rooms in a renovated 19th-century house. The less formal garden room has a fireplace. 🕭 *Hrs: from 6 pm. Closed Mon; Easter–Memorial Day. Res accepted. European, Amer menu. Wine cellar. Prix fixe: dinner $46. Tasting menu $60. Specialties: Vermont lamb and game birds, lobster ravioli, pan-roasted striped bass. Own pasta, pastries. Chef-owned. Totally nonsmoking in dining rm. Cr cds: A, C, D, MC, V*

Ludlow

🏛 ★★★★
GOVERNOR'S
86 Main St, Ludlow VT 05149
☎ *802/228–8830 or 800/468–3766*

Built as the summer residence of former Vermont governor William Wallace Stickney, this house is quintessentially late Victorian. Each room is individually decorated with antiques. 🕭 *9 rms, 3 story. No rm phones. MAP: S $150; D $190–$220; B & B rates avail; higher rates: late Dec, fall foliage season. Adults only. Complimentary afternoon tea, sherry. Dining rm 8–9:30 am sitting, 7 pm sitting. Ck-out 11 am, ck-in flexible. Bus depot transportation. Downhill ski 1 mi; x-country ski ½ mi. Library, sitting rm. Totally nonsmoking. Cr cds: MC, V*

Springfield

INN AT WEATHERSFIELD ★★★★

VT 106, Weathersfield VT 05151
☎ 802/263-9217 or 800/477-4828
FAX 802/263-9219

An inn since 1961, this lodging is built around an historic four-room building that dates back to 1795; it has served as a station on the Underground Railroad, a stagecoach stop and a home for elderly ladies. Public and guest rooms are furnished with antiques; many have fireplaces. The 21 acres at the base of Hawks Mountain include a spring-fed swimming pond and an English garden. 🐾 *12 rms, 2 story, 3 suites. No A/C. July–Mar: MAP: D $185–$225; each addl $75; higher rates hol wkends & fall foliage season; lower rates rest of yr. Children over 8 yrs only. TV in sitting rm. Complimentary full bkfst; afternoon tea. Dining rm 6–9 pm. Rm serv. Ck-out 11 am, ck-in 1 pm. Business servs avail. Gift shop. Game rm. Lawn games. Downhill ski 20 mi. Health club privileges. Sleigh rides in winter; carriage rides in fall. Swimming pond. Cr cds: A, C, D, DS, MC, V*

St Johnsbury

RABBIT HILL ★★★★

VT 18, Lower Waterford VT 05848
☎ 802/748-5168 or 800/762-8669
FAX 802/748-8342

This restored inn (ca 1795–1825) has a country atmosphere. 🐾 *21 rms, 1–2 story. 17 A/C. No rm phones. MAP: S $129–$209; D $179–$259; each addl $70; higher rates fall foliage season. Children over 12 yrs only. Coffee in rms. Complimentary afternoon tea. Restaurant 8:15–10 am, 6–8:45 pm. Bar. Ck-out 11 am, ck-in after 2 pm. Gift shop. Pond, canoes. Golf privileges. X-country ski on site. Lawn games. Some in-rm whirlpools, fireplaces. Porches. Gazebo. Totally nonsmoking. Cr cds: A, MC, V*

WOODSTOCK

Stowe

TOPNOTCH AT STOWE ★★★★

4000 Mountain Rd, Stowe VT 05672
☎ *802/253-8585 or 800/451-8686*
FAX *802/253-9263*

Located on 120 mountain acres, this polished resort has individually decorated rooms and an imposing lobby with a freestanding circular stone fireplace, floor-to-ceiling windows and a cathedral ceiling. *107 rms in main bldg, 15 kit. town houses. Some A/C in townhouses, chalet. Late May–mid-Oct: S, D $186–$236; each addl $45; suites $290–$570; kit. townhouses $250–$550; tennis, ski, spa plans; wkend rates; higher rates winter hols; lower rates rest of yr. Crib free. TV; cable (premium), VCR avail (movies). 2 heated pools, 1 indoor. Supervised child's activities (July–Sept 4); ages 5–12. Dining rms 7–10 am, 11:30 am–2 pm, 5:30–9:30 pm. Complimentary tea & cookies 4 pm daily. Rm serv 6:30 am–9:30 pm. Box lunches. Bar noon–2 am; entertainment. Ck-out 11 am, ck-in 3:30 pm. Meeting rms. Business center. Bellhops. Valet serv. Concierge. Gift shop. Beauty shop. 14 tennis courts, 4 indoor, pro. Golf privileges. Downhill ski 2 mi; x-country ski on site. Ski equipt, instruction. Trail rides, instruction. Mountain bikes. Bike rentals. Movies Sun–Thurs. Full-service spa facilities also include European hydrotherapy, health & fitness programs; special spa menu & spa cooking demonstrations. Exercise rm; instructor, weights, bicycles, whirlpool, sauna, steam rm. Massage. Libraries. Some fireplaces. Some balconies. Sun deck. Cr cds: A, D, DS, MC, V*

Woodstock

TWIN FARMS ★★★★★

Stage Coach Rd, Barnard VT 05031
☎ *802/234-9999 or 800/894-6327*
FAX *802/234-9990*

The secret to this inn's success is its devotion to guest comfort and its unbridled privacy. The setting is magnificent: a 235-acre estate in verdant rolling countryside. The accommodations and public rooms are elegant, the food is excellent and the staff is young and friendly, paying meticulous attention to every detail that makes a guest comfortable. They happily show you about the property, prepare box lunches if you'll be out at midday, help you canoe about the pond or pick you up in Woodstock, 8 miles away, if you have cycled there and prefer a quicker ride back. Rates are steep, but they include all meals, 24-hour open bars, afternoon tea upon request, snacks whenever you want them up to 11 pm, evening cocktails with canapes, use of all recreational facilities (including canoes, bicycles, and a well-stocked trout pond) and even gratuities. In the winter there is on-site ice skating, skiing and snowshoeing. Dress is always casual; you don't come here to be seen. 🐎 9 cottages, 4 rms in 2-story inn. AP (advance payment required): D $700; cottages $850–$1,500; 2-day min wkends. Closed Apr. TV. Complimentary afternoon tea/sherry. Dining rm for guests only. Rm serv. Business servs avail. In-rm modem link. Tennis; pro. Downhill, x-country ski on site. Exercise rm; instructor, weight machine, stair machine, Japanese furo tubs. Rec rm. Totally nonsmoking. Cr cds: A, MC, V

🏨 ★★★★
WOODSTOCK INN

On Village Green, Woodstock VT 05091
☎ *802/457–1100 or 800/448–7900*
FAX *802/457–6699*

At this genteel resort, the lobby has a floor-to-ceiling fieldstone fireplace and a massive wood-beam mantel. The patchwork quilts on the beds dominate the modern guest rooms; some have a fireplace. Antiques are found throughout. 🐎 143 rms, 3 story. S, D $149–$285; each addl $15; suites $391–$499; under 14 free; MAP avail; ski, golf, tennis plans. Crib free. TV; cable, VCR avail (movies). 2 pools, 1 indoor; whirlpool. Dining rm 6–9 pm. Box lunches. Picnics. Rm serv. Bar noon–midnight; entertainment. Ck-out 11 am, ck-in 3 pm. Grocery, package store ½ mi. Meeting rms. Business servs avail. Bellhops. Concierge. Gift shop. Sports dir. Indoor, outdoor tennis, pro. 18-hole golf, greens fee $36–$42, pro, putting green, driving range. Downhill ski 4½ mi; x-country ski ½ mi. Lawn games. Exercise rm; instructor, weights, bicycles, sauna, steam rm. Massage. Sports Center with complete facilities. Some refrigerators. Cr cds: A, MC, V

Virginia

Abingdon

★★★★
MARTHA WASHINGTON INN

150 W Main St, Abingdon VA 24210
☎ *540/628-3161 or 800/555-8000*
FAX *540/628-7652*

Built as a private home in 1832, this historic inn became a girls' school before the Civil War and an inn in the 1930s. Today it is filled with antiques that recall its vivid past.  61 rms. S, D $135-$170; each addl $10; suites $170-$425; under 12 free. Crib free. TV; cable (premium), VCR avail. Pool privileges. Dining rm 5-10 pm. Rm serv. Bar 4:30 pm-1 am. Ck-out 11 am, ck-in 3 pm. Meeting rms. Business servs avail. Bellhops. Airport transportation. Tennis and golf privileges. Lawn games. Bathrm phone in suites. Antique furnishings. Cr cds: A, C, D, DS, MC, V

Alexandria

★★★★
MORRISON HOUSE

116 S Alfred St, Alexandria VA 22314
☎ *703/838-8000 or 800/367-0800*
FAX *703/684-6283*

This elegant redbrick building is furnished in the style of the Federal period throughout. Public rooms include the mahogany-paneled library and a parlor with fireplace. Many of the individually decorated rooms have four-poster beds and fireplaces.  45 rms, 5 story. S, D $195-$295; suites $295-$495; wkend rates. Crib free. Covered parking $10. TV; cable, VCR avail (movies $5). Dining rm 6-10 pm. Afternoon English tea 3-5 pm. Rm serv 24 hrs. Bar 11:30 am-11 pm; entertainment Thurs-Sat. Ck-out noon, ck-in after 3 pm. Meeting rms. Business servs avail. In-rm modem link. Butlers. Health club privileges. Bathrm phones. European-style inn. Cr cds: A, C, D, MC, V

VIRGINIA

Arlington County (National Airport Area)

🏨 ★★★★★
THE RITZ-CARLTON, PENTAGON CITY
1250 S Hayes St, Arlington County VA 22202
☎ *703/415-5000*
FAX *703/415-5061*

The Persian carpets, fine art and 18th-century antiques of this quiet hotel contrast with its surroundings. Guest rooms are lavishly appointed with silk drapes and Federal-style furnishings and have panoramic views of the Capitol and the Potomac River. 🐾 *345 rms, 18 story, 41 suites. S, D $179–$229; each addl $30; suites $289–$1,500; under 19 free; wkend plans. Crib free. Garage, valet parking $20. TV; cable (premium), VCR avail (movies). Indoor pool; lifeguard. Supervised child's activities (hols). Restaurant 6:30 am–10:30 pm. Bar; entertainment. Ck-out noon. Convention facilities. Business center. In-rm modem link. Concierge. Shopping arcade. Free airport transportation. Tennis privileges. Golf privileges. Exercise rm; instructor, weight machine, bicycles, whirlpool, sauna, steam rm. Massage. Bathrm phones, minibars. Luxury level. Cr cds: A, C, D, DS, ER, JCB, MC, V*

Hot Springs

🏨 ★★★★★
THE HOMESTEAD
US 220, Hot Springs VA 24445
☎ *540/839-1766 or 800/838-1766*
FAX *540/839-7556*

Famous for its mineral waters since 1766, this luxurious resort is on a 15,000-acre estate. Spacious guest rooms have Victorian decor. 🐾 *521 units, 4-12 story. Apr–Oct: S $170–$295; D $195–$320; parlor $140–$170 addl; family rates; MAP avail; ski, golf, tennis packages; some seasonal rates; some lower rates rest of yr. Serv charges: 15% daily housekeeping and 15% at all dining outlets. Crib free. TV; cable, VCR avail. 3 pools, 1 indoor; whirlpool, lifeguard. Supervised playground, playroom. Supervised child's activities; ages 3-12. Dining rm 7-10 am, noon-2:30 pm, 7-9:30 pm. Afternoon tea. Box lunches, snack bar. Rm serv 7 am–midnight. Bar 11 am–midnight. Ck-out noon, ck-in 3 pm. Con-*

vention facilities. Business servs avail. Valet serv. Gift shops. Airport, RR station, bus depot transportation. Sports pros. Tennis. Three 18-hole golf courses, greens fee $70–$85, cart $15/person, putting greens, driving range. Downhill/x-country ski on site. Skating. Hiking & horseback trails. Skeet & trap shooting. Archery. Lawn games. Rec rm. Movies. Bowling. Exercise rm; instructor, weights, bicycles, whirlpool, sauna, steam rm. Spa, mineral pool, medical dir. Extra fees for sports facilities. Picnic tables. 5,600-ft airstrip. Cr cds: A, MC, V

Richmond

★★★★
THE JEFFERSON

Franklin & Adams Sts, Richmond VA 23220
☎ *804/788–8000 or 800/424–8014*
FAX *804/325–0334*

This twin-towered landmark about one-half mile from downtown is an immaculately restored illustration of Richmond's rich history. Some guest rooms are small, but they are well furnished with reproductions and have large lighted closets and all other facilities necessary for a comfortable stay. 🚭 274 rms, 9 story. Apr–mid-June & mid-Sept–early Dec: S $140–$180; D $155–$195; each addl $15; suites $225–$825; under 18 free; special package plans; lower rates rest of yr. Crib free. Valet parking $10. TV; cable (premium), VCR avail. Pool privileges. Restaurant 6:30 am–midnight. Rm serv 24 hrs. Bar 11–2 am. Ck-out noon. Meeting rms. Business center. In-rm modem link. Concierge. Shopping arcade. Exercise equipt; weights, bicycles. Bathrm phones, refrigerators, minibars. Some balconies. Cr cds: A, C, D, DS, ER, JCB, MC, V

VIRGINIA

Tysons Corner

★★★★
THE RITZ-CARLTON, TYSONS CORNER

1700 Tysons Blvd, McLean VA 22102
☎ *703/506–4300*
FAX *703/506–4305*

A keynote of this hotel is its superb service. The lobby, furnished with antiques and 18th-century oil paintings, sets a tone of comfort and elegance that is carried through in the generously appointed guest rooms. ✈ *399 units, 24 story. S, D $170–$250; suites $375–$1,400; under 16 free; monthly rates; wkend family package; lower rates some wkends. Crib free. Garage parking $12; valet $4. TV; cable (premium), VCR avail (movies $4). Indoor pool; lifeguard. Supervised child's activities (wkends only). Restaurant 6:30 am–10 pm. Afternoon tea in lounge. Rm serv 24 hrs. Bar 11:30–1 am; entertainment. Ck-out noon. Convention facilities. Business center. In-rm modem link. Concierge. Gift shop. Tennis privileges. 18-hole golf privileges, greens fee $75, pro, putting green, driving range. Exercise rm; instructor, weight machine, bicycles, whirlpool, sauna. Masseuse. Bathrm phones, minibars. Luxury level. Cr cds: A, C, D, DS, JCB, MC, V*

Washington

★★★★★
THE INN AT LITTLE WASHINGTON

Middle & Main Sts, Washington VA 22747
☎ *540/675–3800*
FAX *540/675–3100*

This English-style country inn at the center of a small picturesque village in the Shenandoah foothills—less than two hours from its namesake, Washington, DC—exceeds even extravagant expectations. In 18 years under its current owners, it has been refashioned into one of the country's premier getaways for a superb dinner and overnight stay. Rooms are of different shapes and sizes, and some have balconies overlooking the village's main intersection or a placid, off-street courtyard garden. Almost nothing has been spared (except television, although it may be coming) to pamper guests. Guest rooms are tastefully decorated with antiques and the finest, carefully coordinated wallpapers and fabrics. The staff is largely inconspicuous but always at hand should you need them. 🕭 *12 rms in 2 bldgs, 2 story. D $260–$400; each addl in suite $40; suites $390–$490; higher rates: Fri, Sat, hols & Oct. Inn closed Tues (exc May & Oct); also Dec 24, 25. Complimentary continental bkfst. Restaurant (see THE INN AT LITTLE WASHINGTON RESTAURANT). Rm serv. Serv bar. Ck-out noon, ck-in 3 pm. Business servs avail. Bellhops. Gift shop. Airport transportation. Minibars. Some balconies. Complimentary tea service, fruit and cookies upon arrival. Cr cds: MC, V*

THE INN AT LITTLE WASHINGTON

Middle & Main Sts, Washington VA 22747
☎ *540/675–3800*

Extraordinary dining is found in quietly elegant, intimate surroundings courtesy of Old World decor; impeccable, indulgent service; and especially the remarkable culinary creations of chef Patrick O'Connell. The prix-fixe dinner begins with an off-the-menu taste of such tidbits as a sesame-sprinkled pocket containing spinach and ricotta cheese and a small cup of sorrel vichyssoise sprinkled with chives. Appetizers and entrees are equally intriguing and make use of the freshest seasonal ingredients from the region. Desserts include Seven Deadly Sins, a taste of many of the tantalizing items on the menu. 🕭 *Hrs: 6–9:30 pm; Sat 5:30–10 pm; Sun 4–9:30 pm. Closed Tues (exc May & Oct); also Dec 24, 25. Res accepted; required Fri, Sat. Eclectic regional cuisine. Wine cellar. Prix fixe: dinner $88, Fri $98, Sat $108. Specialties: local rabbit braised in pressed apple cider, native wild rockfish pan-roasted. Valet parking. Chef-owned. Smoking permitted in lounge and garden only. Cr cds: MC, V*

VIRGINIA

Williamsburg

★★★★★
WILLIAMSBURG INN
Francis St, Williamsburg VA 23185
☎ 757/229-1000 or 800/HISTORY
FAX 757/220-7096

Most visitors to Colonial Williamsburg come to relive the 18th century in its quaint shops, taverns and streets, but Williamsburg is also a resort destination. A stay at the elegant Williamsburg Inn can include golf, tennis, swimming, even lawn bowling, as well as afternoon tea served to live piano music in the East Lounge. Guest rooms are of different sizes and shapes and are furnished with Williamsburg reproductions; many face lush gardens. Except for the more formal Regency lounge and dinner in the dining room, the mood is casual and the atmosphere suffused with Southern hospitality. 🐾 *91 rms, 2 story. S, D $245-$325; each addl $12; suites $375-$575; package plans. Crib $12. TV; cable (premium), VCR avail. 3 pools, 1 indoor; wading pool, poolside serv, lifeguard. Supervised child's activities (Memorial Day-Labor Day); ages 4-12. Family activities program summer months & hols. Restaurant 7 am-10 pm. Complimentary tea 4 pm. Rm serv 24 hrs. Bar 11:30 am-11 pm; entertainment. Ck-out noon, ck-in 3 pm. Meeting rms. Business center. In-rm modem link. Airport transportation. Concierge. Tennis, pro. 9-hole & 2 18-hole golf courses, greens fee $95, pro, putting green. Exercise rm; instructor, weights, bicycles, whirlpool, sauna, steam rm. Massage. Lawn games. Bicycle rentals. Card rm. Some refrigerators. Balcony, fireplace in suites. Cr cds: A, D, DS, MC, V*

★★★★
KINGSMILL
1010 Kingsmill Rd, Williamsburg VA 23185
☎ 757/253-1703 or 800/832-5665
FAX 757/253-3993

The weathered-gray buildings and steep, shingled roofs of this resort are typical of those seen frequently in this part of Virginia. 🐾 *407 rms, 2 story. Mar-Nov: S, D $140-$215; 1-bedrm suites $191-$275; 2-bedrm suites $330-$490; 3-bedrm suites $470-$705; family rates; golf, tennis, vacation package plans; lower rates rest of yr. Crib free. TV; cable (premium), VCR avail. Indoor/outdoor pools. Supervised child's* *activities (Memorial Day–Labor Day); ages 5–12. Dining rm 6 am–9:30 pm. Rm serv to midnight. Bar from 10 am. Ck-out noon, ck-in 4 pm. Meeting rms. Business center. In-rm modem link. Concierge. Lighted tennis, pro. Three 18-hole golf courses (1 par 3), pro, driving range, putting green. Paddleboats. Marina privileges. Racquetball courts. Entertainment. Exercise rm; instructor, weights, bicycles, whirlpool, sauna. Massage. Some refrigerators, fireplaces. Picnic tables, grills. Cr cds: A, C, D, DS, JCB, MC, V*

Washington

Bellevue

★★★★ BELLEVUE CLUB
11200 SE 6th, Bellevue WA 98004
☎ *206/454-4424 or 800/579-1110*
FAX *206/688-3101*

This four-story, neo-classical structure with Beaux Arts and Palladian influences is matched with interior spaces enveloped in beechwood paneling with French limestone floors and suspended, curved ceilings. The overall effect is clean, contemporary and inviting. The health-club facilities are outstanding, with everything from indoor tennis courts and two fully equipped weight-lifting and aerobic centers, to an Olympic-size swimming pool and running track. ✈ *67 rms (2 with shower only), 4 story. S, D $150-$205; suites $295-$895; under 18 free; wkend rates. Crib free. Valet parking $3. TV; cable (premium), VCR avail. Indoor pool; whirlpool, poolside serv, lifeguard. Supervised child's activities; ages 1-12. Complimentary coffee in lobby. Restaurant 7 am-1:30 pm, 6-9 pm. Rm serv 24 hrs. Bar 11 am-midnight; entertainment Thurs-Sat. Ck-out 1 pm. Coin lndry. Meeting rms. Business center. In-rm modem link. Concierge. Gift shop. Indoor tennis, pro. Exercise rm; instructor, weights, bicycle. Minibars. Balconies. Cr cds: A, C, D, MC, V*

★★★★ WOODMARK HOTEL ON LAKE WASHINGTON
1200 Carillon Point, Kirkland WA 98033
☎ *206/822-3700 or 800/822-3700*
FAX *206/822-3699*

Guests fish for trout, stroll along a shoreline promenade or lie on the beach and soak in the panoramic views at this contemporary-style resort hotel, the only lodging on the shores of Lake Washington. ✈ *100 units, 4 story, 21 suites. S $155-$200; D $180-$230; suites $260-$1,000; under 18 free. Crib free. Overnight parking $9; valet. TV; cable, VCR (movies). Complimentary coffee in rms, late night snacks.*

Restaurant 6:30 am–10 pm, Sat & Sun from 7 am. Bar 11 am–midnight. Ck-out noon. Meeting rms. Business servs avail. In-rm modem link. Concierge. Health club privileges. Refrigerators, honor bars. Balconies. Complimentary newspaper, shoeshine. Marina; 3 lakeside parks. Cr cds: A, D, MC, V

Issaquah

THE HERB FARM
32804 Issaquah-Fall City Rd, Fall City WA 98024
☎ 206/784-2222

The menu at this formal cottage changes weekly in order to feature the freshest ingredients available. Herbs and vegetables are grown on the property. *Lunch sitting noon, dinner sitting 7 pm. Closed Mon–Wed, some Thurs; Dec 25; also closed Mar. Wine. Res required; res taken every Fri at 1 pm for following wk. Complete meals: 6-course lunch $65, 9-course dinner with wine $125. Parking. Totally nonsmoking. Cr cds: A, JCB, MC, V*

Long Beach

SHOALWATER
WA 103 at 45th St, Seaview WA 98644
☎ 360/642-4142

In this historic building (1896) filled with stained glass, natural wood and antiques, nationally acclaimed Northwest cuisine is served. Ingredients range from the freshest local fish to mushrooms and salad greens gathered from the peninsula's wood and gardens. *Hrs: noon–3 pm, 5:30–9 pm. Sun brunch 10 am–2:30 pm. Closed Dec 25. Res accepted. No A/C. Bar from noon. Semi-a la carte: lunch $3.95–$8.50, dinner $13.50–$24. Child's meals. Specialties: oysters, pasta, salmon. Own breads. Parking. Cr cds: A, C, D, DS, MC, V*

North Bend

SALISH

6501 Railroad Ave, Snoqualmie WA 98065
206/888-2556 or 800/826-6124
FAX *206/888-2533*

Located at the crest of spectacular 268-foot Snoqualmie Falls, the lodge was used in filming of the TV series *Twin Peaks*. Salish is dotted with antiques, and most rooms have a view of river, valley or falls. *91 units, 4 story. S, D $165-$245; each addl $25; suites $500-$750; higher rates Fri, Sat & hols mid-June-mid-Sept. Crib free. Pet accepted, some restrictions. TV; cable (premium), VCR. Restaurant 7 am-10 pm. Rm serv. Ck-out noon. Meeting rms. Business servs avail. In-rm modem link. Concierge. Golf privileges. Downhill/x-country ski 20 mi. Exercise equipt; weight machines, bicycles, saunas. Refrigerators, whirlpools, minibars, bathrm phones, fireplaces. Private patios, balconies. Library. Cr cds: A, C, D, DS, JCB, MC, V*

Port Angeles

DOMAINE MADELEINE

146 Wildflower Ln, on Finn Hall Rd, Port Angeles WA 98362
360/457-4174
FAX *360/457-3037*

This house sits on a bluff providing views of the Strait of Juan de Fuca and mountains. Many amenities are offered here including a gourmet breakfast. *5 rms (1 with shower only), 2 stories. Mid-Apr-mid-Oct: S $125-$150; D $135-$165; each addl $25; wkly rates; 2-day min wkends; lower rates rest of yr. Children over 12 yrs only. TV; cable (premium), VCR (movies). Complimentary full bkfst; tea & coffee in main rm. Ck-out 11 am, ck-in 4-6 pm. Luggage handling. Business servs avail. In-rm modem link. Airport, ferry transportation. Lawn games. Picnic tables. Totally nonsmoking. Cr cds: A, DS, MC, V*

  SC

Seattle

FOUR SEASONS OLYMPIC HOTEL
411 University St, Seattle WA 98101
☎ *206/621–1700*
FAX *206/682–9633*

Housed in a 1924 landmark with elements of Italian and English Renaissance styles and a Spanish ballroom, the Four Seasons Olympic was restored to its original glory in the early 1980s. It continues to hold a central position in the city's social calendar, while treating guest to attentive and personalized service. The spacious 2nd-floor lobby has oak-paneled walls, marble terrazzo floors and antique mirrors; you can look down on it from the curved staircase and balustrade of the Georgian Restaurant, which has chandeliers and graceful arched windows. (A second restaurant, the casual, pub-style Shuckers, is one of Seattle's more notable shellfish and seafood restaurants.) Also off the lobby, the Garden Court Lounge features fully grown trees bedecked with enchanting fairy lights at night, visible from University Street through large windows. The spacious rooms achieve a comfortably residential feel through the use of antiques, artwork and muted color schemes, while a full-service health club features a lap pool, cardio equipment and a separate weight room. 🐾 *450 rms, 13 story. S $225–$255; D $255–$285; each addl $20; suites $275–$1,200; under 18 free; wkend rates. Crib free. Valet parking $15. TV; cable (premium), VCR avail (movies). Indoor pool; poolside serv. Restaurant 6:30 am–2 pm, 5:30–10 pm. Rm serv 24 hrs. Bar 11–1 am; dancing Fri & Sat. Ck-out 1 pm. Convention facilities. Business center. In-rm modem link. Concierge. Shopping arcade. Barber, beauty shop. Airport transportation. Exercise rm; instructor, weight machine, bicycles, whirlpool, sauna. Massage. Bathrm phones, minibars; some refrigerators. Cr cds: A, C, D, ER, JCB, MC, V*

ALEXIS HOTEL
1007 1st Ave, Seattle WA 98104
☎ *206/624–4844 or 800/426–7033*
FAX *206/621–9009*

A charming small hotel, the Alexis is in an artfully restored 1901 building near the waterfront, the Public Market and the Seattle Art Museum. 🐾 *109 rms, 4 story. S, D $175–$210; suites $220–$370; under 12 free; some wkend rates. Crib free. Pet accepted. Covered valet parking $15/day. TV; cable (premium), VCR avail. Complimentary continental bkfst. Restaurant 6:30 am–3 pm. Rm serv 24 hrs. Bar 11 am–midnight. Ck-out 1 pm. Meeting rms. Business servs avail. In-rm modem link. Concierge. Shopping arcade. Tennis privileges. Exercise equipt; treadmill, stair machine. Steam rm. Bathrm phones; refrigerators. Wet bar, minibar, beverages, whirlpool in suites. Some balconies. Rms individually decorated; 8 wood-burning fireplaces. Cr cds: A, C, D, DS, MC, V*

HOTEL VINTAGE PARK

1100 Fifth Ave, Seattle WA 98101
☎ *206/624–8000 or 800/624–4433*
FAX *206/623–0568*

Built in 1922, this European-style lodging combines the luxury of an upscale hotel with the personality of a bed-and-breakfast. Guest rooms are named for Washington wineries and decorated in rich vineyard shades of dark green, plum and gold. 🐾 *126 rms, 11 story. S $175–$205; D $190–$220; under 12 free; suites $205–$375; wkend rates; honeymoon, Seahawks football, theater plans. Crib free. Valet parking $16. TV; cable, VCR avail. Complimentary coffee in rms. Restaurant 7–10 am, 11:30 am–2:30 pm, 5–10 pm. Rm serv 24 hrs. Ck-out noon. Meeting rms. Business servs avail. In-rm modem link. Concierge. Exercise equipt delivered to rms. Health club privileges. Bathrm phones, minibars. Wine tasting (Washington wines) in lobby Mon–Sat. Cr cds: A, C, D, DS, ER, JCB, MC, V*

INN AT THE MARKET

86 Pine St, Seattle WA 98101
☎ *206/443–3600 or 800/446–4484*
FAX *206/448–0631*

Adjacent to the Pike Place Market, this small, deluxe hotel emphasizes the informality of the Pacific Northwest rather than the amenities of a big hotel. Rooms are spacious, have contemporary furnishings and ceramic sculptures, and look out on the city, the market, the hotel courtyard or Elliott Bay. 🐾 *65 rms, 4–8 story, 10 suites. May–mid-Oct: S, D*

SEATTLE

$140–$205; each addl $15; suites $250–$325; under 16 free; some wkend rates; lower rates rest of yr. Crib free. Parking $15; valet. TV; cable (premium), VCR avail. Complimentary coffee in rms. Ck-out noon. Meeting rm. Business servs avail. Shopping arcade. Beauty shop. Health club privileges. Bathrm phones, refrigerators. Cr cds: A, C, D, DS, JCB, MC, V

[D] [≥] [🔥] [SC]

SORRENTO

900 Madison St, Seattle WA 98104
☎ *206/622–6400 or 800/426–1265*
FAX *206/343–6155*

Designed in 1909 to resemble an Italian villa, this deluxe hotel offers wonderful views of downtown and the waterfront. Standard rooms are quiet and comfortable; spacious corner suites have antiques and oversize baths. 🕸 *76 rms, 6 story, 42 suites. S, D $160–$220; each addl $15; suites $200–$1,200; under 16 free. Crib free. Covered parking; valet $15. TV; cable (premium), VCR avail. Restaurant 7 am– 2:30 pm, 5:30–10 pm. Bar 11:30–2 am. Ck-out noon. Meeting rms. Business servs avail. In-rm modem link. Concierge. Airport transportation. Exercise equipt; weight machine, treadmill. Refrigerators; many bathrm phones. Complimentary shoeshine, newspaper. Cr cds: A, C, D, DS, JCB, MC, V*

[D] [🏃] [≥] [🔥]

FULLER'S

In the Sheraton
1400 6th Ave, Seattle WA 98101
☎ *206/447–5544*

Original works by Northwest artists are found throughout the restaurant on permanent display. A marble pool and fountain decorate the center of the dining area. 🕸 *Hrs: 11:30 am–2 pm, 5:30–10 pm; Sat from 5:30 pm. Closed Sun; most major hols. Res accepted. Bar. Wine list. A la carte entrees: lunch $8–$16, dinner $18–$28. Child's meals. Specialties: Northwest seafood, fowl, Ellensberg lamb, herb-crusted sea scallops. Own soufflés, sauces. Valet parking. Formal dining. Totally nonsmoking. Cr cds: A, C, D, DS, ER, JCB, MC, V*

[D]

Winthrop

SUN MOUNTAIN LODGE
★★★★

Patterson Lake Rd, Winthrop WA 98862
☎ 509/996-2211 or 800/572-0493
FAX 509/996-3133

This resort on 2,000 acres of wilderness features stone fireplaces, handcrafted furniture and a lake with a beach. 102 rms, 2-3 story, 13 kit. cottages. Mid-June-Sept: S, D $140-$230; each addl $18; suites $240-$300; kit. cottages $150-$175; under 13 free; higher rates: wkends (2-night min) & hols (3-night min); lower rates rest of yr. Crib free. Pool; poolside serv. Playground. Supervised child's activities (July-Labor Day); ages 4-10. Dining rm 7-11 am, 11:30 am-2 pm, 5:30-10 pm. Rm serv. Bar; entertainment Wed-Sun. Ck-out noon. Meeting rms. Business servs avail. Bellhops. Concierge. Sundries. Gift shop. Local airport transportation. Tennis. X-country ski on site. Exercise equipt; weight machine, bicycles, whirlpool. Rec rm. Lawn games. Many refrigerators. Balconies. Picnic tables. Cr cds: A, MC, V

West Virginia

Shepherdstown

★★★★
BAVARIAN INN AND LODGE
WV 480, Shepherdstown WV 25443
☎ 304/876-2551
FAX 304/876-9355

Situated above the Potomac, this inn includes a gray stone main lodge and chalets reminiscent of old Bavarian inns. The luxurious guest rooms have canopy beds. *71 rms, 2 in main building, 1-3 story, 4 chalets. S, D $85-$160; each addl $10; suites $195-$275; under 12 free; wkday package rates; golf package. Crib $10. TV; cable (premium), VCR avail. Pool. Complimentary coffee & tea avail. Dining rm 7:30-10:30 am, 11:30 am-2:30 pm, 5-10 pm. Bar 5 pm-midnight; Sun from 1 pm. Ck-out noon, ck-in 3 pm. Meeting rms. Business servs avail. In-rm modem link. Tennis. Golf privileges, putting green. Exercise equipt; weight machine, bicycles. In-rm whirlpools, fireplaces. Balconies. Cr cds: A, C, D, DS, MC, V*

White Sulphur Springs

★★★★★
THE GREENBRIER
300 W Main St, White Sulphur Springs WV 24986
☎ 304/536-1110 or 800/624-6070
FAX 304/536-7874

The 7,000-acre Greenbrier, one of America's premier resorts, offers gracious hospitality, elegant accommodations and a broad range of recreational facilities and opportunities—even falconry. You can drink the waters that made White Sulphur Springs popular more than 200 years ago and unwind in a 1990s spa. This is a popular site for large meetings of business executives, but it's big enough and diverse enough for all. The decor is striking and the maintenance immaculate. Rates include breakfast, tea and dinner in a grand dining room (a gourmet dinner in the Tavern, where all entrees are cooked to order, is extra). *699 rms in hotel, 6 story, 103 guest house rms. MAP, Apr-

WEST VIRGINIA

Oct: S, D, guest rms, cottages $215–$310/person; each addl $125; family rates; tennis, golf, wkend package plans; lower rates rest of yr. Service charge $18 per person daily. Crib free. TV; cable, VCR avail (movies $2.50). 2 pools, 1 indoor; whirlpool, wading pool, poolside serv, lifeguard. Playground. Supervised child's activities. Dining rm 7:30 am–9:30 pm; restaurant 7:30–10 am, 6:30–9 pm. Box lunches, snack bar. Rm serv 24 hrs. Private club noon–1 am; entertainment. Ck-out noon, ck-in 3 pm. Convention facilities. Business center. In-rm modem link. Airport, RR station, bus depot transportation. Sports dir. 5 indoor, 15 outdoor tennis courts, pro. Lighted, heated platform tennis. Three 18-hole golf courses, greens fee $92, cart $34, pro, 2 putting greens, driving range. X-country ski on site. Ice-skating. Horse-drawn sleighing & carriage rides. Fitness trail. Bicycling. Lawn games. Trap shooting. Hunt club and game preserve. British regulation croquet court. Stables; English saddles. Soc dir; movies, dancing, entertainment. Bowling; indoor games. Full-service health spa. Exercise rm; instructor, weight machines, bicycles, sauna, steam rm. Massage. Some refrigerators; fireplace in cottages. Private patios, balconies. Cr cds: A, C, D, DS, MC, V

Wisconsin

Milwaukee

SANFORD
1547 N Jackson St, Milwaukee WI 53202
☎ 414/276–9608

This is an elegant restaurant set in a remodeled grocery store and named for the chef, Sanford D'Amato. The cuisine is a mix of Western and Asian influences and has won national acclaim. 🚭 *Hrs: 5:30–9 pm; Fri, Sat to 10 pm. Closed Sun; major hols. Res accepted. Serv bar. Wine cellar. Semi-a la carte: dinner $23.95–$29.95. Specialties: seared sea scallops, grilled breast of duck, cumin wafers with grilled, marinated tuna, provincial fish soup. Valet parking. Totally nonsmoking. Cr cds: A, C, D, DS, MC, V*

[D]

Rice Lake

CANOE BAY INN & COTTAGES
W 16065 Hogback Rd, Chetek WI 54728
☎ 715/924–4594 or 800/568–1995
FAX 715/924–2098

This inn offers luxury and pampering in an unspoiled wilderness environment. The Frank Lloyd Wright-inspired architecture is the perfect complement to the tranquil, forested setting. Accommodations include any of a combination of whirlpools, fireplaces, private decks, convenience bars, video and audio systems and fabulous lake views. 🚭 *15 units, 6 rms in inn, 4 rms in lodge, 5 cottages. Rm phone avail. S, D $145–$245. Adults only. TV; cable (premium), VCR (movies). Complimentary bkfst served in rm. Complimentary coffee in rms. Restaurant sitting 6–8 pm. Rm serv noon–8 pm. Ck-out 11 am, ck-in 3 pm. Luggage handling. Concierge serv. Business servs avail. 9-hole golf privileges. Downhill/x-country ski on site. Ice skating. Refrigerators. Picnic tables. On 2 lakes. Totally nonsmoking. Cr cds: DS, MC, V*

WISCONSIN

Sheboygan

★★★★
THE AMERICAN CLUB
Highland Dr, Kohler WI 53044
414/457-8000 or 800/344-2838
FAX *414/457-0299*

The same people who make plumbing in a huge factory across the street have created a delightful resort hotel in a 3-story, Tudor-style, rambling, redbrick building that originally housed the plant's immigrant workers. In 1981 it was converted into the American Club, with tastefully furnished guest rooms; a large, cozy, book-lined lounge; a superb gourmet restaurant among several dining choices; many recreational and fitness opportunities nearby; and four elaborately planted courtyard gardens, each with a different theme. 236 rms, 3 story. S $165–$595; D $195–$595; each addl $15; under 10 free. Crib free. TV; cable (premium), VCR avail (movies). Heated pool. Supervised child's activities; ages 4–teens. Restaurants 6–10 pm. Rm serv 24 hrs. Complimentary afternoon tea & coffee. Bar 11:30–1 am; entertainment. Ck-out noon. Airport, RR station, bus depot transportation. Meeting rms. Business center. In-rm modem link. Concierge. Gift shop. Indoor tennis, 2 pros. 36-hole golf, 3 pros, par course. X-country ski on site. Exercise rm; instructor, weight machines, bicycles, whirlpool, sauna, steam rm. Massage. Complete spa services. Health club privileges. Trap shooting. In-rm whirlpools, wet bars, honor bar; some bathrm phones, refrigerators. Carriage rides; bicycles; trolley. Cr cds: A, C, D, DS, MC, V

Wyoming

Grand Teton National Park

⭐⭐⭐⭐
JENNY LAKE LODGE
Jenny Lake Rd, Moran WY 83013
☎ *307/733–4647*
FAX *307/543–3046*

Restored 100-yr-old homesteader cabins moved from all around the area to the base of the Grand Teton range accommodate guests at the property. Homemade quilts and electric blankets are representative touches. ✈ *37 cabins. No A/C. No rm phones. MAP, late May–early Oct: S, D $265–$340; each addl $105; suite cabins $470–$480. Closed rest of yr. Crib free. Restaurant 7:30–9 am, noon–1:30 pm, 6–8:45 pm. Serv bar. Ck-out 11 am, ck-in 4 pm. Bellhops. Airport transportation. Bicycles; trail rides. Some refrigerators. Wood stove in suites, lounge. Private patios. Golf, tennis & swimming privileges nearby. Cr cds: A, D, MC, V*

⭐⭐⭐⭐
LOST CREEK RANCH
N on US 26/89, 2 mi E on gravel rd, Moose WY 83012
☎ *307/733–3435*
FAX *307/733–1954*

Tiled and carpeted cabins, some with wood-burning fireplaces, nestle on 110 acres thick with pine and aspen. Animal heads and original artwork in the lodge vie with views of the Grand Teton Mountains for guests' attention. ✈ *10 cabins (7 with kit.). No A/C. AP, June–Sept, wkly rates: 1–4 persons $3,835–$8,675; each addl $800; under 6 free. Closed rest of yr. Crib free. Heated pool; whirlpool. Supervised child's activities (June–Aug). Coffee in cabins. Dining rm sittings: bkfst 7:30–8:30 am, lunch 12:30 pm, dinner 7 pm (children's dinner at 6 pm if desired). Coffee & tea service in cabins. Ck-out 10 am, ck-in 3 pm. Complimentary lndry serv. Meeting rms. Business servs avail. Airport transportation. Tennis. Hayrides. Lawn games. Entertainment (evenings). Game rm. Scenic float trips. Riding instruction avail. Wkly trips to rodeo. Yellowstone Natl Park tour. Hiking in Grand Teton Natl*

Park. Refrigerators, fireplaces. Private porches. Picnic tables, grills. Fresh fruit in rms. No cr cds accepted.

Jackson

★★★★
RUSTY PARROT
175 N Jackson, Jackson WY 83001
☎ 307/733–2000
FAX 307/733–5566

Three blocks northwest of the town square, this log-and-riverstone getaway offers easy access to shops and restaurants. Antiques and a roaring fireplace set a romantic tone. 32 rms, 3 story. No elvtr. S, D $165–$225; each addl $30; suite $450; ski plans. Crib free. TV; cable (premium), VCR avail. Complimentary full bkfst. Afternoon tea service. Rm serv. Ck-out 11 am, ck-in 4 pm. Bellhops. Valet serv. Concierge. Downhill ski 12 mi; x-country ski 15 mi. Whirlpool. Spa, massage therapies avail (fee). Balconies. Fireplace in 13 rms. Library/sitting rm. Totally nonsmoking. Cr cds: A, C, D, DS, MC, V

ALPENHOF
In the Alpenhof
Teton Village Rd, Teton Village WY 83025
☎ 307/733–3462

Etched glass, wood beams and lots of greenery paint a pretty Alpine picture. More than half of the pink-clothed tables look out on Jackson Hole ski base. Hrs: 7:30–10:30 am, 6–9:30 pm. Closed early Apr–mid-May & mid-Oct–early Dec. Res accepted. No A/C. Continental menu. Bar 11:30–2 am. Wine list. Semi-a la carte: bkfst $3–$7.95, dinner $13.95–$24; special dinner for 2, $45–$59. Child's meals. Specializes in pasta, wild game, fresh seafood. Own baking. Tableside preparation. Parking. Totally nonsmoking. Cr cds: A, C, D, DS, MC, V

Canada

Edmonton, Alberta

★★★★
HOTEL MACDONALD

10065 100th St, Edmonton, Alberta T5J 0N6
☎ *403/424–5181 or 800/441–1414*
FAX *403/424–8017*

Restored to its 1915 glory, this chateau-like property on the North Saskatchewan River features ornamental plasterwork and original artwork in the lobby. Gardens and gazebo grace the spacious grounds. *198 rms, 8 story. S $139–$220; D $159–$240; each addl $20; suites $300–$2,500; under 18 free; wkend rates. Crib free. Pet accepted, some restrictions. Valet parking avail. TV; cable (premium). Indoor pool; wading pool, poolside serv. Restaurant 6:30 am–10 pm. Rm serv 24 hrs. Bar 11–1 am. Ck-out 1 pm. Meeting rms. Business servs avail. In-rm modem link. Concierge. Gift shop. Exercise rm; instructor, weight machine, bicycles, whirlpool, sauna. Massage. Sun deck. Game rm. Minibars. Cr cds: A, C, D, DS, ER, JCB, MC, V*

Montréal, Québec

★★★★
LOEWS HÔTEL VOGUE

1425 rue de la Montagne, Montréal, Québec H3G 1Z3
☎ *514/285–5555*
FAX *514/849–8903*

This small luxury hotel in the heart of Montréal has an elegant facade of polished rose granite, trimmed in aqua, with tall windows. Guest rooms are decorated with satiny duvets on the beds and striped silk. *126 rms, 9 story, 16 suites. Mid-May–mid-Oct: S, D $195–$255; each addl $20; suites $350–$1,500; under 18 free; wkend rates; lower rates rest of yr. Crib free. Pet accepted. Garage; valet parking $15. TV; cable, VCR (movies). Restaurant 7 am–11 pm. Rm serv 24 hrs. Bar 3 pm–1 am. Ck-out 1 pm. Meeting rms. Business servs avail. In-rm modem link. Concierge. Gift shop. Exercise equipt; weight machine, rowers. In-rm whirlpools. Minibars. Cr cds: A, C, D, ER, JCB, MC, V

THE RITZ-CARLTON, KEMPINSKI MONTRÉAL

1228 Sherbrooke St W, Montréal, Québec H3G 1H6
☎ *514/842–4212 or 800/363–0366*
FAX *514/842–2268*

Opened in 1912 by a group of local investors who wanted an elegant hotel in which to woo their rich European friends, the Ritz-Carlton Kempinski has been the backdrop for many noteworthy events ever since. Guest rooms are decorated in Edwardian style; service is impeccable. 🍽 230 rms, 9 story. May–Oct: S $190–$205; D $215–$230; each addl $35; suites $525–$750; under 14 free; wkend package; lower rates rest of yr. Crib free. TV; cable. Restaurants 6:30 am–10 pm. Rm serv 24 hrs. Bar 11:30–2:30 am; pianist. Ck-out noon. Meeting rms. Business servs avail. In-rm modem link. Barber. Exercise equipt; bicycles, treadmill. Valet parking. Minibars. Cr cds: A, C, D, ER, JCB, MC, V

THE BEAVER CLUB

In the Queen Elizabeth Hotel
900 Rene Levesque Blvd W, Montréal, Québec H3B 4A5
☎ *514/861–3511*

Founded by fur traders during Montréal's colonial days and serving as a social club for the city's elite during the 19th century, the Beaver Club maintains the august atmosphere of a men's club. Pelts of bear, buffalo and beaver still line the walls with members' engraved copper plates, but antique chairs and stained-glass panels also mark the decor. Having become Canada's first luxury restaurant in 1958, it still turns out classic haute cuisine, complemented by an extraordinary wine cellar. Add to that a few low-fat, low-salt, low-calorie plates and the result is one of the most unusual and best dining rooms in North America. 🍽 Hrs: noon–3 pm, 6–11 pm; Sat from 6 pm. Closed Sun & Mon eve; also July. Res accepted. Continental menu. Bar. Wine cellar. A la carte entrees: lunch $15.75–$19.75, dinner $23.50–$29.75. Complete meal: lunch $16.75–$29, dinner $29.75–$35. Child's meals. Specialties: steak Charles, hare *velouté, pan-fried duckling foie gras. Valet parking. Antique chairs, stained-glass panels. Jacket. Cr cds: A, C, D, DS, ER, JCB, MC, V*

✕ ★★★★★
NUANCES
In the Casino de Montréal
1 ave de Casino, Montréal, Québec H3C 4W7
☎ 514/392–2708

In a city noted for fine restaurants, this is one of the best. It's location on the casino's fifth floor yields stunning views, matched by the elegance of the high-ceilinged dining room. The contemporary French cuisine, awesome wine list and seamless service create a superlative dining experience. 🕊 *Varied hrs. Res required. French menu. Bar. Specialties: coriander-flavored rabbit stuffed with scampi, medallions of salmon topped with a scallop mousse, smoked duck with cardamom sauce. Cr cds: A, D, ER, MC, V*

Ottawa, Ontario

🏨 ★★★★
CHÂTEAU LAURIER
1 Rideau St, Ottawa, Ontario K1N 8S7
☎ 613/241–1414 or 800/441–1414
FAX 613/592–7030

Built in 1912, this is one of Canada's great railroad hotels. The Château, as it's known, is one of Ottawa's must-see sights. 🕊 *435 rms, 8 story. S, D $131–$231; each addl $25; suites $290–$470; under 18 free. Crib free. Garage parking (fee). TV; cable (premium). Indoor pool; lifeguard. Supervised child's activities (summer). Restaurant 6:30 am–11 pm; dining rm (summer) 11:30 am–10 pm. Rm serv 24 hrs. Bar noon–1 am. Ck-out noon. Convention facilities. Business center. In-rm modem link. Concierge. Shopping arcade. Downhill/x-country ski 12 mi. Exercise equipt; weights, stair machine, sauna. Rec rm. Minibars. Luxury level. Cr cds: A, C, D, DS, ER, JCB, MC, V*

CANADA

LE CHÂTEAU MONTEBELLO
★★★★

392 Rue Notre Dame, Montebello, Québec J0V 1L0
☎ *819/423-6341 or 800/441-1414*
FAX *819/423-5283*

Some 10,000 logs were used in the construction of this unique resort on 65,000 acres. Dating from 1930, it consists of several log buildings, each with its own design. *210 rms, 3 story. Mid-May–mid-Oct, MAP: S $1,658–$1,870; D $2,107–$2,420; each addl $769; under 4 free; lower rates rest of yr. Crib free. TV; cable. 2 pools, 1 indoor; lifeguard. Playground. Supervised child's activities (mid-June–early Sept); ages 3–12. Dining rm 7 am–3 pm, 5:30–10 pm. Rm serv to 11 pm. Bar 11–1 am; entertainment Fri-Sat. Ck-out noon, ck-in 3 pm. Meeting rms. Business center. In-rm modem link. Bellhops. Valet serv. Gift shop. Sports dir. Tennis. 18-hole golf, pro, greens fee with cart $54, putting green. X-country ski on site (rentals). Sleighing. Curling. Bicycles. Horseback riding. Lawn games. Soc dir. Dancing. Rec rm. Game rm. Squash courts. Exercise rm; instructor, weight machines, bicycles, whirlpool, sauna, steam rm. Massage. Fishing, hunting guides. Minibars. Marina. Cr cds: A, C, D, DS, JCB, MC, V*

Sherbrooke, Québec

AUBERGE HATLEY
★★★★

325 Virgin St, North Hatley, Québec J0B 2C0
☎ *819/842-2451*
FAX *819/842-2907*

This Victorian-style mansion (1903) on Lake Massawippi features antiques and a sitting room. *25 rms, 3 story, 5 suites. MAP: D $200–$340; each addl $65–$75; wkly, wkend rates; ski plans. Heated pool. Complimentary full bkfst. Dining rm 8–10 am, 5 pm-closing. Rm serv to midnight. Ck-out noon, ck-in 4 pm. Business servs avail. Downhill ski 1 mi; x-country ski ¼ mi. Many fireplaces, some in-rm whirlpools, balconies. Lake opp; swimming, boats avail for guest use. Cr cds: A, MC, V*

Toronto, Ontario

★★★★
THE BRISTOL PLACE HOTEL
950 Dixon Rd, Toronto, Ontario M9W 5N4
☎ *416/675-9444 or 800/268-4927*
FAX *416/675-4426*

This traditional hotel has a small waterfall in the main lobby, and guest rooms are individually decorated. ✈ *287 rms, 15 story. S, D $185-$210; each addl $15; suites from $275; under 18 free; wkend, package plans. Crib free. TV; cable (premium). Indoor/outdoor pool; poolside serv. Playground. Supervised child's activities; ages 2-16. Restaurant 7 am-11:45 pm. Rm serv 24 hrs. Bars 11-1 am; entertainment. Ck-out 1 pm. Convention facilities. Business center. In-rm modem link. Concierge. Valet parking. Free airport transportation. Exercise equipt; weights, bicycles, sauna. Minibars; bathrm phone, whirlpool in some suites. Some private patios. Cr cds: A, C, D, DS, ER, JCB, MC, V*

★★★★
FOUR SEASONS
21 Avenue Rd at Bloor St, Toronto, Ontario M5R 2G1
☎ *416/964-0411 or 800/268-6282*
FAX *416/964-2302*

This fashionable, elegant hotel has a prime location in Toronto. ✈ *380 rms, 32 story. S $240-$275, D $275-$305; each addl $25; suites $360-$2,400; under 18 free; wkend rates. Crib free. Pet accepted. Garage $16/day. TV; cable (premium), VCR avail (movies). Indoor/outdoor pool; poolside serv, lifeguard. Restaurant 6:30 am-11 pm (also see TRUFFLES). Rm serv 24 hrs. Bar 11:30-2 am; entertainment exc Sun. Ck-out 1 pm. Convention facilities. Business center. In-rm modem link. Concierge. Barber, beauty shop. Valet parking. Exercise equipt; weights, bicycles, whirlpool, sauna. Bathrm phones, minibars. Some balconies. Cr cds: A, C, D, ER, JCB, MC, V*

CANADA

INN ON THE PARK

1100 Eglinton Ave E, Toronto, Ontario M3C 1H8
☎ *416/444–2561 or 800/268–6282*
FAX *416/446–3308*

This hotel is set in a 600-acre park just 15 minutes from downtown Toronto. Guest rooms are decorated in American colonial style, and the lobby is rustic with abundant touches of wood, a large fireplace and a marble front desk. *568 rms, 2–23 story. S $115–$175; D $135–$195; each addl $20; suites $225–$750; under 18 free; wkend package. Crib free. TV; cable (premium), VCR avail. 2 heated pools, 1 indoor; lifeguards. Free supervised child's activities (May–Oct); ages 5–12. Restaurant 6:30 am–midnight. Rm serv 6:30 am–midnight. Bar 11:30–1 am; pianist exc Sun. Ck-out noon. Business servs avail. Concierge. Barber, beauty shop. Valet parking. Lighted tennis, pro. X-country ski ¼ mi. Exercise equipt; weights, bicycles, whirlpool, sauna, steam rm. Rec rm. Lawn games. Some minibars. Some private patios, balconies. Cr cds: A, C, D, ER, JCB, MC, V*

INTER-CONTINENTAL

220 Bloor St W, Toronto, Ontario M5S 1T8
☎ *416/960–5200 or 800/327–0200*
FAX *416/960–8269*

Edwardian and art deco touches embellish public spaces and guest rooms of this post-modern structure. *209 rms, 8 story. S $195–$275; D $215–$295; suites $325–$1,150. Crib free. Valet parking $21.40. TV; cable (premium), VCR avail (movies). Indoor pool. Restaurants 7 am–11 pm. Rm serv 24 hrs. Bar noon–1 am. Ck-out 1 pm. Meeting rms. Business center. In-rm modem link. Concierge. Gift shop. Exercise equipt; weights, treadmill, sauna. Bathrm phones, minibars. Cr cds: A, C, D, ER, JCB, MC, V*

TORONTO, ONTARIO

KING EDWARD
37 King St E, Toronto, Ontario M5C 1E9
☎ *416/863–9700 or 800/225–5843*
FAX *416/367–5515*

Built in 1903 and remodelled in the early 1980s, this stately and attractive hotel has a vaulted ceiling, marble pillars and palm trees in its lobby. *299 rms, 9 & 16 story. S $229–$289; D $249–$309; suites $300–$500; under 17 free; wkend package plans. Crib free. Covered parking, valet $24. TV; cable (premium), VCR avail. Restaurant 6:30 am–2:30 pm, 5–11 pm (also see CHIARO'S). Bars noon–1 am. Rm serv 24 hrs. Ck-out 2 pm. Convention facilities. Business center. Concierge. Shopping arcade. Beauty shop. Exercise equipt; weights, bicycles, whirlpools, sauna. Bathrm phones, minibars. Cr cds: A, C, D, ER, JCB, MC, V*

CENTRO GRILL
2472 Yonge St, Toronto, Ontario M4P 2H5
☎ *416/483–2211*

The facade of etched glass, granite and marble may seem hard-edged, but the interior is as warm as the folksy blow-ups of owner Franco Prevedello's home town of Asolo. Massive columns that seem to hold up a bright blue ceiling and salmon-colored walls lined with comfortable banquettes help to create an intimate setting. *Hrs: 5 pm–1 am. Closed Sun. Res accepted. Italian, Amer menu. Bar. A la carte entrees: dinner $20.95–$29.95. Specialty: rack of lamb with tomato, garlic, Spanish capers, eggplant and salsa. Own baking. Pianist. Cr cds: A, D, ER, MC, V*

CHIARO'S
In the King Edward
37 King St E, Toronto, Ontario M5J 1W2
☎ *416/863–9700*

Located in the opulent King Edward Hotel, this softly lit, plush dining room in shades of gray serves superior French-and-other-inspired cuisine. *Hrs: 6–10 pm. Closed Sun. Res accepted. Continental menu. Bar to 1 am. Wine cellar. Semi-a la carte: dinner $27–$38. Child's meals. Specialties:*

rack of lamb, Dover sole, New York steak. Valet parking. Cr cds: A, C, D, DS, ER, JCB, MC, V

✕ ★★★★
NORTH 44 DEGREES
2537 Yonge St, Toronto, Ontario M4P 2H9
☎ *416/487-4897*

North 44°, Toronto's latitude, is the restaurant's logo and an oft-repeated visual refrain. The trendy atmosphere is fostered by a metallic, modern look, but chef Mark McEwan's dishes more than hold their own in this singular decor. ✈ *Hrs: 5 pm-1 am. Closed Sun; some major hols. Res accepted. Bar. A la carte entrees: dinner $23.95-$33.95. Child's meals. Specialties: mixed appetizer platter, angel hair pasta, rack of lamb. Entertainment Wed-Sat. Wine bar on upper level.* Cr cds: A, D, ER, MC, V

✕ ★★★★
SCARAMOUCHE
1 Benvenuto Place, Toronto, Ontario M4V 2L1
☎ *416/961-8011*

This is Toronto's most luxurious French restaurant. Superb service and delicious food are served up in an atmosphere of understated elegance. ✈ *Hrs: 6-10 pm; Sat to 11 pm. Closed Sun; major hols. Res accepted. Continental menu. Bar to midnight. A la carte entrees: dinner $19.75-$29. Pasta bar $12.75-$21.75. Specialties: grilled Atlantic salmon, roasted rack of lamb. Own baking. Valet parking. View of city.* Cr cds: A, D, ER, MC, V

TRUFFLES
In the Four Seasons
21 Avenue Rd at Bloor St, Toronto, Ontario M5R 2G1
☎ *416/964-0411*

The wine list offers rare European and North American vintages in this formal, contemporary restaurant with bay windows and a high ceiling. Mirrors, murals, paintings and ceramics by local artists decorate the room. ✈ *Hrs: 6-11* *pm. Res accepted. Provençale cuisine. Wine cellar. Semi-a la carte: dinner $26–$38. Table d'hôte: dinner $75. Child's meals. Specialties: Québec duck, rack of lamb with mustard seed sauce. Own pastries. Valet parking. Jacket. Cr cds: A, C, D, ER, JCB, MC, V*

Vancouver, British Columbia

FOUR SEASONS
791 W Georgia St, Vancouver, British Columbia V6C 2T4
☎ *604/689-9333*
FAX *604/684-4555*

Tasteful pastel-hued decor, outstanding service and large, luxurious rooms create an atmosphere of calm in this bustling high-rise above the Pacific Centre shopping mall, adjacent to the Vancouver Stock Exchange. Notable are the glamorous atrium bar/restaurant and a partially covered pool on a sun terrace. 🚭 *385 rms, 28 story. May–Oct: S $340–$399; D $360–$419; each addl $25; suites $450–$2,200; under 18 free; special wkend rates; lower rates rest of yr. Crib free. Pet accepted. Garage $20/day. TV; cable (premium), VCR (movies). Heated pool. Restaurant 6:30 am–11 pm. Rm serv 24 hrs. Bar 11:30–1 am. Ck-out noon. Meeting rms. Business center. In-rm modem link. Concierge. Shopping arcade. Tennis privileges. Downhill ski 10 mi. Exercise rm; instructor, weights, bicycles, whirlpool, sauna. Massage. Shuffleboard. Minibars. Cr cds: A, C, D, ER, JCB, MC, V*

PAN PACIFIC VANCOUVER
300–999 Canada Place, Vancouver, British Columbia V6C 3B5
☎ *604/662-8111 or 800/663-1515*
FAX *604/685-8690*

Dramatically positioned at the cruise-ship complex, looking over the bay toward Stanley Park and the mountains, this ultra-modern luxury hotel has comfortable Asian-accented rooms with fine views. There's a well-equipped gym and sports center and several bars, cafes and restaurants. 🚭 *506 rms, 23 story. Mid-Apr–late Oct: S, D, studios $400–$430; each addl $30; suites $800–$2,000; under 18 free; wkend rates; lower rates rest of yr. Crib free. Pet accepted.*

Garage $20; valet. TV; cable, VCR avail. Heated pool. Restaurant 6:30 am–11 pm. Rm serv 24 hrs. Bar 11:30–1 am. Ck-out 1 pm. Convention facilities. Business center. In-rm modem link. Concierge. Shopping arcade. Barber, beauty shop. Exercise rm; instructor, weights, bicycles, whirlpool, sauna, steam rm. Massage. Bathrm phones, refrigerators; some in-rm steam baths. Cr cds: A, C, D, ER, JCB, MC, V

SUTTON PLACE

845 Burrard St, Vancouver, British Columbia V6Z 2K6
☎ *604/682–5511 or 800/961–7555*
FAX *604/682–5513*

This European-style hotel has a lively late-night bar and a restaurant that serves afternoon tea. Compact rooms have Regency-style furnishings and skyline views. 🐾 *397 rms, 21 story, 47 suites. Mid-Apr–Oct: S $195–$375; D $215–$395; each addl $20; suites $370–$1,500; under 18 free; lower rates rest of yr.* Crib free. Garage, valet parking $15. TV; cable (premium), VCR avail (movies). Indoor pool; poolside serv. Restaurant 6:30 am–11 pm. Rm serv 24 hrs. Bar 11:30–1:30 am; entertainment. Ck-out noon. Convention facilities. Business center. In-rm modem link. Concierge. Gift shop. Courtesy car. Exercise rm; instructor, weights, bicycles, whirlpool, sauna, steam rm. Massage. Bathrm phones, refrigerators. Sun deck. Cr cds: A, C, D, DS, ER, JCB, MC, V

THE WESTIN BAYSHORE HOTEL, VANCOUVER

1601 W Georgia St (BC 99), Vancouver, British Columbia V6G 2V4
☎ *604/682–3377*
FAX *604/687–3102*

The closest thing you'll find to a resort in the downtown area, the elaborately landscaped Bayshore is perched on the harbor, five minutes away from Stanley Park. Rooms in the newer tower section are largest and offer water views. 🐾 *517 rms, 9 & 20 story. Apr–Oct: S $199–$265; D $224–$299; each addl $25; suites $335–$1,600; under 18 free; lower rates rest of yr.* Crib free. Parking $11/day. TV; cable (premium), VCR avail. 2 pools, 1 indoor; poolside serv. Complimentary coffee in rms. Restaurant 6:30 am–10 pm. Rm *serv 24 hrs. 2 bars 11:30–1 am; entertainment exc Sun. Ck-out 1 pm. Convention facilities. Business servs avail. In-rm modem link. Concierge. Shopping arcade. Barber, beauty shop. Valet parking. Complimentary shuttle to shopping ctrs. Exercise equipt; weights, bicycles, whirlpool, sauna, steam rm. Massage. Bathrm phones, refrigerators. Balconies. Cr cds: A, C, D, DS, ER, JCB, MC, V*

[D] [≈] [🏃] [⛷] [🚭] [🔥] [SC]

Victoria, British Columbia

★★★★
EMPRESS

721 Government St, Victoria, British Columbia V8W 1W5
☎ *250/384–8111 or 800/441–1414*
FAX *250/381–4334*

The Empress, first opened in 1908, dominates the Inner Harbour area and is the city's primary meeting place for politicians, locals and tourists.  *475 rms, 7 story. No A/C. Mid-May–Sept: S, D $255–$315; each addl $25; suites $405–$1,700; under 18 free; lower rates rest of yr. Crib free. Garage $14.50. TV; cable (premium), VCR avail. Indoor pool; wading pool. Restaurants 6 am–10 pm. Bar 11:30–1 am; entertainment exc Sun. Ck-out noon. Convention facilities. Business servs avail. In-rm modem link. Shopping arcade. Exercise equipt; weight machine, rowers, whirlpool, sauna. Mini-bars; some refrigerators. Cr cds: A, C, D, DS, ER, JCB, MC, V*

[D] [≈] [🏃] [🚭] [🔥]

★★★★
SOOKE HARBOUR HOUSE

1528 Whiffen Spit Rd, Sooke Harbour,
British Columbia V0S 1N0
☎ *250/642–3421*
FAX *250/642–6988*

This elegant country inn by the sea offers all the amenities of an exclusive resort with a homey, yet elegant, atmosphere. All 13 rooms have an ocean view, balcony or terrace and fireplace. Staff will arrange everything from scuba diving excursions to fishing charters. *13 rms (1 with shower only), 2 story. No A/C. Apr–Oct, MAP: S, D $225–$295; each addl $35; under 12 free; lower rates rest of yr. Closed 3 wks Jan. Crib free. Pet accepted; $20 nonrefundable. TV avail; cable (premium), VCR avail (movies). Whirlpool.*

CANADA

Restaurant (see SOOKE HARBOUR HOUSE). Rm serv 24 hrs. Ck-out noon, ck-in 3 pm. Luggage handling. Business servs avail. In-rm modem link. Free airport transportation. Lawn games. Refrigerators. Balconies. Picnic tables. On ocean. Totally nonsmoking. Cr cds: A, ER, MC, V

SOOKE HARBOUR HOUSE
1528 Whiffen Spit Rd, Sooke Harbour, British Columbia V0S 1N0
☏ *250/642-3421*

Well worth a trip from Victoria, this restaurant in a 1931 clapboard farmhouse uses just-caught seafood and some 200 varieties of herbs grown on the property. Sitting on the terrace on a summer evening, you may catch a glimpse of the sea mammals that play nearby. *Hrs: 5:30-9:30 pm. Res accepted. Continental menu. Bar. Semi-a la carte: dinner $40-$45. Specializes in fresh seafood. Cr cds: A, MC, V*